A Firm Guiding Hand

"Saturn is a planet that is looking out for our highest good at all times. It acts as our Cosmic Parent who prevents us from hurting ourselves any more than our own self-ignorance would readily allow."

—from the Introduction

"We treat knowledge with reverence and view it as a power tool regarding our overall success. We feel it is almost our duty to turn out brainy."

—from Saturn in Gemini

" ... we shouldn't get too upset when metaphysical astrologers speculate on how unloving and mean we were in past lives, or how we did a masterful job using people selfishly and then disposing of them like Kleenex! Our present situation may not necessarily be punishment for being a real stinker in those bygone days during the Dark Ages."

—from Saturn in the Seventh House

"We can become very hard taskmasters, almost incapable of giving in to weaknesses and vulnerabilities. Nobody gets to see the tiny cracks in our fortress walls: we make sure they see the intimidating mesh of barbed wire instead."

—from Saturn in Scorpio

"For some reason, a few of us were taught to either fear or loathe anything or anybody different or foreign. We may have been told not to trust folks from abroad—not their culture, not their religion, and certainly not their weird food!"

—from Saturn in the Ninth House

ABOUT THE AUTHOR

Bil Tierney, at age 21, was one of the youngest astrologers to be certified for professional practice by the Atlanta Board of Astrology Examiners. Since invited by Isabel Hickey to lecture at The Star Rovers Conference in New Hampshire, Bil has spoken at major astrological conferences across the United States and Canada.

He has served several times as the newsletter/journal editor of the Metro Atlanta Astrological Society, contributing many articles throughout the years. His writings have also appeared in astrological publications such as *Aspects* and *The Mercury Hour*. In 1975, he self-published two books: *Basic Astrology For A New Age* and *Perceptions In Astrology* (which is now available in an expanded edition titled *Dynamics of Aspect Analysis*).

Bil currently limits his practice to working with clients, lecturing, occasionally tutoring, and writing articles and books. Clients are impressed with his analytical and intuitive abilities. They also appreciate his warm, vibrant, and humorous personality.

TO CONTACT THE AUTHOR

If you would like to contact the author or would like more information about this book, please write to him in care of Llewellyn Worldwide. All mail addressed to the author is forwarded, but the publisher cannot, unless specifically instructed by the author, give out an address or phone number. Please write to:

Bil Tierney
c/o Llewellyn Publications
P.O. Box 64383, Dept. K711-0
St. Paul, MN 55164-0383, U.S.A

Please enclose a self-addressed, stamped envelope for reply or $1.00 to cover costs. If ordering from outside the U.S.A., please enclose an international postal reply coupon.

Llewellyn Worldwide does not participate in, endorse, or have any authority or responsibility concerning private business transactions between our authors and the public.

TWELVE FACES OF
SATURN

Your Guardian Angel Planet

Bil Tierney

Llewellyn Publications
P.O. Box 64383-0383
St. Paul, MN U.S.A. 55164-0383

FIRST EDITION
First Printing, 1997

Cover design: Anne Marie Garrison
Editing and book design: Ken Schubert

Library of Congress Cataloging-in-Publication Data

Tierney, Bil.
    Twelve faces of saturn : your guardian angel planet / Bil Tierney.
--   1st ed.
        p.   cm.
    Includes bibliographical references.
    ISBN 1-56718-711-0 (pbk.)
    1. Saturn (Planet) -- Miscellanea.   2. Astrology. I. Title.
BF1724.2.S3T54   1998
  133.5 ' 37--dc21   97-38822
                                                        CIP

Printed in the United States of America

Llewellyn Publications
A Division of Llewellyn Worldwide, Ltd.
P.O. Box 64383
St. Paul, MN 55164-0383, U.S.A.

DEDICATION

I dedicate this book to my honored colleague
and good buddy Jeff Jawer. I am so glad our
paths have crossed in this lifetime.

ACKNOWLEDGEMENTS

I want first to thank Llewellyn's Acquisitions and Development manager Nancy Mostad for her quick response and positive interest in my manuscript. Her upbeat correspondence was an encouragement. Bright blessings to you too, Nancy!

Maybe you can't judge a book by its cover, but you may not even pick up the book if the cover is dull as old dishwater. Senior Creative Designer Anne Marie Garrison made sure none of us would get bored with the book's eye-catching cover. Thanks so much, Anne Marie, for those warm, appealing colors and your striking use of different fonts. Your Piscean magic worked—and rumor has it that Saturn's refusing to go back to its old mustard-streaked look! Now see what you've started? My thanks also go to Art Director Lynne Menturweck for helping to make sure everything turned out so well!

Last but not least, a big thanks to my fine Editor, Ken Schubert, for allowing me to tell what I know about Saturn in my own "gotta be free" Uranus-in-the-Third-House way. I appreciate you, Ken, for being so sensitive to that. I didn't want *Twelve Faces of Saturn* to sound too stiff and conventional, and it sure doesn't! I am especially happy that you left in all my good-natured humor (we are not used to smiling, much less laughing, when reading books about Saturn). Anyway, Ken, you are a pleasure to work with and you've given me a few good tips on how to even better edit my future manuscripts before they're sent off.

Thanks to all at Llewellyn Publications for making this educational experience an enjoyable one for me!

TABLE OF CONTENTS

Chapter Eight

Chapter Nine

Chapter Ten

Chapter Eleven

Chapter Twelve

Chapter Thirteen

SMARTIES WILL READ THIS FIRST (THAT'S YOU)

Twelve Faces Of Saturn provides a detailed report of prime features I associate with Saturn's natal sign and house. Some Saturn issues have understandably been left uncovered (particularly those regarding the myriad situational affairs linked to each house). I have chosen to focus on Saturn themes and challenges that most interest me. For example, Saturn in the Fourth House could be interpreted from a business real-estate angle (as in leasing/buying office space). But I am more interested in how we feel "at home" within ourselves security-wise. Saturn in Virgo might indicate issues involving "trouble with hired help." Yet for me the shortcomings of intellectually over-compartmentalizing life—while failing to feel unified with others emotionally—are more relevant concerns. You will find this book to be a worthy supplement to other fine texts on this subject. Benefit yourself by reading all you can about Saturn. It would be especially wise to read Liz Greene's *Saturn: A New Look At An Old Devil*[1] for a fascinating Jungian perspective. Most seasoned astrologers already own a copy.

A helpful way to use my material is to first read your natal Saturn sign—let's say it's Aquarius. See how you relate to what's being said (due to your unpredictable human complexity, only certain themes will apply to you while others may not). Then look for any extra insights by reading Saturn in the Eleventh House (even if your Saturn is in a different house), and finally review the Saturn/Uranus natal/transit material. Next, read about your Saturn house position—maybe it's in your Eighth House. But don't stop there. Also read Saturn in Scorpio and what I've said about Saturn/Pluto aspects.

Pooling all this information together, you should be able to develop a better feel for the overall texture of any Saturn placement operating through the twelve principles of astrology. Zip Dobyns has called them the alphabet "letters"[2] of the zodiac, while Jamie Binder prefers the term "traits".[3] But I refer to them as Principle One (Aries, First House, Mars), Principle Two (Taurus, Second House, Venus), and so on. Whatever terminology you choose, these basic twelve building blocks of consciousness manifest from the more sublime levels of awareness down to the denser material realms of worldly experience. Astrology—and life itself—is held together and made meaningful by our manifestation of these twelve creative principles. Metaphysically, I'm not too sure if I would even call them universal principles in the broadest sense of that term, since other beings inhabiting faraway solar systems probably have "zodiacs" and planets whose life functions we'd find totally alien and bizarre. They may not even need a Saturn-like principle. But we earthlings apparently do.

When I first conceived this book, I was planning to only write about Saturn from a natal sign and house perspective. Eventually I decided to include Saturn's aspects in order to further demonstrate one more layer of Saturnian themes at work. Thus Saturn/Venus becomes another example of Principle Ten blended with Principles Two or Seven. I have used separate chapters to interpret Saturn and Principle Two (earth Venus) vs. Saturn and Principle Seven (air Venus). I've taken the same approach when addressing Saturn with Principle Three (air Mercury) vs. Principle Six (earth Mercury). Also included is a look at Saturn through each element and quality (the modalities of cardinal, fixed, mutable), as well as interesting miscellaneous information about this Mother (Father?) of All Ringed Planets. A bit of Saturn's astronomy, mythology, and metaphysics is included. Plus a look at what some famous names in psychology might have associated with the Saturn principle.

My information on aspects will touch upon basic inner issues common to all aspects of the planetary pairing in question. If I sometimes briefly mention natal conjunctions, sextiles, squares, trines, quincunxes, or oppositions, I do so randomly. I did not wish to undertake the mammoth effort required to give fuller details of each and every possible aspect. This would have been too exhaustive a task, and more deserving of analysis in another book. But not this book (Saturn means being mindful of sensible limits— plus all that detail can become mind-numbing after a while). And so, my main thrust covers basic concerns common to Saturn aspecting any particular planet rather than individually addressing the ramifications of, for example, Saturn quincunx Jupiter or Saturn semi-square Neptune.

However, besides natal aspects, I have included a look at Saturn's transits to our natal planetary positions. You may find it valuable to apply some of this transit information to your natal interpretation, and vice versa.

There is no mention of Saturn retrograde or unaspected, and that's because I have covered each at length in my book *Dynamics of Aspect Analysis.*[4] Please read or reread what I've said in its chapters regarding these conditions. Also not included are delineations of transiting Saturn through the houses plus the transits of everything else to our natal Saturn; that also deserves another book.

I purposely have done here what some astrologers warn against: personifying the planets and implying that they are doing "this" or "that" to us rather than through us. But in my world of astrology, allowing planets to behave and interact like real people helps me to see their processes as less abstract (even the interior world of the psyche and the unconscious can seem very remote and impersonal at times). Maybe Saturn *is* trying to have an intimate relationship with me, telling me in a very personal way what its guidelines are all about. Maybe Capricorn *is* pulling me aside to offer cautious advice, while Pisces is tempting me to peek through its magical kaleidoscope. Who knows for sure how all this actually works upon our consciousness?

We call astrology a language, but perhaps it is at least a tool for speaking with the "gods" within and listening to their wiser, timeless counsel. Jungian-oriented astrologers would agree. It doesn't detract from my own sense of free will and self-determinism to view astrological factors in this picturesque way. It holds a certain charm for me and helps the experience of my birthchart seem more vivid (as my Scorpio Mercury would want me to feel—see, there I go again). So I hope this doesn't get in the way of you benefiting from studying the principles at play in my interpretations.

In my earlier writings (especially during the 1970s) I used the pronouns "he" and "his" exclusively when making references to an individual. My consciousness was raised during the mid-1980s when a feminist colleague gave me a book that instantly and happily opened my eyes to the power of gender-applied words in our culture: *The Handbook of Nonsexist Writing.*⁵ I am not crazy about using the optional he/she or s/he formats, and so my workaround is to use the less specific, more inclusive "we."

What's also good about using "we" is that it might help readers temporarily identify with those natal Saturn positions they technically do not have. We get to have a vicarious experience of what it might be like for someone else to have Saturn in the Twelfth House or Saturn in Leo, or even a Saturn/Uranus transit. This identification is probably not going to be conscious, but I'm hoping some part of our inner self will resonate to the material being read. With such momentary identification can come understanding and empathy, which should help raise our sensitivity level when reading another person's chart as well as our own.

Finally, it is important to note that I will be writing about, let's say, Saturn in Aries without any of the modifying features we all have to this planet in our actual charts. For the most part, I'm trying to describe how Saturnness mixes with Ariesness without any third factor included to alter this mixture. In reality, a chart may have Saturn in Aries trine Mars, with Mars ruling the Tenth

House. This would imply that Saturn has an easier time working with Aries' psychological response to life (as here Principles One and Ten work well together). Sometimes my delineations may seem mostly structured by an adherence to astro-logic. Even so, you can fill in certain subtleties and nuances about your Saturn experience in light of your own life's development. This book cannot flesh out those kind of uniquely personal details. Beginners especially need to keep this in mind when reading about their natal Saturn placements. And no matter what I've written, your own self-knowledge and a measure of common sense can better guide you when evaluating specific Saturn issues described.

Astronomical Saturn is a gaseous planet whose density is about 13% of our Earth's[6] (and so why do we still insist on making Saturn act as "the big heavy" when even physically it is not?). Therefore, I decided to approach writing about this planet with an occasional touch of humor. Saturn needs us to lighten up the traditional, worn-out image we have of it. Thus expect every so often to read something that will at least make you grin! And don't be guilty thinking that grim-faced ole Saturn has heard you giggle and will thus drop a ton of woe on your shoulders as punishment for such impudence and disrespect! That's more the portrait of the creepy looking, scythe-wielding Saturn of centuries ago ("yes, ladies and gentlemen, he slices...he dices...he mows down your ego and nails your coffin shut..."). Ah, such fun times in those days of yore.

Anyway, put on your seat belt, check your rear view mirror, slowly pull out of your spot, look both ways at the stop sign on the corner, and after making sure the wipers work, you are free to cruise through this book at a sensible speed. Enjoy the ride.

Preface Endnotes

1. Liz Greene, *Saturn: A New Look At An Old Devil,* Samuel Weiser, Inc., 1976.
2. Zipporah Dobyns, *Expanding Astrology's Universe,* ACS Publications, Inc., 1983, pp. 23–47.
3. Jamie Binder, *Planets in Work*, ASC Publications, Inc., 1988, pp. 43–89.

4. Bil Tierney, *Dynamics of Aspect Analysis,* CRCS Publications, 2nd revised edition, 1993, 277 pp.

5. Casey Miller and Kate Swift, *The Handbook of Nonsexist Writing,* Barnes & Noble Books/Division of Harper & Row Publishers, 1981, softbound, 134 pp. A second edition of this book was released in 1988 by Harper & Row, Publishers, 180 pp.

6. Jeff Mayo, *The Astrologer's Astronomical Handbook,* L. N. Fowler & Co. LTD, England, 1972, p. 65.

INTRODUCTION

LET'S GET ESOTERIC

Throughout centuries of astrological evolution, the ponderous ringed planet Saturn has had the heady role of governing a process in consciousness that humanity must undergo to attain self-mastery within the structured laws of the physical plane. This apparently is a slow but thorough unfoldment, ensuring the proper development of each individualized being. Considered esoterically as the guardian planet of our particular solar system, Saturn is given charge over the careful, methodical organization of formative principles inherent in matter. Saturn furnishes the spiritual life force with appropriate vehicles for material expression. Spirit needs a suitable shell to ensoul; Saturn provides this.

Saturn also supplies the cohesive substance needed to hold the structural integrity of all separate units of consciousness in their place. It's the cosmic version of collagen. Because of this, human beings are able to think in terms of "me" versus "you" or "us" versus "them." It's a pretty neat trick that only works on the physical plane. Saturn's esoteric association with the Lords of Karma (always a tough group to please) is due to its special binding power: actions taken are forever bound to consequences. In this respect, Saturn symbolizes the operation of law on all levels. It regulates the fundamental laws of atomic density (the hardening of atoms) and thus directs the composition of each separate yet interwoven plane of consciousness, allowing us to build protective and meaningful layers of awareness that assist our spiritual evolution. These levels of awareness are to be kept separate for the sake of our sanity (severe mental illness may be partially due to a lack of such protective boundaries in consciousness).

Without the support of Saturn, humanity would have trouble breaking itself up into a multitude of distinct individuals, each with his or her unique ego-structure. Things could get messy. Actually, without Saturn, all would operate as one undifferentiated life form (which it may have done in the beginning). Saturn is behind our capacity to make the human experience real and lasting in the sense of having material purpose and direction. Without it, an unstructured state of chaos would prevail on end—and then how would you find your car keys? And so Saturn can be viewed as a cosmic container or (as friends of mine who practice Kundalini yoga have called it) the "urn of Sat"[1] holding the otherwise overwhelming, incomprehensible spiritual outpourings of the Godhead—that font of unconditional love, creative power, and wisdom made manifest by Deity.

BACK DOWN TO EARTH

This book is about coping with certain realities we all face in life. It's about growing up in a world where limitations abound and external authorities lay down rules, regulations, standards, procedures, or whatever else it takes to keep billions of people under control and held accountable for their actions. Without the organization many of these rules enforce upon a mass level, society would never be able to build the collective structures needed to ensure its long-term security and continuity. Saturn provides humanity with the materials required to create enduring frameworks for stable living. And by urging us to collect and sort out useful life experiences that seemingly get better with repetition (up to a point), Saturn gives birth to traditions and cyclic social rituals that we eventually cherish and depend on.

Oddly enough, the observance of holidays (as festive as some are) is tied in with Saturn, which in turn is linked to the predictable changes of the seasons. The observance of the passage of time and thus the aging process itself is also a Saturn theme. The regularity of our body clocks and the necessity of even using mechanical clocks are Saturn issues. The list could go on and on regarding the things associated with this planet we earthlings need to function. Even dirt and the ground we walk on are Saturn-related; we trust walking on the ground when it's solid but universally fear it when it becomes as unstable as quicksand, thanks to Saturn. But this book isn't about dirt, except for spilling the "dirt" on what life can be like when we mismanage our natal Saturn. We may overdo it, under-emphasize it, attempt to ignore it, or occasionally get it just right after many tries at bat. The key is not to ever quit swinging at the fast balls life pitches to us. But just don't let the ball hit you and knock you down so many times. And always wear your safety helmet, for Pete's sake!

One last thing: we have made in the last half of this century a welcomed attempt to redeem the Saturn principle (even if only to claim truth in saying "no pain, no gain" rather than "lotsa pain, a-gain and a-gain"). Saturn is a planet that is looking out for our highest good at all times. It acts as our Cosmic Parent who prevents us from hurting ourselves any more than our own self-ignorance would readily allow. We often are stopped in our tracks, while we curse the Fates for being so cruel as to keep us from what we want now. But Saturn knows we will enjoy reaching our goals all the more at a later time, after we've pumped up our psychological muscles, gained needed spiritual weight, and developed a sturdy backbone of maturity to help us continue on our path to self-awareness. I say, "Good work, Saturn!"

Introduction Endnote

1. Sat is "being," one aspect of God (Brahman).

CHAPTER ONE

SATURN IN THE MODES

Just a quick note: I've noticed many astrologers aren't referring to Cardinal, Fixed, and Mutable as "qualities" these days. Instead, they call them modalities (or "modes" for short), so that's what I'm calling them here.

CARDINAL SATURN

Saturn has ambition and cardinality has a lot of push and kick. Cardinal energy is forward thrusting, so Cardinal is a determined and enterprising mode for Saturn. We may have a strong urge to keep proving ourselves to others in terms of our persistence, gumption, determination, and drive to make it all the way to the top. Cardinal Saturn, like all cardinal placements, has a no-nonsense "let's get the job done" quality about it, but Saturn adds the need to get the job done *right*. Our big tests are often in the area of the competence and timeliness of our actions. We aren't given a life where moping around or sitting on issues is allowed. We have to take responsibility and move with much strength of conviction and decisiveness. It won't always be easy to feel we're doing what's best, but we certainly know what we feel when we opt to do absolutely nothing—Guilt City.

2 • CHAPTER ONE

Cardinality is excellent at meeting challenges head on. Even Cancer the Crab, which, when moving sideways, can make it to the shore line lickety-split. It zeros in on its desired direction quickly once it feels completely safe. The Cardinal signs like hands-on involvement, and don't tolerate being delayed from taking action when ready. Saturn is a planet that spurs us to grow by facing tough, testing challenges. Hands-on involvement for Saturn means more direct control. However, delays are often the best way for Saturn to slow us down and make us produce better results in the long run. Wanting quick achievements makes us push too hard at times, and our frustrations are acute when we are thwarted in action. But the Cardinal mode means we don't get stuck in ruts for too long. We will move on to new projects that will work for us. Our innate executive ability is something that needs further development. Mainly, we need to learn to supervise without becoming too pushy and insistent on immediate results from others. Even though cardinality demands fast resolutions, nothing about Saturn is immediate. We will be disciplined enough to forego shortcuts and learn to take sufficient time to plan out our strategies before taking the plunge.

FIXED SATURN

Most of Saturn's typical traits are already very similar to the fixed mode: steadfastness, endurance, careful planning, purposeful action, rigidity, and resistance to change. The danger here is overdoing our fixity and becoming too inflexible. Delays do not bother fixed Saturn like they do cardinal Saturn. Not being able to act quickly is less a source of frustration, since we tend to feel we are not ready until we've had ample time to organize and prepare. Responsibilities suddenly thrust upon us are not welcomed and probably feel like intrusions. Our need to control everything seems to be strong (though perhaps a bit less so in Aquarius, which is partly Uranian in behavior). Saturn can resort to domineering tactics in order to establish reliable structures. We can be unbending in how we wield authority, a trait that becomes oppressive in relationships. Determination is very strong, helping us plod on in the face of seemingly insurmountable obstacles. But without adequate adaptability, we can become stubborn and consequently rut-bound. It is important that we know when to stop pursuing unworkable objectives.

Fear of change is common with fixed Saturn (whereas fear of not changing would better describe cardinal Saturn). We want security to last, so we do whatever it takes to preserve what we value to protect it from being altered. But sometimes that is not realistic, and therefore the effort won't be totally supported by Saturn. When a loss or a defeat is experienced it can be devastating for us because we have allowed ourselves to become too attached to whatever is no longer ours to own and control. Our inner resistance can make for a stiff approach to life, and such stiffness can even manifest bodywise (tight muscles, stiff joints, an arthritic predisposition). Going with the flow is a major lesson for us, since our tendency is to become too fixated on having everything predictable and unchangeable. The drive for power can be strong, and that power is not easily shared with others. We feel we must always be in charge—but life will probably say otherwise. Our conflicts are worked out less through action and movement than through inner reaction and reflection (much of Saturn energy here turns inward; control is to be applied toward the self rather than the external environment). Our reliability and dutiful nature motivate us to complete our tasks.

♍ MUTABLE SATURN

Completing tasks and finishing projects may be trickier for mutable Saturn (the exception here is Saturn in Virgo). Staying power is not a strong mutable trait. But under the right conditions, mutability offers the last-minute adjustments and alterations that can make for successful results. Mutable Saturn is challenged to trust adaptability. It's prone to be a smarter Saturn, thinking twice before taking on responsibilities (Cardinal Saturn wants to act first and review later while Fixed Saturn doesn't want to veer off course and make any changes once committed). The one mutable sign that may not detach or analyze issues as well is Pisces. Saturn in this sign can make some of us feel obligated to respond to the call of duty even when it is not always sensible to do so—and that's often due to the unconscious needs inherent in water signs. The nervous temperament typical of mutability needs to be harnessed by mental discipline to prevent a scattered waste of energies. Saturn wants clarity and concentrated focus to help us better structure our thinking process. This can help us become more selective and discriminating regarding what we mentally take in and digest.

Two of the mutable signs are highly rational (Virgo/Gemini) and two are intuitional (Sagittarius/Pisces). Mutable Saturn helps us bridge the gap between applying logic and following hunches. Both approaches supply us with a complete picture regarding whatever we're dealing with, which can, in turn, help us with our decision making. Being overly rational can narrow our perspective and make us overlook subtleties, yet being too faith-driven can make us fail to analyze essential details in favor of sweeping generalities. Saturn is teaching us to decide when to be reasonably skeptical and when to deeply believe in something. Ongoing education seems very important to us, but at some point we need to realize that reality is not something that lives only in our minds. Life will push us to apply practical mental skills to the concrete needs of the real world.

CHAPTER TWO

SATURN IN THE ELEMENTS

ℳ FIRE SATURN: STEADY FLAME OR SLOW BURN?

Practical, cautious Saturn seldom finds harmony when blended with the high-spirited, risk-taking fire signs. Contrasting themes between planet and element abound. Filtered through heavy, ego-crystallizing Saturn, the driving, vital energy of colorful and vibrant fire is typically denied its full range of expressiveness. Also, fire seeks action without regard to consequences, but Saturn won't take any action until it's reviewed all the probable results.

Fire will not tolerate blockages and initially becomes intensely frustrated, but soon can destructively erupt and lash out against all restraining factors. For better or worse, fire resorts to emotive, passionate outpourings. Saturn symbolizes both resistance and the pressure it builds, operating in a manner alien to fire. Thus it is important that such Saturn placements be handled with much patience and level-headed understanding if they are to benefit our growth process.

Fire's volatile temperament contrasts markedly with Saturn's inclination to take the logical, carefully considered, and well-timed approach to life. Saturn requires a practical sense of planning to ensure stability and predictable outcomes before it commits to action. Fire disregards mundane security in favor of adventurous exploration. The unknown beckons fire, but threatens Saturn.

Possessing a high degree of impulsiveness and daring, fire signs attempt to defy life's limitations in an assertive, untempered manner. Yet when combined with Saturnian principles, many fire traits are notably dampened, subdued, or generally held back from their full effect. Saturn curbs fire's natural instinct to freely burn off its energy. This could constructively result in a slow, steady output of fire energy (more like the natural endurance of fixed Leo when well handled) without unnecessary flame-outs. However, repression of fire energy can create potent resentments that take time building up before they do surface and lash out in full force (if they ever do).

Although the vitality, enthusiasm, and animated spark of enlivening fire is kept in check by reserved, energy-conserving Saturn, both planet and element share a need to exercise autonomy. Both need to free themselves from external controlling factors by taking full charge of their personal affairs without intrusion. Like fire, Saturn is motivated to establish a conscious awareness of itself as a self-contained, separate entity. In this regard, fire signs evoke and accentuate the self-deterministic facet of Saturn. Saturn prefers distance, not intimacy. Yet since fire is an element of (innocent) self-interest, fire emphasis may unfortunately over-energize Saturn's self-preservation streak. The problem with this is that Saturn can turn selfish and fearful of giving itself freely to the world. Independent fire in this case only reinforces a loner tendency, with Saturn feeling cut off from human connection and often much too self-preoccupied.

Fire Saturn highlights an ambitious drive to achieve and be recognized, but self-centeredness, egotism, and insensitivity to others may become problematic. Basically, what is required is a safe harnessing of the creative power of Will. Ego drives need careful, practical channeling so that we don't squelch our spirit or bulldoze our way through life. Saturn typically represents well-defined energy. It also symbolizes life's safety brakes, preventing fire's high-powered vitality from destructively burning itself up in an impetuous, non-productive manner.

Perhaps karmically, we have over-extended ourselves in past lives, much to the detriment of our ego development. As a result, we now are forced to get a grip on the pros and cons of self-will, especially when taking action. Saturnian lessons involve the wholesome expression of fire. Saturn in fire combines vitality and strength of will with a purposeful sense of control and direction, often in a manner enabling personal objectives to be executed with sound judgment and creative flair.

EARTH SATURN: SOLID ROCK OR OLD FOSSIL?

Saturn exhibits its most natural traits when operating in earth signs. Common denominators between planet and element are easy to establish. Earth Saturn puts its central focus on the practical use of time, space, and energy. It loathes wasting anything unnecessarily, but also hates hanging on to useless things. Both Saturn and earth urge us to master the tangible components of life. Both seek to deal squarely with the daily necessities that make living so thoroughly mundane. Each recognizes and accepts that which solidly "exists" according to the perceptual framework provided by our five senses (when unimpaired). Both planet and element seek to comprehend the reality principle as manifested through material form and structure. Saturn in earth must work slowly and with much effort and persistence to physically master and control such form, partly due to the strong resistance factor inherent in earth. Saturn seeks to actualize itself through well-organized, purposeful activity in this pragmatic element.

Carefully fortified structures can be built, ensuring their long-lasting stability. Functional durability and permanent worldly value are also important. Main themes are the realistic application of effort, efficiency, orderly routine, proper maintenance, and the general preservation of resources.

Earth Saturn wants to be very grounded in the world. It adeptly attends to everyday tasks and labors consistently until concrete results are effectively obtained. Saturn and earth are very much concerned with safety, stability, and preserving the status quo whenever possible. This is not an adventurous combination of principles—both are pro-caution and anti-risk. The unknown, with its potential for uncertainty, becomes intimidating rather than exciting. However, Capricorn can be relatively enterprising when it feels solid about its objectives, due to its cardinal drive to move forward into experience.

Earth Saturn is instinctively good at wall-building in a protective, survival-conscious manner. This does not have to always suggest outright defensiveness, although when mismanaged, earth Saturn can value security at all cost in favor of spontaneity. The expression of our individualism is less important to us than feeling assured that the outer environment will not impose changes on us. Saturn and earth want things to remain intact in familiar ways, but this could lead to being rut-bound or stifled to the point that true growth becomes impeded. Earth Saturn needs to be careful not to become too comfortable being boxed in a safe little world devoid of stimulating challenges. The cultivating of adaptability is very important to prevent stagnation. When well managed, earth Saturn denotes much common sense and practical know-how in dealing with everyday living—but the drive for security could lead to monotony and the mindless repetition of habits.

While life's more painful elements are apt to be less vividly felt on the emotional level, this Saturn is motivated to know why things hurt and what can be sensibly done to relieve discomfort. It looks to the world for solutions rather than reflecting within. Dilemmas that cause pain typically involve a lack of some needed external resource. Saturn in earth does tend to tackle problems in the present, usually by dealing with one issue at a time until all issues are resolved. Obstacles within a reasonably immediate grasp are the focus, not vague intangibilities in some unspecified future. Patience is a must, as well as timing and hard work. A certain degree of stick-to-it-iveness is also required. This Saturn can endure delays fairly well, knowing it will eventually turn goals into concrete actualities.

The game of life can be more of a chore than an exploration for earth Saturn. Life can seem very heavy in those same situations where others easily float along with little care and worry. Saturn is a planet associated with perfection and excellence, yet to expect perfection on earthly levels is unrealistic. While Saturn seeks permanence in perfected form, life continues to be in a constant state of flux and change. Karmically, we are to learn that perfection as an ongoing dynamic process and that static conditions can be paralyzing. We also run the risk of being too rigid in our handling of change. This could make for an unadaptable temperament that can turn brittle and become dried up in old age. We calcify when we refuse to be flexible in spirit. Saturn can be an introvert, suggesting moody self-inspection. Under stress, it can withdraw and become depressed. But earth, even under great stress, doesn't cave in—it plods on (as if numbing itself to certain unpleasant realities in order to function). And so this could be a point of contrast between planet and element.

There is also something very sensuous about earth that Saturn may have trouble accepting. Earth deals with all the functions of our body, which include our pleasurable experiences. Saturn is more likely to target the painful, limiting facets of being in a body and not feel at home with physical comforts. Saturn obviously thinks there are laws against feeling too good (typically a Judeo-Christian bias). Learning to relax and not always push ourselves physically to the point of exhaustion is good advice.

AIR SATURN: DEEP THINKER OR DOUBTING THOMAS?

Air Saturn's brain tends to work overtime, deep in thought. Yet how we communicate to the world sometimes makes others question our intellectual strength. Insecure Saturn can clam up when in air and appear not as smart or as observant as it really is. Realistic Saturn often operates in a highly logical yet aloof manner when in cerebral, objective air. Rational, scientific-oriented air coordinates well with purposeful, truth-testing Saturn. Saturn helps this normally diffusive element harness its mental power with an uncommon degree of concentration, discipline, patience, and stability. Restless, hard-to-contain air is thus better regulated, allowing thought processes to consolidate rather than to randomly disperse or scatter. Saturn provides needed direction and focus, even though air may not necessarily apply itself in practical or worldly ways. The abstractions of air are more easily converted into intelligent structures, made concrete and workable with organized Saturn.

Air desires no set limitations or permanent structure. It naturally wants to be free to circulate and disperse its thoughts outwardly into the social environment. This encourages a wide and stimulating range of relationships plus a greater, more encompassing understanding of life's diversity. In contrast, the often reserved and exclusive Saturn establishes protective boundaries in order to preserve itself from potential chaos. It fears the lack of control that could occur from being too open and responsive to the variety of stimuli that curious air requires. Saturn puts limits on air's adaptability, restricting its social inclination. Air Saturn is less likely to encourage social exchange, shared closeness, or deep intimacy. The separative quality of Saturn is further accentuated by the impersonality of detached air. We can therefore appear friendly and humane, but cool, unemotional, and undemonstrative. If stress patterns are involved, indifference or callousness can be a way to prevent vulnerability on the one-to-one level.

Although it is concerned with achieving control and stability in the intellectual realm, Saturn here seldom trusts the native intelligence of the instincts or intuitive urges, repressing or blocking their spontaneous release while reinforcing air's reasoning power. Perhaps at the root of this is a profound fear or denial of that which appears irrational, unknowable, or beyond the logic of the mind. Mental perspective can become narrow due to firm insistence on the factual rather than the speculative if Saturn squelches air's theoretical interests. However, the mind can also be disciplined and sharpened until it becomes a useful, productive tool to evaluate life without bias or distorted emotional coloration.

Air is less free to travel far and wide due to Saturn's restraint. Without adequate circulation or ventilation, air can grow stale, losing much of its vitality. This can result in a dry, pedantic intellect devoid of imagination and color (perhaps explaining why it at least is better suited for the rigors of scientific pursuits and technical applications). Air's natural urge is to uplift awareness through expanded mental comprehension. It is innately buoyant, boundless, and pervasive. But Saturn's gravity keeps air from skimming the surface of things, which could prove depressing and deflating to air's temperament. Nevertheless, Saturn adds a measure of depth and substance to lightweight air, and tones down this element's potential for superficiality.

When well managed, air Saturn exhibits an above average degree of mental discernment, coherence of thought, impartiality, consistency of reasoning, and clarity in communication. Saturn effectively steadies this restless, fickle element, enabling ideas to lead to workable results. Fairness and justice seem to be important to both planet and element. Air Saturn looks at issues objectively with an interest in getting down to the solid facts of any matter by eliminating the superfluous. It's somewhat like Virgo in this respect. Saturn helps trim excess, preventing air from becoming windy. Saturn cools so-called "hot air" and trains the mind to express itself with greater simplicity (which is not to be confused with simple-mindedness). But air, like fire, has to work harder to appreciate Saturn's discipline and need for routine. Consistency is required if air is to be really efficient in life. Otherwise, it merely has fun dabbling and trying out a little bit of everything, but not enough to excel in any one thing.

Karmically, this combination indicates that we are to use our mind like a fine tool. Constantly educating ourselves is one way to give our brains needed tune-ups. But being responsible with words and thoughts is also part of our karma. Maybe we said the wrong thing last time around that ended up bringing others down with us. Or maybe we fabricated falsehoods and got others in lots of trouble. However it all played out way back then, we now are to choose our words carefully and do our homework before communicating what we think we know. This Saturn would agree that a mind is a terrible thing to waste, and thus treats the learning process with great honor and respect.

WATER SATURN: SECURITY GUARD OR FRAIDY CAT?

Saturn typically responds in a hypersensitive, untrusting manner when operating in the easily threatened water signs. The safety urges of both planet and element are highlighted—often negatively so. Water Saturn tends to retreat behind barriers that provide protection from attack or harm, whether real or imagined. Both Saturn and water are cautious and self-preserving. Defensive Saturn combined with strongly instinctual water implies a deeply ingrained vulnerability. A feeling of being somewhat naked and exposed on some inner level is strong, and this can provoke an irrational response of fear. Due to water's unconscious nature, such fears are more likely to manifest as complex phobias and/or "intimacy anxieties," since water puts us in touch with the pros and cons of emotional closeness, which can be comforting or can threaten to drown us. The persistence of these fears is often due to our tendency to not allow such feelings to surface, ventilate, and be consciously analyzed. (Quick, anyone have a can of air Saturn handy?)

Saturn and water both share an interest in the past. For Saturn, the past connotes an orderly and dependable sequence of activity—a purposeful continuity that proves reliable in terms of achieving sound results. In other words, a tried-and-true pattern. Expect Saturn to always strive to produce tangible results, to manifest something whenever possible. However, water Saturn might view parts of the past as entrapment, with painfully remembered failures and defeats embedded in the confines of a introspective and sometimes troubled psyche. For water Saturn, the past can be a nagging source of unresolved guilt and regret, providing no quick or satisfying way to erase past mistakes. For water in general, the past often represents vividly sensed impressions of previous lives or early childhood experiences, especially those involving either a deeply gratifying assimilation or a profound sense of loss. Water symbolizes the end of a cycle, resolved or unresolved.

Proper digestion of past experiences gives water built-in strength, resilience, and an uncanny ability for self-renewal. Water knows how to lay low, hide out, or just go within to refresh itself on inner levels. But under certain situations, Saturn could trigger a personal sense of deprivation, which in turn brings out water's more negative traits: helplessness, defensiveness, over-dependency, weakness of will, and feelings of being too socially isolated or cut off to cope with life's touchier challenges. Mismanaged, Saturn in water can trigger inner blockages concerning former experiences we have trouble owning up to, even in this lifetime.

Such a double dose of past orientation can foster current inertia (we're afraid to make a move), stagnation (we're not motivated to make any moves), a sense of fatalism (moves will be made on us we won't like), or even chronic timidity regarding our future, especially in terms of emotional expectations (we will regret the disappointing moves we are bound to make). All this can leave water Saturn very unfulfilled and lacking in self-assurance. We are too scared to confront issues in the present. But only by doing so will we be truly able to cope better with life. Taking personal responsibility for the restructuring of distorted feeling and images dwelling within is the first step.

When well managed, water Saturn denotes emotional mastery as a result of our in-depth sense of self-control and discipline. Such equilibrium is needed before we attempt to do too much spiritual exploration. It is often assumed that a chaotic personality will achieve emotional discipline and inner peace after engaging in enough spiritual techniques, but sometimes such mental disorganization can merely end up magnified instead. Stable earth temperaments, ironically, are better suited for spiritual practices because they are great at remaining grounded in all the right ways—once they are convinced there is something real to all this otherworldliness. Saturn in water can award us with an uncommon ability to provide ourselves with our own security needs. We thus do not feel defensive because we see the world we encounter as less able to throw us off emotional balance. We don't have to be on guard or act like a scared rabbit all the time. We can be emotional in a deeply caring way that can even help others who are instead plagued by destructive emotionalism.

Such Saturnian placements suggest inner stamina during tension-ridden times when our most protective psychological resources are actively put to the test. Emotional energy can be held within, but that may indirectly help it become a concentrated power—especially if we have Saturn in Scorpio. The result of such concentration (or compression) can be either hard-to-comprehend fixations or a mature gut-level intuitiveness that gets us through difficult times again and again. Water Saturn means we can learn to inwardly pull ourselves together when we most need to and root ourselves in the strength of a well-nourished feeling nature.

We with Saturn in water may not appear warm on the surface. In fact, some of us can seem crusty, grouchy, remote, and unapproachable—especially Cancer and Scorpio, symbolized by creatures that have claws that snap and pinch. (Pisces isn't so grouchy, but its quick defense is swimming away from direct encounter on all levels.) A few of us may not even seem particularly maternal or eager to do care-giving. Yet with time, patience, and a good measure of maturity, we water Saturn types are very capable of making the rest of the world feel solidly sheltered and supported. We can put people under our fin and convince them (since our powers of persuasion can be strong) that the sky is not falling and that they will, by having faith in themselves, be able to overcome any hardship or obstacle (such as addictions or other forms of self-abuse). Nurturing the soul of others is also part of our karmic challenge, something we learn to approach from a very knowing inner place.

CHAPTER THREE

SATURN'S NATAL SIGN AND HOUSE

SATURN'S NATAL SIGN

Saturn will generally show ways we can ambitiously strive to use the more relevant, stabilizing qualities of its natal sign, but it can also reveal how we defensively block and hamper the needs of that sign in ways that handicap our development. We may also overemphasize its traits in ways that inadvertently frustrate us when we become too driven in our Saturnian expression. Life will require that we honestly analyze the pros and cons of this sign. There are obviously many things about it we dislike or feel uncomfortable with, especially when we perceive others applying these traits in a manner that feels controlling to us. There are also qualities of this sign that offer us much security, usually as a result of discipline and hard work. Very little about our Saturn sign comes to us easily, even when our natal Saturn forms several sextiles and trines. Saturn is in this particular sign because we have something here to pay close attention to in this incarnation. Life and karma will slowly let us know what that "something" is.

The intensity of our dislike, fear, or avoidance of our Saturn sign reveals the necessary degree of self-examination regarding its life themes. If some of us remain overly vulnerable to that sign's weaker points or blind spots, we could stunt our ego-growth and thus find ourselves having a difficult time fulfilling our solar potential. Saturn provides the ego (Sun) with protective structures it needs to manifest its essence. A faulty Saturnian structure interferes with our ability to become individualized, which in turn thwarts our Sun's optimum unfoldment. A mismanaged Saturn affects the Sun much like a blocked artery impairs the heart's healthy functioning. By openly and earnestly accepting our Saturn sign challenges with greater self-discipline and less anxiety, we can learn to operate beyond the restraining psychological rings of the Saturn principle within and free ourselves from the ego-bondage by which we have unwittingly limited ourselves. We then become better able to safely and directly experience the realms of transpersonal awareness natural to the Outer Planets (Uranus, Neptune, and Pluto).

It really doesn't help to bad-mouth the traits of our Saturn sign (such as hating Cancer's hypersensitivity or loathing Libra's indecisiveness). Many of the qualities we like least are nevertheless ingrained in our psyche. Maybe we only hate such traits because we don't do them as well as we know they can be done. Our Saturn sign shows us how we have to work hard to understand the meaning of that sign, and our challenge is to attempt to express the virtues of that sign consistently in our daily lives with a measure of self-reliance. Saturn's sign offers behavioral traits that can give us much inner security and stability; they help anchor us in the real world by guiding our material/career direction. No matter what that sign is, we will need to find practical outlets for its expression. Saturn will malfunction if we don't come up with workable solutions. We can ground ourselves by using psychological material from Saturn's sign. Escapist attitudes lead nowhere fast wherever our Saturn is natally. This sign is showing us how we can best get a grip on life. So be careful what you think about the traits of your Saturn sign. You need many of them very badly.

SATURN'S NATAL HOUSE

If our Saturn sign explains what we must learn and how, our Saturn house points us to where we most often need to target our developing awarenesses. This is the area in our life where we are to directly play out our Saturn energy. Our Saturn themes are also indirectly connected to houses with Capricorn (primarily so) and Aquarius (secondarily so) on the cusp (or intercepted in that house). For example, if your Saturn is in the Eleventh House, think of how its drives and urges relate to issues of Capricorn on the Fifth House cusp. These two houses are linked by more than just being polar opposites. Saturn affects the dynamics of both. Something in the Eleventh House teaches us to cope with matters of the Fifth House. If the Fifth House becomes our children, the awareness of a Saturn nature operating through the socially expansive atmosphere of the Eleventh House (a fairly impersonal house) influences how we view our kids, attempt to raise them, and even what we project onto them, which they then mirror back to us. In this case, we probably help our offspring feel responsibly involved in the larger social patterns of living; and so they may eventually wish to contribute something of social relevance, something progressive and humanitarian. When a child later goes on to win the Nobel Prize, we inwardly know we had something to do with promoting his or her special vision of the collective future. Of course, the sign Saturn falls in must be added to the picture. It can get pretty complex.

In our Saturn house, we meet the circumstantial consequences of our own ego insecurity. Long-standing vulnerabilities are typically found here. Yet this house also promises (to those who work at it) a tremendous amount of inner strength and outer self-assurance. This is often our "ugly duckling becomes beautiful swan" life sector where time and patience are on our side. Never give up on your Saturn house, for it gets better with age. This is an area where we can slowly but thoroughly build an enduring sense of who we are. We get to test our competence in honorable, worldly ways. Here is where we best ground ourselves in the necessities of mundane reality and social responsibility. We are challenged to apply our focused energies in a sensible, level-headed manner if we are to make the most of this house. Consistent, careful attention is required.

Our Saturn house deals with learning about appropriate structures that support meaningful growth. Whatever we build here is meant to be workable and stabilizing. This is an area where we cannot afford to remain unconscious of what we are doing, especially if we are already doing it badly. We cannot get away with leaving loose ends unattended, for this only results in chronic frustration. Saturn demands that we bring a measure of order and maturity to the affairs of this house—but it is imperative that we discipline ourselves without degenerating into patterns of rigidity and monotony (and that goes double for those of us with a fixed Saturn).

It's always good to remember the value of common sense when dealing with this life area. We need to give our Saturn house issues time to properly unfold. Things seem to happen slowly here. Situations typically involve delays, obstacles, postponements, and baffling reversals no matter how hard we try to get things off the ground. Why are we thwarted here so? While it appears that unfortunate outside circumstances are to blame, we are often the ones who inwardly conspire to block our intentions. If we try to escape from Saturn's life lessons due to our ignorance of their importance to our overall fulfillment, life puts protective hurdles in our path to prevent us from straying too far from what we ultimately need to accomplish. We try to weasel out of learning things here, but seemingly are roped back again and again.

Saturn thus plays more of a "guardian angel" role than we realize or appreciate, yet we often give it nothing but bad reviews until maybe around the second half of our lives—and hopefully by the time we get old enough to enjoy the "wisdom years" of our life and our hard-earned consciousness. Saturn makes more sense to us the older we get.

THREE
SATURN TYPES

SELF-INHIBITORS

We are into a "self-inhibitor" mode when we let ourselves get so intimidated by Saturn's implied limits that we never strive to overcome even ordinary obstacles in our path. We assume it will be too hard, too impossible, or too futile to try to accomplish such demanding Saturn tasks. We can easily tell ourselves and others that we are just not ready yet—so stop pushing and pressuring us! We let self-doubt rob us of the gumption to accomplish what is probably well within our grasp. Our Saturn muscles are puny and weak, and it shows, even though some of us are convinced our fearfulness is our own little secret. Our basic problem is more than surface shyness or a low-key personality.

A lot of us self-inhibitors get by doing the minimum and making sure we set up monotonous, unchallenging routines for ourselves. The more predictable our lives, the more we avoid surprises that could pressure us to change. Zip Dobyns and Maritha Pottenger have used the term "self-blocker"[1] to similarly describe some of these tactics (although these astrologers apply self-blocking to more chart factors than just

21

a mismanaged natal Saturn). We Saturn self-inhibitors do not relish being in the spotlight where others get to see how much we have to struggle to get what we want. Open competition is out of the question, unless we are operating under very controlled circumstances where nothing gets too much out of hand. A chess match might be acceptable, but forget mud wrestling! We are self-conscious about showing off our skills, which can lead to performance anxiety.

Because we don't take potentially advantageous risks when we could or should, we never get to know our true capacity to achieve. We impose restrictions on ourselves much too soon—and often needlessly. We reveal who we are with self-depreciating phrases like "Oops, there goes clumsy me again!" or "Now don't make fun of my singing (or whatever) or I won't even begin!" A fear of failure is obviously one reason we refuse to initiate a lot of things—we think we already know ahead of time what the results will be (even though self-inhibitors are not necessarily more psychic than anyone else). For whatever reason, we are just too sensitive to the potential judgment of others to be willing to make mistakes. Yet mistakes are often a natural consequence of trying to do something new and unfamiliar. We assume others will criticize us, but it's clear we are already much too self-critical and harsh in our self-judgment. We can project some of the worst traits of this planet onto others, but also save a lot of them for purposes of self-identification.

Self-inhibitors often fail because of a lack of effort or an unwillingness to have certain experiences associated with the sign or house in question. We just don't give the potentials indicated our best shot. A variation on this type is the self-inhibitor who tries and tries, but fails and fails. Some of us claim we just can't do anything right, that we are jinxed, or that the world is not giving us a fair chance. Everyone else is making things difficult for us and we are getting "no respect" at all. It's all their fault. We thus may quit trying altogether, and end up feeling frustrated and resentful regarding our Saturn areas and issues. Are we trying for all the wrong reasons? Are we doing things to please someone else (parental figures, perhaps)? Are we really even committed to the goal to begin with? If we self-blockers try to reach a goal and are denied, thwarted ambition is not so much the cause as is inner ambivalence about our direction. Subconsciously, we may not give ourselves full permission to succeed. We generally tend to hesitate and mull things over rather than act decisively. This can throw off optimum timing, which in turn can foil opportunities.

Sometimes we keep trying to do things by coming at them from the wrong angle. This will probably also guarantee not getting what we want. An example is Saturn in the Seventh House: We are afraid nobody will want to ever get close and intimate with us, so we reluctantly go to a friend's party not even looking our best. We sit in a corner, grip our drink and avoid eye contact. If we want to encourage a serious love relationship, is this the right approach? We are longing to meet the right person, but we may not make ourselves emotionally accessible once we have. It's the wrong technique—trying to "charm" people with our cool facade or using aloofness as a flirting strategy. But this realization is nothing to get defensive about. Changing our approach to getting whatever it is we want makes sense when our old ways of doing things do not work for us. Such change is good, and self-inhibitors must learn this.

The above gives you a feeling of what we self-inhibitors often do with our Saturn energy. However, it's too downbeat and alienating to operate in this mode forever, and sometimes we instead feel an urge to do what often comes easier for the next type—the "over-achievers." While self-inhibiting resembles mishandled mutable Saturn, over-achieving seems very much like mismanaged cardinal Saturn.

OVER-ACHIEVERS

What I am calling the over-achiever type is what Dobyns and Pottenger have referred to as the "overdriver."[2] They focus on many different factors that contribute to over-driving (even cultural ones that go beyond the chart). What makes us a qualified Saturn over-achiever is our refusal to look at life as a series of never-ending stumbling blocks. We feel very capable when meeting our Saturn challenges, and will attempt to plow through any obstacles. Put up a roadblock and watch us try to knock it down with all the force of our will and determination. Why waste time with self-defeating attitudes? This approach sounds a lot like Mars. However, Saturn is all about knowing our limits. Self-inhibitors may not know their limits, since they give up too soon to find out, but we over-achievers tend to ignore limits, or we push these so-called limits to see how far we can get, because ambition is very strong in us.

Active ambition sounds like a good thing until we realize that we are talking about Saturn ambition, which, when unchecked, can have a take-over quality. Hitler and Napoleon had great ambitions with their Saturns in the Tenth House, but they each took a conquerer's approach to fulfilling their appetite for control. The results made history. I'm not implying that we over-achievers are dictators at heart, but we do wish to dictate our own moves and are probably anti-authority (whereas self-inhibitors sometimes depend on authorities too much for direction). Breaking rules or acting unlawfully could result when some of us resist all forms of authority too blindly or stubbornly. We often learn the hard way that laws and limits imposed upon us by society are to be obeyed if we wish to remain reasonably autonomous. Saturn in over-achiever mode can also suggest we can be very task-focused and driven in reaching our goals. We don't necessarily seek short-cuts, because we have the stamina and determination to plod on until victory is ours. Still, we are likely to be impatient. When we don't get results as quickly as anticipated, we could feel very frustrated and anxious.

We over-achievers overdo Saturn's more assertive qualities. Saturn can work hard, but over-achievers can overwork (while self-inhibitors can't get organized momentum and thus tend to put things on hold). We need to realize that too much work and no play can be stress-producing. It's no big surprise that over-achievers can get a lot done in short periods of time, because they know how to effectively focus and utilize their time. Super-efficiency may be a common trait, but in our attempt to manage everything we could exhaust ourselves and eventually burn out. Saturn means work and productivity, but it also means high quality rest and stillness. Signs that are more prone to support over-achiever behavior than others when it comes to "busyness" are Aries, Virgo, Capricorn and obsessive, indefatigable Scorpio.

One thing we typically don't do is over-obligate ourselves to others, since that could slow us down with a pile of commitments (although signs like Cancer, Virgo, or Pisces might feel a high degree of responsibility when serving the needs of others). In general, we try to do things that keep us from getting stuck in ruts. Saturn over-achievers can be highly self-sufficient. We'd rather take charge than wait for others to get the ball rolling or depend on them to get the job done (again, very cardinal-sounding). Some of us start showing our best Saturn attributes at an early age—we are not late bloomers, but early risers. Not easily satisfied with just attaining our immediate goals, we are always moving on to bigger and more challenging ones. The problem is that this can put too much pressure on us to be competent in everything we tackle. When do we get a chance to enjoy what we've already accomplished?

Over-achiever Saturn also displays some less attractive traits. Reasonable management of people and situations becomes oppressive control. Normal concerns for safety become paralyzing fears. Fair judgment becomes harsh condemnation. Healthy skepticism becomes outright cynicism. These are examples of more Saturn than is necessary to satisfy a need. It is hard to imagine how we could be happy and content behaving like this, since we sound quite uptight and tension-riddled. It seems that operating somewhere between the self-inhibitor and the over-achiever modes would be our best bet for a workable, balanced life. I call those who achieve this equilibrium the "moderates."

MODERATES

Saturn believes moderation in all things holds the key to true success in life. We learn to find a proper time and place for all our needs, not just those few we fixate on. We moderates learn at different life stages to balance our energies with just the right amount of work and rest, work and play, give and take, etc. A clue to this ability is shown by our natal Saturn sextiles (if we have any). The sextile aspect feels stimulated to learn new things and try out several options available. It is open to suggestion. Sextiled Saturn keenly observes what has worked before, what can work now, and what has not and never will work properly by watching others strive and struggle. The typical strategy of the sextile is to let others first get the energy going and then decide if it will participate in or duplicate the experience. Sextiles are not driven to act, they just prefer to do so when they sense an opportunity at hand that will involve nothing too laborious. Saturn sextiles feel that there is a way around any barrier that blocks its path.

I'm not sure if any of us are allowed to jump right into moderation mode soon after our birth. This is something we must slowly and thoughtfully cultivate. The path of the moderate is a wisdom path, and will not come without first experiencing the contrasts of self-inhibiting and over-achieving. Plus we have all those authority figures to psychologically process in our early years before we can even get a glimpse of the power of our own inner authority. For many of us, it takes a mid-life crisis to get all this to kick in, so I'm assuming that we moderates are older but wiser people. Our feet are firmly planted on the ground, yet we are open to expansive but realistic ideals. We feel we have a future worth living. We also are grateful we have learned from our past mistakes, seeing them as necessary stepping stones. We know we are not perfect, but we no longer make reaching such a state of perfection our ultimate goal.

A secret to our success lies in our ability to realistically know when to be self-reliant and do something by ourselves and when to trust the expertise of others and allow people to help us. We learn that when we put the burden of doing everything on our own shoulders we overtax our energies and can run a greater risk of not succeeding. We also learn to work effectively with others without unduly leaning on them. This is a juggling act that can take years to master for those of us who've been addicted to self-inhibiting or over-achieving.

Now, in the real world beyond the shores of theoretical astrology, people are not as neatly divided into the above three camps. We have some Saturn experiences where we take the self-inhibiting route. Whether due to unresolved childhood hang-ups or some other reason, we still freeze in our tracks and fail to meet these issues head on (maybe we are afraid to dance in public). Yet we also have shown the world how good we are at over-achieving. In those areas where we have always felt competent and confident, we have accomplished things that have gotten other people's attention and praise (even though we still won't dance in public, we win the Pulitzer Prize after years of hard work in journalism). On the job, we can walk in the office with the worried frown of a self-inhibitor one day and the beaming smile of an over-achiever the next. (It might depend on what assignments the boss has asked us to do that week.) A few of us have learned the ropes early on, enabling us to play the moderate sooner than others. Learning from our mistakes and not blaming others for our shortcomings can speed up this process.

Anyway, please use all this as a guideline for interpreting Saturn behavior. Squares and oppositions are not automatically the red flags of a self-blocker (study the charts of the truly great in history and see). And trines or sextiles may not offer enough push to help us accomplish at the pace of an over-achiever. The chart alone can't tell us all this. Real people's life decisions can.

Chapter Four Endnotes

1. Maritha Pottenger, *Complete Horoscope Interpretation,* ACS Publications, Inc., San Diego, CA., 1986, p. 473.
2. Ibid., p. 474.

CHAPTER FIVE

OUR SATURN TRANSIT

Saturn's purpose by transit is to pressure us to fix what is broken, to attend to what we've long neglected, to restore order to whatever has become chaotic or out of control, and to reclaim what is intrinsically valuable to our core development. It also insists we let go of anything or anybody that unduly weighs us down or thwarts our ongoing growth. Saturn is one of our "terminator" planets (Pluto is the other). It undertakes to rid us of all impeding non-essentials, uncluttering and simplifying our lives.

Saturn offers us the chance to know when and why things we've outgrown must come to an end. We mature by recognizing those specific relationships and conditions in our life that have become unworkable. To reduce further pain and frustration, we need to allow such matters to come to a well-defined close. Saturn assures us that this can be done with a measure of level-headed resolve on our part, based on a pragmatic assessment of the issues.

Patience is always required, while a stubborn refusal to allow for needed change is to be avoided. The Saturn principle is a fair and even-handed one (traditionally symbolized by its exaltation in Libra). It will work with us no matter how deep a self-created hole we find ourselves in, but we need to commit to the required tasks at hand without looking for escape hatches, lapsing into long stretches of denial, or projecting blame onto others.

Saturn transiting a natal planet or house represents a timely opportunity to take stock of ourselves by carefully weighing the pros and cons of any course of action we have undertaken. Saturn will reward us in small but steady ways for our solid, well-grounded efforts to wisely structure our goals, particularly long-range ones. Saturn phases, when well managed, can help us preserve or restore "sanity" and usher in a welcomed measure of continuity to our lives. They help us get back on track.

Its tempo may appear a tad dull and predictable at times, but getting on the good side of a Saturn transit also means not having "the bottom falling out" in our lives. We're not hit with out-of-the-blue jolts that disorient our steadier rhythms. Even when problems arise, nothing is really sprung on us at the last minute with this planet. Problems we become mired in have slowly taken root long before our present state of frustration or fear.

Fear can indeed be a vivid Saturn reality, but so can a sense of wasted time, regret, and shame. Difficult Saturn transits can suggest a period when we are thin-skinned and very sensitive to criticism and judgment. We half-expect to be scolded or rejected for revealing any of our shortcomings, and we often attempt to hide our feelings of failure by wearing a suit of psychological armor or by staying clear of people and intimate situations altogether.

It is often true that we may be or at least feel alone during our pivotal Saturn transits (Saturn/Moon and Saturn/Venus phases invite such solitude and reflection), but this doesn't have to feel like loneliness. Think of it as an opportune time to carefully measure our degree of self-sufficiency and willingness to better focus on our own self-contained consciousness for a while. We will probably feel separate and apart from the frenetic world around us, but this is quite appropriate.

Quietness is important for Saturn to do its best magic, and solitude is one way to achieve such stillness. This could be a well-needed period of rest and repose for those of us who are approaching burn-out, so we should appreciate this slower phase and curb any inclination to fritter away our energies on superficial, non-productive matters.

Saturn transits often call for a review of our work attitudes and our material ambitions (or the lack thereof). Are we on the right track professionally? Are we on *any* realistic track, or are we just floundering in an anxious but aimless manner? Saturn terminates by putting the brakes on our ability to muck up our affairs with unexamined self-destructive impulses (those Plutonian/Neptunian demons within). It hits us with an attack of clarity, which may not always make us feel at ease or secure.

Saturn loves to take over what is malfunctioning. Perhaps with a little help from Uranus or Pluto, it assists us in getting fired from dead-end jobs, ending estranged or love-starved marriages, or even halting body-destroying habits by creating serious health "scares." We can expect certain elements of ourselves or our environment to go on strike and refuse to feed illusionary pursuits or stagnating conditions. If we choose not to cooperate, situations force us to bring such matters to a halt. Sometimes authorities step into the picture and take control over our disorganized circumstances. Things needing final closure can "up and die" on us, even if we do not recognize the importance of ending such experiences.

Saturn seeks to grow deep, strong roots and build fortified structures that insulate our strengths rather than trap our inner weaknesses. Successfully surviving a potent Saturn transit means consolidating all those parts of our being that are durable enough to withstand the future. We weed out the sabotaging facets of our psyche. We restore order and purpose to our life direction. We are mercifully cut off from the power of destructive attachments to our past, and this alone may require time for healing (wound-covering scabs are ruled by Saturn) and for a slow rebuilding of healthier new patterns.

The outcome can be an authentic awareness of who we really are at this point, and a concrete sense of where we are really meant to go. Saturn will slowly continue to aspect our natal planets or visit our houses to assess any damage we have incurred. What we have already gained from its past cycles will become the effective life-tools we can use with conviction. While Saturn's wisdom seems to come from attending classes in the school of hard knocks, we end up feeling content knowing we've earned self-respect plus the deserved honor of others in the process.

SATURN IN ARIES

THRUSTERS ON HOLD

Aries' energetic theme of outward push and forward drive can coordinate well with Saturn's organizational power and executive ability. One result is an alert and ready sense of purposeful enterprise. The natural initiative of Aries is combined with an extra measure of common sense and long-range planning strategy. All our new endeavors thus have a better chance at productive outcomes, but we must feel ourselves to be in the driver's seat rather than steered by others.

This may be one of the few Aries' placements less plagued by impulsiveness, hasty action, or short-lived self-interest. Staying power is not an innate Aries quality, but Saturn can provide a degree of steadfastness and concentration atypical of this hyperactive, often impatient sign if we consciously apply a measure of self-control, discipline, and patience. Saturn is telling Aries to slow down its life process to the point where assertive action becomes workable, putting our thrusting power on hold until we learn to effectively cooperate with the process. Aries also teaches Saturn to meet life head on without the fears or anxieties common to this planet.

The essential method of cardinal Aries is the vigorous expenditure of raw energy in an attempt to move out into life while remaining unhampered by any external conditions. Aries desires complete freedom to act on its spontaneous, self-generated desires and impulses—often without concern for the consequences of its actions. It is not motivated to accept responsibility for itself. In this regard, Aries is glaringly at odds with the basic principles of conscientious, dutiful Saturn. Saturn's cautious nature vastly contrasts this impetuous sign of new starts, unplanned beginnings, and immediate self-willed response.

No Boss Needed

Saturn's ambitious, self-striving qualities are favorably evoked due to the forward momentum of headstrong, challenge-ready Aries. This sign can provide uncertain, hesitant Saturn with just the right amount of personal courage and pioneering spirit. Aries' added degree of self-reliance and dynamic vitality helps us take immediate advantage of here-and-now opportunities. We can thus accomplish our more serious objectives through direct, unambiguous action. Aries offers a helpful dose of fire to encourage doubtful Saturn to adopt a positive, optimistic outlook based on an open acceptance of self-interest (Saturn normally has a problem perceiving itself as selfish). Aries thus conditions denial-prone Saturn to be straightforward regarding its objectives, rather than to mask its true intentions. Aries may help reduce the guilt factor in Saturn.

Both Saturn and Aries suggest we want to feel independent from the control of outside authority. We may have a fundamental "anti-boss" attitude. No person or social system is to unconditionally rule and regulate us. Perhaps this comes more so from our Aries side than our Saturn urge. Still, as both planet and sign are self-contained and self-motivated, we typically dislike being ordered around by the "powers that be." We do not want to be controlled by any kind of Daddy-figure types.

We do better when launching a project, enterprise, or a business on our own instead of having to kowtow to head honchos in conservative, established companies where all the protocols are clearly spelled out and are not to be ignored. This would feel very confining and may eventually arouse degrees of hostility within us, and a clash with the Boss or the Board is likely. In fact, we are at odds with society's laws in general. We may not deliberately break laws, but we probably abide by them grudgingly when they seem to impede our interests. When they block our impulsive, strong-willed attempts to "do our thing," we become determined to defend our autonomy against authoritative control.

LONE WOLFISM

Saturn in Aries teaches us to attempt to properly harness and manage much of the raw energy within ourselves before we begin to focus attention on the environment. With such a highly personalized orientation, we might feel awkward and hypersensitive about how we project ourselves until proper inner integration is achieved. We are to learn to become less fearful (Saturn) about acting out our vital, subjective impulses (Aries). Otherwise, inhibitions gain the upper hand. Once we recognize even having such desires, we are in a better position to eventually find appropriate ways to maturely fulfill them. Denial of these impulses keeps them beyond our conscious control and blocks their expression.

Both Saturn and Aries share a common need to do things solo, without interference. The concept of sharing is not as well developed. The natural inclination is to wing it alone, tap into our own abilities, and do whatever it takes to avoid other people's intrusion in our space. This can be one of Saturn's strongest positions when it comes to pure survival ability. We believe that we can do a lot of things by ourselves. We don't easily run with the pack. Regardless of pressing circumstances, we can concentrate on being who we are in a forthright, no-excuse manner, since deep inside may lie a

solid core of steely individualism, well fortified from the
indoctrinations of mass socialization. But this attitude sometimes makes us seem standoffish and can prove alienating, so
we may end up feeling cut off from others on some level.

TRUSTING THE NOW

Aries urges Saturn to act in the now from a point of pure innocence mixed with primal urgency. This is difficult for Saturn
the strategist, who cannot help but become anxious about the
often unpredictable results of impetuous action. Although
Saturn insists on guarantees of safety and security before initiating action, such surety is impossible when the Aries principle is involved. This is actually a good thing, because always
playing it safe doesn't get us in touch with our true grit. We
need to overcome our fears and self-doubts and develop the
internal strength and conviction required to bravely face up to
the world's challenges. Then we can test the choppy waters
while staying afloat.

Aries is a sign associated with our developing self-image.
Saturn in Aries implies a well-defined, well-preserved identity
that provides the security we need to keep from feeling overly
threatened and vulnerable. This positive sense of identity
ensures the protective psychological buffer we seek. But herein
lies a major problem for some of us with Saturn in Aries—
struggling with a weak and negative self-concept that stifles
spontaneous personal expression in the early years of life.

SLOW STARTER

Having Saturn in Aries often means we may undergo many
personal limitations early in life, and this can cause us to feel
acutely inadequate or unsure of ourselves. Obstacles may
occur that squelch our immediate desires or our will while
growing up. We may rigidly pit ourselves against perfectionist
(Saturn) standards of conduct and behavior that are too strenuous and confining for us to live up to. This can result in a

sense of constant personal frustration and disappointment. Self-resentment due to our failings may also become an issue.

Should we adopt an inflexible or overly self-conscious approach, we are apt to be too harsh with ourselves concerning our apparent deficiencies. (Saturn in Virgo seems to have a similar problem, although without the fiery inner clashes, struggles, and battles Aries stirs up.) Perhaps we were raised by a demanding, unyielding authority figure (not always our father, the traditional Saturn parent) who treated us harshly or with cold indifference, effectively invalidating who we were. As a result, we may not be very supportive or nurturing of ourselves, and (with egocentric Aries involved) we may become too wrapped up and absorbed with such early negative impressions to be able to take an objective look within. While we might feel defenseless against apparent outside threats to our identity, we may also defensively compensate by assuming a guarded, impenetrable, chip-on-the-shoulder attitude toward the world and everyone who dares to confront us. We may try to shield ourselves from feeling inner frustrations by adopting an uncaring, hard-nosed disposition, making us appear anything but vulnerable to others, and may aggressively shut others out of our life or at least keep folks at a safe and controllable distance. Accordingly, intimacy can become difficult to achieve (similar to Saturn in the First House, especially when conjunct the ASC).

ATTACK MODE

We can also project authoritarian traits on our immediate environment, and then forcefully attempt to defend ourselves against what we perceive as hostility, antagonism, or power plays (especially if Saturn is under a stress aspect from either Mars or Pluto). The self-preservation instincts of Saturn combined with the militant force of Aries impels us to strike first before the assumed opposition can get an upper hand and overwhelm us. Unfortunately, once we have succeeded in pushing supportive people away by our actions, our frustration might incline us to turn back against ourselves. Thus, self-defeatism can be one of the pitfalls of this Saturn placement. Mismanaged Saturn in Aries can also manifest as a dilemma in which we withdraw from accepting any assertive challenges. Some self-inhibitors may manifest an almost conspicuous display of meekness, timidity, and self-effacement. We have allowed forces in our environment to dominate us—yet underneath our seemingly calm and passive exterior may dwell deep seething anger and even physically violent tendencies.

AGAINST ALL ODDS

Planets in Aries function better when their energies are thrust out towards the world and challenged, rather than inhibited and shielded from confrontation. Saturn in Aries enables us to energetically operate from responsible positions with self-reliance. The driving force of bold Aries plus the stamina of ambitious Saturn keeps us from giving up, giving out, or being sidetracked in our goals. We have the will to overcome all odds and succeed at any cost. Sometimes the ends justify the means for us. Sometimes it's how tough we play the game that counts. Still, it is best that we draw on the wisdom of Saturn to sensibly direct our strengths.

Saturn characteristically seeks, in an unhurried manner, a thorough understanding of whatever it concentrates its attention on. It wants to go beyond the superficial and focus on the relevant and essential. Thus, we need to take a serious, in-depth look at ourselves and steadily work at structuring a self-image that we can truly respect and feel fortified by. This allows us to exercise the vibrant power of our being in a masterful manner. Our presence can then naturally command, not defensively demand, recognition from others who genuinely admire our inner strengths. Proper self-discipline rather than rigid self-control will allow us to earn such stature. By adopting a positive attitude concerning our urge to act and our will to do, we also become more ready to accept the consequences of our actions with greater courage. As we no longer intimidate ourselves in this regard, we find we are less directly stymied in our actions by conditions in the outer world.

A WILL TO SURVIVE

When well integrated, Saturn in Aries suggests we can energize people with the power of our self-sufficiency. We can be role models for those who feel too scared to stand up for themselves during critical periods in their lives. We are survivors, not quitters. When the going gets tough, we get even tougher. But we also learn to feel secure with our ability to bring spontaneous warmth (Aries) into any life situation. We no longer subvert our passion for living. As much of our Ariesness has been held back for many years, we may now discover we can direct our fire wholeheartedly and positively towards people. Saturn in Aries teaches us to share our strengths rather than use them as weapons. Saturn urges us to bring out the most excellent qualities of the sign it is in. In Aries, it instills the positive facets of self-focus, action, and direct movement toward immediate and long-range goals. The challenge to initiate becomes something we master rather than dread.

Astro-lebrities with Saturn in Aries

George Washington   Lee Harvey Oswald
Ulysses S. Grant   Helen Keller
Isadora Duncan   Mary Baker Eddy
Joseph Stalin   Julia Roberts
Bette Davis   Grace Slick

SATURN IN THE FIRST HOUSE

BE HERE NOW?

The closer Saturn is to the ASC, the more it suggests we may start off in life with an uncomfortable self-image. An unchildlike uptightness is suggested. We have learned at a very tender age to hold back from taking spontaneous action due to basic insecurities about ourselves. Our instinct is to hesitate rather than self-assuredly mobilize our energies. Cautiousness and an air of reserve are often evident in our youth, reflecting an apparent degree of maturity in at least some of us. But because we naturally consider the consequences of our actions before initiating them, we readily keep most impulses in check. We at least are able to wait until we can calculate a better sense of timing before attempting to fulfill our urges. We seldom assertively or boldly move out into our environment. Patient restraint and a wait-and-see attitude are typical ways we face life.

Some astrologers suggest our circumspect disposition was linked to a difficult birth. Maybe some of us with Saturn in the First House were indeed reluctant to be born, thus making the birth process laborious. Perhaps our soul somehow felt it was not ready to incarnate—a stage fright of sorts. While astrologers cannot easily explain why any soul would think it was not ready to emerge into the world, the sign Saturn inhabits may give us a few clues.

It's My Karma & I'll Cry If...

Karmic astrologers would perhaps speculate that our resistance to be born could be in direct reaction to past life body trauma, severe abuse, or even torture. Imagine if you were burned at the stake for whatever sick reason by a jeering mob of half-wits; would you willingly want to make another debut into this potentially threatening, cruel world? At the least, Saturn near the ASC suggests we might have been personally subjugated to physical restraint or confinement of some sort. For some reason, we probably suffered in the hands of authority by trying to simply be ourselves and follow our impassioned impulses.

Those interested in exploring former incarnations by analyzing Saturn's natal position should read Jeanne Avery's

Astrology And Your Past Lives.[1] Granted, many were con-fined in the past in varying degrees for a wide range of rea-sons. Such past life experiences related to Saturn in the First House could now manifest as an obstacle to the devel-opment of a secure sense of identity and self-will in action. Our uncertainty about re-entering this world results in a ponderous, guarded nature. We observe our surroundings from a safe psychological distance. We may even tend to frown a lot. Since the First House deals with our body lan-guage, we may hold a lot of tightness in our physical frame, making us look stiff.

My Body Blues

Our physical appearance is usually a sensitive issue. We don't seem to feel at home with our shape, size, or overall structure. Saturn traditionally symbolizes that which is slim, slender, thin, reed-like, under-abundant, or downright skinny. Those of us who fit this description have unconsciously been bought into the Saturn archetype quite literally. Yet there also are some of us here who struggle with chronic obesity: the dilemma implied here is quite complex.

Self-loathing may actually have nothing to do with why we are overweight. Most likely, a heavy individual with a First House Saturn is psychologically using excess weight as a way to create symbolic insulation from a potentially harm-ful, unkind world. The extra fat in this instance becomes a ready defense against pain and rejection. Ironically, we are further judged negatively for such a physique. Society assumes we have gotten so heavy because we really don't care about ourselves, otherwise why have we allowed our-selves to balloon to such a degree? As the social environment continues to dump on us, we put on more pounds, and the vicious cycle continues.

Whether too fat or too skinny, our outward disposition is rarely vibrant or brimming with liveliness. We may rarely be physically animated, since Saturn can impose a body heaviness (not to be confused with weight) as if we were very much operating under the laws of gravity. Some of us may attempt to resist the pull of gravity by training our body to go beyond average physical limits and restrictions, perhaps by participating in ballet or weightlifting. Graceful lightness or imposing strength thus become physical ideals to aspire toward. Realize that planet Saturn in the sky is gaseous and that it could float upon water if the Earth had a large enough ocean. Sadly enough, it is human ignorance that creates undue Saturnian weightiness in our psyche. We often make Saturn heavier in temperament than need be.

HAPPY FACE?

Due to Saturn's expert talent for self-inhibiting, some of us do appear to be light, vivacious, and even superficial on the personality level—so much so that astrologers are tempted to immediately rectify our natal chart (I'm half-joking here). We can act chipper, as if we do not have a care in the world. Maybe those of us here who express ourselves with an uncommon sense of flair and pizzazz are really trying to distract critical observers from detecting just how much we inwardly feel instead like unlovable loners. It's just that we do not want people to realize we can actually be too easily hurt and made to feel unworthy. To avoid public judgment, we try very hard to appeal to and gain approval from anybody and everybody. This becomes our best defense against personal attack. We normally think of Neptune as having chameleon-like qualities. But apparently so does Saturn when under an intense pressure to fit in and be accepted. Remember this when you meet someone with a First House Saturn who instead behaves like a person with Venus or Jupiter rising in a fire or air sign.

UPHILL CLIMBING

Because we often perceive the harshness of life's uncompromising realities very personally and directly, we tend to feel it's all a big struggle to even exist. We may also make things harder for ourselves by going down more difficult paths to begin with. Yet maybe in the process we discover we have a keenly ambitious drive to handle adversity and eventually achieve more than was ever expected of us. We have had to continuously meet up against many forms of authoritative backlash—from father to boss to our own rigid sense of inner authority. This can be a hardy placement for Saturn, once thin-skinned hypersensitivity has been replaced with unflinching determination and confident self-clarity. Although our actions appear level-headed, we seem to want to prove our inner strength by putting ourselves in situations where we have a chance to mow down obstacles and overcome hurdles.

STILL HURTING

Our childhood years were seldom free from inhibiting factors. We most likely attracted at least one parent who presented authority to us in a fear-provoking manner. Feelings of personal inadequacy were typically due to some early deprivation. Economics may or may not play a role here (Saturn has traditionally been associated with poverty and physical want), but a greater sense of lack can revolve around the matter of not receiving sufficient personal attention. We may have been ignored too much and not held or comforted enough.

We might grow up much too sensitive to criticism, rejection, or neglect from others (whether real or imagined). We probably also were affected by adult power and its abuse. At least one of our parents (daddy?) was apparently good at showing us all about wielding power at the social level. Authoritarian control, or at least a general strictness, was probably applied to us at too young an age. Whatever the scenario, we eventually learned to become vulnerable to coldness, indifference, or a lack of sympathy from others—especially from those who become our replacement authority figures during our adult years. Such surrogate parental types can be our coach, our doctor, our therapist, our business mentor, our employer, even our judge should we have our day in court.

How Do I Look?

Perhaps we have been made to feel like ugly ducklings while growing up. We could have a lot going for us, but still can get hung up on our appearance. Self-criticism regarding our looks can become a huge roadblock. Our assumption that we are basically unattractive can leave us feeling awkward and undesirable when making physical/sexual contact with others. Some of us may even downplay our physical attributes and shun direct attention from admirers. Lavish praise and enthused compliments can make us feel uneasy. Do we really want to endure an entire life span looking frumpy or even unkempt? Saturn in the First House means our outer packaging can, although functional, be much too plain, like the dull label on a generic product in the supermarket. Maybe we need to hang out with a few Neptunians, who know an imaginative thing or two about make-over magic.

Big Chill

Should our self-concept remain weak and unclear, we may exhibit self-doubt concerning our ability to both give and receive warmth, closeness, intimacy, and basic human connection. Our fear of disapproval may force us to assume a guarded appearance. We become skillful at covering up our wounded inner nature. On the surface, we may appear aloof and independent. This is a guise that can often work well in the professional zone, where we appear to have it all together as a self-made person. But we also need to review ourselves and determine whether or not we physically give off the (mis)impression that we are cool, composed, and a tad too unfriendly to get to know well. Maybe some of us really are indeed this way all the time. But the rest of us can be someone quite different deep inside. It is our self-uncertainty that makes us mistrust the intentions of others. We must learn that we live in a world that is not seeking to put us down or demean us, and that there are supportive people out there who can bolster our identity in life-affirming ways.

Getting to know us will probably take time. Once people attempt to go beyond our sometimes chilly facade—which can be intimidating at first encounter—they might just discover that we have a lot of depth. We give thoughtful consideration to others and want the same in return. However, we do seem to have a hard time allowing people to penetrate our personality. Those barricades we psychologically construct around us work against us by further increasing our sense of isolation. They will need to be broken down by the power of intimate relationships. One good thing astrologers love to say about Saturn, because it rings true, is that "Saturn gets better with age." All is not lost. We simply need those vital lessons only maturity can provide. We with Saturn in the First House need to keep this is mind.

WHO'S IN CHARGE HERE?

One of the attributes of Saturn in the First House is the ability through sustained effort to convert a frustrated sense of self-will into a more effective sense of self-mastery. We have the strength to transform ourselves into very capable, very adept individuals who can control and manage life quite well. Our inborn sense of orderliness and purposefulness enables us to keep our life active yet stable and productive. When well managed, this Saturn denotes we can begin new projects with more sure-footedness and single-mindedness than most. We are inclined to evaluate all realistic limits involved and make necessary adjustments before or after we've started our project. Our ASC's sign takes on more power with Saturn placed in the First House, even if that sign is not the same as Saturn's. The ASC sign has the responsibility of channeling Saturn's energy out into external experiences, and tends to mature and deepen in its expression as a result.

We are likely to feel more competent regarding worldly matters as we get older. We can become quite solid and grounded as we unfold ourselves and trust spontaneity. We learn to deal with the consequences of our actions courageously. Inner fortification can become well developed in our old age. The key to much of this is learning not to become so crystallized and brittle that making changes becomes a painful ordeal for us. Keeping flexible attitudes and assumptions about life is the key. We need to continuously moisturize our consciousness with a sense of hope and faith, believing that our rut-bound patterns can always be modified, and that it's never too late to inaugurate new beginnings. The reward of a well-handled Saturn in the First House is a well-defined, workable sense of individuality. We can resiliently cope with whatever life presents to us. We can have a lasting feeling of inner security and the satisfying sense that our life is truly significant.

Astro-lebrities with Saturn in the First House

Mary Shelley	John Lennon
Nikolai Lenin	Edward Kennedy
Johnny Carson	Princess Diana
Cher	Henry David Thoreau
Fred Astaire	Karl Marx

SATURN/MARS ASPECTS

NATAL

Mars and Saturn seem to be planets with very different agendas. Fiery Mars is self-willed with highly personal desires to fulfill, while Saturn is a social planet (society-oriented, that is—not gregarious) with a strong sense of duty and responsibility for more than just itself. Saturn doesn't satisfy its personal needs easily due to feelings of guilt or undeservingness. Mars simply rushes in and grabs what it wants: I see, I desire, I get. Mars takes a very direct route while Saturn holds back and rationalizes why it probably will not be able to have what it wants, at least not without struggling or playing the waiting game. It can even talk itself out of wanting anything that may initially be a vigorous challenge to get. Inhibition is seldom a Mars problem, but Saturn is reluctant to expose its desires as openly and boldly. So what do these planets have in common?

Both underscore the drive to act in a self-sufficient manner, without support from others. Both can show the determination to persist in the face of opposition. Both can be tough, with strong survival abilities. We with Saturn aspecting Mars seem to be focused on testing the limits of our own strengths while also sometimes being thwarted by the strengths of our own limits. Mars fuels whatever planet it contacts, for better or worse, so Saturn's less attractive traits can also be energized and made more problematic.

But in general, Saturn is the one trying to temper our Mars potential so that it becomes a workable force for practical activity. Mars has energy to burn but needs sensible channeling to vent its aggressive power. Saturn attempts to control how our Mars will act out its passions. We may first have to deal with the many contrasting themes shared between these planets.

Saturn-based fear can block much of the typical sense of courage and daring natural to Mars. Fear of failure as well as fear of success become issues. We may be afraid not only to act for ourselves and meet challenges, but also may find that others can attempt to dominate and take charge over what we do and how we do it. Identifying more with Saturn means we repress the instinctive Mars drive to destroy the "enemy" who dares to outwardly overpower us, but this passive approach ends up in bitter resentment and grudge-holding instead of a confrontational face-off. Not being able or willing to act upon our inner impulses, we slowly seethe. We need to look at life's challenges as situations we can handle, given enough time and experience, rather than as threatening and overwhelming. Resisting the testing of our capabilities through such challenges only blocks our growth in the long run.

If we identify more with feisty Mars and are actively willing to express its needs, any fear of being opposed can lead to open combat against the control tactics imposed by others or society at large. Great inner fortitude is denoted, because we have the gumption to stand by our convictions and hold our ground in life. We just need to make sure we are not being too defensive and intractable in our stance. Defying needed restraints can create conflicts that have long-term detrimental consequences, depending on how much we are willing to break laws (including the internal law of our conscience) in order to do what we want. Trouble with authority leading to confinement or penalties is commonly noted with mismanaged Saturn/Mars aspects. A struggle with structuring a sense of inner authority can also ensue. Life is teaching us to fend for ourselves while not over-stepping legal boundaries.

Competition is not something we lightly engage in. Saturn is a sore loser, and not winning after expending a lot of energy can make Mars see red. We either play the game of winning much too seriously and cannot appreciate the healthy spirit of competitive interplay, or we refuse to play at all and avoid pitting our skills against someone whose performance may outshine our own—or we work hard to reach our ambitions until we near the point where we might succeed, only to give up and drop out of the race. Mars may start with great enthusiasm, but Saturn "chokes" before the goal is completed. This observation is particularly true with squares and oppositions. When it comes to success, we can sabotage ourselves by denying our need to be on top and in charge. Much self-examination is needed here to determine why we do not give ourselves permission to conquer, to win, to feel victorious, or to finish whatever projects we have initiated.

Of course, if the over-achieving side of both planets is operating, then Saturn/Mars comes on like a bulldozer, trying to flatten any and all opposing forces. Ambition becomes mixed with anger or control with violence. We can become a formidable powerhouse with a single-minded desire to have our way. Don't forget, Hitler had his Saturn square his Mars and was capable of a maniacal sense of purpose. Such a Saturn/Mars manner of expression suggests a bully who picks on the weak to prove his or her supposed strength but is too insecure to pick on someone equal or greater in power. Most of us could probably use this energy to help us not give in to fear or weakness, and to instead demonstrate our (often physical) ability to undergo difficult feats of endurance. I would imagine many Olympic athletes have Saturn/Mars or other Saturn/Principle One themes in their charts.

Any Saturn/Mars aspect means we can work long and hard on a project or job, although we need to make sure that our efforts are not too mentally strenuous or physically taxing. These planets are not good at relaxing or taking it easy—their driven natures makes them push too intensely. We can accomplish a lot with Saturn/Mars aspects, assuming we are disciplined, clear about our direction, and aware of sensible limits. Well handled, Mars energy gives Saturn the guts and boldness to fight off fear and self-doubt. Mars urges Saturn to take decisive action rather than stall or delay. This aspect becomes a highly organized, purposeful power source for those of us who allow the structuring side of Saturn to best manage the martial impulses of Mars through sustained application, the acceptance of routine, and a realistic understanding of how much can be accomplished.

TRANSIT

A Saturn/Mars transit can denote a period when we need to take a thoughtful look at how we have been acting or not acting on life issues up to this point. Saturn by transit tests how well any planet in question is serving our current needs (actually, how we are internally processing what that planet symbolizes regarding our self-awareness). Saturn will either attempt to give that planet a needed tune-up or will shut down those planetary facets that are no longer working for us. We have the option to repair something here if that is within the realm of realism. Otherwise, the unhealthy parts of the natal planet are to be thrown out of our consciousness once and for all. Saturn and Pluto both serve as trash collectors of the psyche. Saturn usually gives fair warning that something is malfunctioning, since we can see signs of it way before we are forced to deal with the matter. Pluto is more intense and overwhelming, like a sudden avalanche that releases tremendous forces of destruction. Such Plutonian periods of high drama during our life span are few. Saturn, however, makes us take out the trash more regularly.

With Mars, this Saturn transit puts pressure on our need to take action based on exclusive self-interest. If we've been overdoing our Mars side and making rash moves that are uncontrollably impulsive or too fitful to manage, Saturn slows us down or denies us mobility at some level. We can feel stuck, as if "put in our place" by unsympathetic forces that deny us autonomy.

Such "stuckness" can mean breaking a leg (maybe we should have taken more lessons before attempting to ski down that big hill) or even having problems with the brakes in our car (and now we can't hop into our auto and whiz around like we used to until we can afford the costly repair job). Saturn aspecting Mars is this case makes us feel slightly punished, as if "grounded" by the Cosmos. Yet when we are forced to slow down and move about less, we can attend to other life issues we have ignored. Rather than feel trapped in our home (with no car and a bum leg), we need to clean closets, or go from room to room organizing our space-hogging junk and planning to unload it (have a yard sale). Maybe we also can put quality time/energy into relating more to others in our household.

There are innumerable scenarios showing the dynamic of transiting Saturn to natal Mars, but it's more important to get in touch with the underlying principles than to try to predict the outer situations. Realize that we are now pressured to find better ways to do things, with an emphasized focus on finishing up worthwhile matters rather than starting new projects of unknown value. It's not that we can't succeed with new ventures, it's just that we had better do our homework first and carefully weigh the pros and cons of taking action now. Any delays are instructive in that they imply a better timetable awaits us in the future. Why fish when it's low tide? asks Saturn. This transit can be a great period to tie up loose ends and put a stop to time-wasting procrastination. We must act, but with a structured sense of order and planning.

Mars deals with how we vent anger and other turbulent passions like jealousy. Saturn contacting Mars can turn any pent-up or repressed anger into a conscious experience. Saturn makes things concrete. Our anger now takes on form through its direct release. No more sitting on it, while stewing and quietly steaming. This is especially true should our Mars be placed in a water sign. However, Saturn abhors over-reaction (unlike cataclysmic Pluto, a planet that also helps us release deeper material within). Rather than eruptively explode and try to annihilate conditions with our temper unleashed, we probably are filled with a sense of righteous anger that keeps our grievances focused and firmly directed. When it's over, practical Saturn urges us to move on and rebuild a new, sturdier framework for dealing with such future confrontations. We thus may learn to mature in this area of Mars expression.

We just need to know who not to get angry at. Self-attack is not the best way to use a Saturn/Mars transit (although self-examination leading to the weeding out of our defects is to be encouraged). Getting mad at the boss is seldom helpful, even if we intend to quit (Saturn wants us to leave in a way that ensures us a letter of recommendation by our former boss to bring to our interview for the new job—shrewd Saturn is always thinking ahead). But not voicing our feelings at all to our employer is also an unwise thing to do: congested Mars can rob us of the physical energy we need to do effective work, plus it can make us feel down, devitalized, and powerless (then the boss suspects we have an attitude problem, and thus we still have a Saturn/Mars dilemma on our hands). Also, don't kick the cat or have a fender bender (dents are ruled by Saturn) since cruelty and carelessness will not appease the Saturn principle nor will it make the Mars part of ourselves feel on top of things. Writing a few angry letters (carefully edited) will fulfill Saturn's need to control how Mars vents, but maybe you should rip them up after getting things off your chest, or file them away for later review before mailing them.

So what's so good about having Saturn transit Mars? We can find ourselves being very industrious and productive during this period if we are first willing to reorganize life where needed and work hard when required, and to work consistently, which may be more the secret to our eventual success. We need to harness vital Mars energy and pool it into a few carefully considered areas rather than to scatter our forces. Maybe we could get away with putting most of our eggs in one basket, if we are first sure the basket is well fortified and able to hold the load. We can get something accomplished now that may have long-range purpose in our life. Usually with Mars, no matter what planet is transiting or what aspect is being formed, doing something is better than doing nothing. Stagnation would be an awful way to handle Saturn/Mars, since both planets push for self-interested action.

This could also be a good time to empower our bodies through regular exercise and whatever else it takes to ensure physical fitness, as long as we don't strain our muscles (Mars) or do activities that can be bad for our back or spine (Saturn). Brisk walking would be a good thing to do now, since it would symbolize self-directed forward movement at a pace we are free to determine. Any vigorous action involving repetition would be fine. For some of us, perhaps under expert guidance (such as a professional trainer), weightlifting would be an apt activity symbolizing the merging of the Saturn/Mars interplay. The key thing is to not force anything like this until we feel confident and ready, and then to go at it slowly but consistently.

A Saturn/Mars transit need not be dreaded if it helps us get back on the track and refresh our total being with renewed strength and purpose (at least in small, measured doses). We feel we can target what must be done with greater clarity and a better sense of economy. Some things that never quite got off the ground in the past may have to be let go now or and finally put to rest, but they probably were keeping us from succeeding and even robbing us of vitality in the process. We will look back later and realize that this Saturn transit did us a favor by stopping us from going nowhere fast. Cars and human psyches come with brake systems for good reasons.

Chapter Six Endnote

1. *Astrology and Your Past Lives* by Jeanne Avery, Simon & Schuster, 1987.

CHAPTER SEVEN

SATURN IN TAURUS

STRONG, LIKE BULL

An earthy planet and an earth sign will obviously share several common denominators. The conservative nature of pragmatic Saturn is well attuned to stable, sensible Taurus. Both planet and sign seek to work with solid, well-formed structures (even dull ones) rather than abstractions. Saturn and Taurus are each dependable and able to stick to routines without complaint. Saturn can endure in its tasks while Taurus is known for its physical stamina. That so-called "lazy" side of Taurus has been exaggerated, because this is also the sign of the yoked bull (or water buffalo) plowing the fields (or rice paddies), and that implies hard work. When Saturn is involved, Taurus will exhibit its tougher cowhide qualities. Saturn and Taurus have strong survival instincts, suggesting a knack for self-preservation even under strenuous conditions. They can consolidate their energies, galvanize their inner strengths, and prepare well for potential hardships even before such difficulties arise. Saturn in Taurus suggests a strongly realistic, gritty strategy for living in a world it assumes to be harsh and unyielding at times. This is a very grounded, level-headed Saturn.

ROCK SOLID

We typically adopt a serious, no-nonsense approach toward securing tangible personal assets and resources. Saturn pressures us to establish productive values regarding the basic material and financial elements of our life. Saturn's innate respect for the fulfillment of duties and obligations complements Taurus' steadfast determination to fulfill valued commitments. This psychologically sturdy, headstrong placement grants us the inner strength to plod on during arduous times without being thrown off course by circumstantial delays, obstacles, or setbacks. We typically do not accept responsibilities easily (Taurus slowly evaluates and digests while Saturn doesn't take anything lightly). We may even permit ourselves to endure much personal discomfort (probably the only Taurus position to do so) to assure that all tasks are properly completed before we allow ourselves to rest.

The staying power of Taurus combines well with the perseverance of self-reliant Saturn. Both display a strong work ethic. When well managed, Saturn in Taurus drives us to work long and hard, with a sense of order, purpose, and practical timing once realistic objectives have been clearly defined (and usually not before). We tend to patiently strive toward that which is attainable without giving up or permitting ourselves to be sidetracked. This tenacity reminds me of Joan Baez (born with Saturn in Taurus), famous for her rendition of "We Shall Overcome."

Typical of all the earth signs, Taurus plans its action before making sustained efforts. Saturn reinforces this. We are willing to be very accountable for our actions, as long as nobody pushes us into doing things that are not of our choosing. We can show an amazing resistance when others attempt to force us to do something. But generally, expect many of us with Saturn in Taurus to be "Rock-of-Gibraltar" types—you can count on us to deliver the goods in a timely fashion!

ALL THE WAY TO THE BANK

The quietly ambitious nature of Saturn (less assertive than Capricorn's ambition) easily expresses through the material-istic nature of capable Taurus, accentuating an ability to con-centrate on a mature, skillful handling of the mundane necessities of life. Taurus' form-building urges are here taken very seriously. This placement often denotes excellent busi-ness acumen. We achieve concrete goals by remaining faith-ful to traditional methods of procedure. There can be a marked degree of self-sufficiency regarding our basic tangible sustenance. We simply want stable, solid results and guaran-tees of security.

However, an underlying fear of deficiency or deprivation on the material survival level may foster an above-average drive to retain goods and possessions at all cost. Thus, the security of total personal ownership, control, and manage-ment is highlighted. Saturn's safety urge coupled with Taurus' retention ability suggests that we are likely to keep a tight grip on our private financial affairs, and it is likely that we become increasingly well-disciplined and organized here as we mature. We are serious about our money issues and spend cautiously with much concern for an object's true value.

LOSING MY "MINE"

In our somewhat anxious attempts to become materially well insulated and self-sufficient, we can be overly cautious and uncertain about the value of periodically letting go of what we own and what we have carefully safe-guarded and stock-piled, even if our cherished possessions prove to be burdensome from time to time. As acquisitiveness is fortified with this placement, we may want to firmly hang on to all that we have earned and accumulated. We might even be reluctant to share our goods with others. The fear of physical/material loss can be one of our greatest self-imposed limitations. Thus we will often be tested (Saturn loves to give exams) in life to see if we can recognize and weed out our potential miserly streak, selfish hoarding instinct, or basic lack of generosity—the shadow parts of our grasping nature. Having little faith in taking economical risks and gambles, some of us will eventually learn the necessity of releasing a few of our resources back into the mainstream of life for the welfare and support of others, since Saturn emphasizes social responsibility more than personal self-gratification. A danger here is that we may exclusively seek to become completely settled (consciousness-wise) in the realm of earthly attachments while also becoming increasingly desensitized to more encompassing spiritual values.

SIMPLE VIRTUES

The down-to-earth attributes of Saturn in Taurus are frugality and a sensibly organized material outlook. Smart shoppers or bargain hunters could easily have Saturn in Taurus (or Saturn in the Second House, or Saturn-Venus aspects). We are able to maintain what we own over long periods of time in near-perfect condition because Saturn adds an element of reverence and respect for all those well-made objects Taurus enjoys owning. Both Saturn and Taurus lean toward functional simplicity in taste. For us, beauty and design (Taurus) should also serve a practical, useful purpose (Saturn). But there may be some frustration here, since Taurus' naturally sensual orientation can be in conflict with Saturn's fear of indulging the senses. Taurus sometimes wants to own things because they are aesthetically pleasing, while not necessarily serving any practical function. Saturn could be an inhibiting factor in this regard.

Saturn is driven to always work at something, push against inertia, and never completely rest or relax. For Saturn, enjoying the fruits of accomplishment is not as rewarding or stimulating as striving to further accomplish. Yet we probably need to know when to give in to our natural Taurus urges to stop being so productive and to instead unwind through a lack of "busyness." Taurus knows the value of resting or stopping motion. It doesn't like overstraining itself. Saturn is thus made to realize the virtues of stillness and the appreciation of energy economy. Hopefully, both planet and sign teach us to appreciate the wisdom of patience and thoughtful timing.

RUT-BOUND BLUES

Psychologically, the natural fixity of Taurus reinforces the potential rigidity of Saturn. Therefore, Saturn in Taurus indicates inflexible patterning on some level. Taurus' general resistance to external changes implies that Saturnian structures may be too rooted and rigid to allow for sufficient new growth and improvement. Because of this, any self-limiting values we may develop can become entrenched. They could remain as permanent character flaws unless we objectively estimate their actual worthiness. Due to Taurus' semi-conscious desire mechanisms, we may have difficulty understanding the rationale of modifying (particularly at the last minute) our set plans of action. While we should learn to capitalize on our ability to endure and wait for the most propitious moments to execute major moves in life, we also need to realize that such beneficial timing often involves a willingness to yield to the unplanned alternatives new conditions present to us. Both Saturn and Taurus rarely embrace anything "unplanned," but perhaps real life is demanding that we do so from time to time.

GOING BROKE

Since Saturn denotes blockages as well as the ambition to overcome hurdles and obstacles, you'll sometimes come across a self-inhibitor with Saturn in Taurus who flatly resists the required lessons of proper self-sustenance in the real world. This most obviously shows itself through chronic money mismanagement or insufficiency. It superficially appears to be general "rotten luck" on the financial level. Some of us might also have a tough time efficiently maintaining what we do own, neglecting to properly protect our property and as a result suffer losses and/or damages in this area. If frustrated with our own incompetence, we may become envious or bitter regarding the material successes of others while we are just barely getting by (Saturn is prone to chilly resentments and grudges). A poor sense of self-value is often the core problem.

Am I Worth It?

If we are unable or unwilling to establish our sense of inner worth (Taurus) in our own eyes, we may have trouble appreciating ourselves and feeling self-content, at least subconsciously. In general, if we are not at peace with the quality of our self-image (Aries), such dissatisfaction reveals itself in the manner in which we work with the laws of attraction (Taurus). This dynamic can also be shown through the interplay of Mars and Venus in our chart. Undervalued Mars activity impedes the proper expression of Venus qualities, and vice versa.

How did we get into such a dilemma? As Taurus is a Venus-ruled sign, there may have been some denial of demonstrative affection, physical touch, or emotional security in the early years. This may have led us to feel worthless in the eyes of authority/parental figures (Saturn) with whom we desired intimate rapport. Or, perhaps due to harsh economical difficulties in our family while growing up (with its attendant social implications), we may have learned to associate money with stress, frustration, burdens, emotional disharmony, and pain. Having to later deal with material realities as an adult may still strike a frictional chord within, or stir up unresolved fears and unsettling anxieties. We may even harbor an unrecognized dread of accumulation, sensing that owning material things will trap us into restrictive patterns of mundane settledness, especially if Uranus is strong in our chart and/or if planets in Aquarius square our Saturn position.

APPRECIATING OURSELVES

Ironically, faulty management of our resources is often the surest way of being forced to get stuck in the center of one financial crisis after another, which keeps us feeling anything but free. A blocked Saturn operating through fixed Taurus can remain quite an unshakable problem for some of us. However, any astrologer reading the chart of those of us with this Saturn in Taurus predicament should use a gentle and tactful approach (since we already anticipate being further devalued) to help us get in touch with here-and-now applications of our underdeveloped talents and assets. We need to understand the futility of living in some frozen past that has no tangible basis in the present—now, how practical is that? We also need to have faith that new worthy values can be developed and supported by life. Of course, no astrologer is expected to perform miracles, and professional therapy may be needed to help those who are deeply blocked to dig into the roots of any core problems.

Often, a clue that psychological conflicts in this area have not been maturely dealt with and resolved would be the existence of chronic health problems in any of the Taurus parts of the body (throat, ears, neck muscles, thyroid, tonsils, gagging reflex, etc.). Since Taurus is a sign that can channel blocked energy into physical structure, the body often becomes a target for such unrelieved inner stress and tension. Energy blockages could make for an overall physical tightness, which massage therapy could help.

Astro-lebrities with Saturn in Taurus

Pablo Picasso	Ringo Starr
Joan Baez	John Lennon
Ronald Reagan	Lucille Ball
Barbra Streisand	Aretha Franklin
Louis Pasteur	Bob Dylan

SATURN IN THE SECOND HOUSE

FOR RICHER OR POORER?

A standard definition of Saturn in this house suggests that restrictions imposed on our earning and spending power exist until we have learned how to better handle finances in a mature and responsible manner. Life will pressure us to establish sound and sensible material values. People who amass great fortunes can have this position, especially those who've earned their riches instead of having simply gotten lucky. A certain shrewdness is implied, as Saturn can calculate and carefully assess its options. What needs to be emphasized with this Saturn position is the proper and timely utilization of all personal resources. Until then, some of us with this placement are either going to feel insufficiently funded or may actually undergo monetary hardships.

Saturn in the Second House, however, is more complex in meaning than this typical interpretation. When we discover that both the destitute and the affluent can have this position, we can't help but wonder what made the difference between one condition and the other. It appears to be a case of either feeling defeated on a mundane level of self-provision or feeling challenged to the hilt to master material affairs and obtain full control over personal resources. On a deeper level, our outer Second House experiences become symbolic of inner (emotional) conditions involving our sense of personal worth. Saturn here implies a psychological blockage in our early development of self-value. This can mean we grow up having trouble appreciating ourselves and finding sources of material contentment in our lives.

Such devaluation can often be traced back to economic tensions experienced in childhood, whereby authority figures in the home were unable or unwilling to provide a comfortable, secure environment. Our basic needs may not have been adequately met, making us now feel anything but relaxed, trusting, and expansive. A sense of lack and of being short-changed by an inhospitable world can develop. We need to ask ourselves whether such early denials have fostered resentments and the fear that our sought-after physical comforts will never be had. Are inner doubts allowing us to give up any hope of ultimate prosperity and financial mastery? Why should we instead tolerate just barely getting by, opting for a meager living devoid of those material things others take for granted? Conversely, this same fear of not having things can also manifest as an all-consuming desire to accumulate and maintain the objects of our attraction. Saturn can be doggedly persistent in the pursuit of making a buck and owning the best that money can buy.

BEING STINGY

Saturn in the Second House can mean strong acquisitive leanings that can turn into a grasping, hoarding tendency backed by a single-minded attitude of self-preservation. Yet Saturn's holding power in this area is more likely due to anxiety rather than the emotional pleasure of owning valued things. In fact, pleasure and sensual enjoyment are not as often associated here with possessions as are prestige, power, security, authority, and a sense of social achievement. The challenge of a Second House Saturn has little to do with money and what it can buy. It instead has a lot to do with understanding what we indeed value and why. We will need to abide by some measure of self-control and discipline of desire, regardless of how successful we are.

Do we truly identify with what we own? Are our possessions a tangible expression of our inner self? Or do we compulsively attract things, then hold onto them due to an unresolved fear of loss? If we choose to take the passive approach (as self-inhibitors do), we are prone to play out a victim role, justifying our difficult material life by blaming situations in the external world for our frustrating condition. If our family neglected us or failed to provide, we may tend to expect the world itself to make up for such unfair deprivation. Ironically, we suspect we are dealing with a cold and uncaring world to begin with, from which we nevertheless expect basic support. Still, we really don't trust anybody to come forth with the things we need, and thus we unintentionally may thwart our capacity to receive what others would willingly give us.

A Second House Saturn suggests we can be opportunistic at the material expense of others. Some of us can maneuver conditions so that others take over our debts. This might be a more tolerable arrangement for those who help us with our mundane necessities if we at least give them sincerely warm, emotional parts of ourselves in return. But that's also a problem. We tend to be emotionally stingy as well, giving of ourselves to others only when we know we'll be getting back what we want. Saturn in the Second House can be one of the more subtle indicators of manipulation, but only when we are vastly out of touch with what it's trying to teach us. We need to discourage ourselves from using greed as a defense mechanism, or as a way of dealing with the pain of feeling worthless.

PAYING BILLS ON TIME

Constructively, we can use the financial restrictions of our past to spur us to better structure a self-reliant material lifestyle. We learn what it takes to help us feel consistently secure. We seldom put ourselves in predicaments where we have to lean on anyone for our sustenance. If anything, we are prone to occasionally take responsibility for the material welfare of our valued loved ones. When we take an active approach (as over-achievers do), we are driven to want power and control in all our Second House situations. While the passive route means we give away much of that power to others, thereby remaining in a chronic state of material vulnerability, a more self-motivated attitude implies we will do our darndest to pay our own bills on time. We do not wish to collect a pile of "past due" notices.

Saturn's house position is often an area of life where we need to take charge of ourselves and assume greater degrees of self-reliance. The Second House is a life sector that cannot successfully be lived out only in our heads (unlike the Ninth or Twelfth House). It demands our worldly involvement in finding concrete solutions. Outcomes here need to become physical realities. Saturn underscores these needs as a planet very much connected with our sense of here-and-now reality. Perhaps all potential financial setbacks, delays, obstacles, and frustrations that occur depend much on how we avoid level-headed, no-nonsense self-confrontation. Is our own handling of our talents, natural skills, and other personal assets too ineffective to support our need to materially and emotionally ground ourselves in the "real" world?

CHEAPSKATE

Any sense of material lack is often related to a hidden (or sometimes not so hidden) sense of worthlessness. This is probably something we learned in our early formative years rather than being something deeply (karmically) ingrained. However, there will be those astrologers who'll say we were slaves or lowly serfs in past lives and never knew what it was like to totally own anything for ourselves. We didn't have the freedom to claim something as exclusively ours. That would indeed be one reason we may now convince ourselves we are not meant for this demanding materialistic world, since we never seem to have the practical know-how required to aggressively or competitively handle money-making and asset-building opportunities.

Should some of us feel this way, we need to work at learning how to evaluate ourselves in a positive light, giving ourselves permission to have things worth having. We need to go first class, splurge a bit, and not be cheap with ourselves. This is easier said than done (we may have great hurdles of guilt to overcome first), but nevertheless it's a step in the right direction. When we feel unworthy and unrewardable, we are prone to live a Spartan existence. But when we feel worthwhile, we are simply pragmatic and thrifty; we refrain from asceticism or severe material denial. Negatively, Saturn is austere.

Positively, Saturn is moderate, which helps us tap into the benefits of our Saturn house. Extremism seems to create the imbalance that further leads to conditions of self-limitation.

LAW OF GIVE & TAKE

As we are likely to be cautious and guarded in how we protect what we own, some of us appear reluctant to share our goods with others. That's too bad, because this house teaches us about give and take (along with the Eighth, its polar opposite house). It metaphysically works this way: When we totally refuse to psychologically let go of our possessions, the universe has a way of reclaiming these things in a manner beyond our control. While often anxious and untrusting, we need to first learn the lesson of the responsible outpouring of our material goods—even just money itself—into a world that in turn supports our existence. Miserly attitudes only thwart our security needs in the long run. We only get back what we've willingly given out, whether that's money, physical objects, or even a big heartfelt hug and kiss.

Saturn in the Second House suggests that we tend to unwisely trap a lot of our energy in such give-and-take matters (similar to when Saturn is in the Seventh or Eighth, but on a different level). We can become too self-absorbed with what we are getting or think we are not receiving from others. What we are most disturbed by are people who give us something and later want to have it back, for whatever reason. Yet we could have the same inclinations, which may explain why some of us do not give in the first place.

Although life requests that we be in full control over our assets, we can be fixated on how much or how little we are being supplied. We typically attempt to amass more than is actually needed for true self-satisfaction. Are we developing a hard-nosed approach to materialism? Will financial stability be preserved at all cost? Will the reality of our spiritual selfhood be less valued as a result? If so, the cost can be great, for we have then sold our soul to a materialistic mindset that promises to keep us running on a consumer treadmill until we expire. Few actually take this path, and that is probably because Saturn hammers away at us until we learn to deepen our value system. We have some wonderful resources to give to the world: endurance, common sense, exacting attention to detail, organizational ability, executive drive, and the ability to simplify matters by eliminating the superfluous. We often find we have a good head for business. If we learn to consciously develop these assets with patience and a respect for proper timing, they can turn into profits that first benefit us and then the world at large. Our environment may eventually expect us to capitalize on these assets in a way that enriches the environment—but usually once our own needs have been met.

APPETITE CONTROL

The Second House deals with our "animal" appetites and creature comfort needs. Our basic experiences with the realm of the five senses in general are suggested. We tend to underplay this facet of the Second House in favor of money and ownership themes. Yet how we enjoy our physicality and allow it to be part of our worldly experience can be a Second House challenge. Remember, the symbol of its associated sign Taurus is not a money mogul busily at work wheeling and dealing, but instead a bull in a meadow ready to graze or fertilize something. The earthy desires of the Second House can be very much wrapped up with beauty, especially in its more physical forms, as well as our sexual instincts. This is not a sex house per se, but it clues us as to what we are willing to arouse inside ourselves sexually (those potential sexual resources we store up while waiting for the right Fifth or Eighth House scenario).

Saturn in this house can suggest a puritanical streak. By its own nature, Saturn is afraid of being overpowered. In this house, we may find we are good at putting limits upon our ability to receive sensual gratification. We might restrict our capacity to respond to the impact of the sensory world, which thus denotes we have trouble accepting the pleasure principle. Indeed, this also sounds like Saturn in the Fifth or Eighth House. But the difference here is that a Second House Saturn tends to have a blockage on an instinctual level in a way that is often unrecognized. The Fifth or Eighth House Saturn is more concerned with performance anxieties or fears of what others expect from us sexually, whether warranted or not.

It could be that Saturn in the Second House tells us we need to be more selective concerning how we develop our sensuous self. The sign on the cusp should also tell us plenty. Gemini, Virgo or Aquarius here normally doesn't worry about overdoing the sensual side, because each sign basically doesn't do so! But Taurus, Leo, Scorpio, and sometimes Pisces may be another story. We will have to learn to properly make inner adjustments to be sure we are not overly depriving or overly accentuating the gratifications our senses can provide.

Astro-lebrities with Saturn in the Second House

Prince Charles	Yogananda
Grace Kelly	Barbra Streisand
Clint Eastwood	Joseph Stalin
Friedrich Nietzsche	Vivien Leigh
Steven Spielberg	Paul McCartney

SATURN/EARTH VENUS ASPECTS

NATAL

The Taurus side of Venus depicts the urge to gratify the five senses. How we register physical body sensations is represented by this facet of the Venus experience. Venus seeks to enjoy nature and helps us inwardly balance ourselves through our ability to establish relaxing, peaceful inner/outer environments. Saturn in aspect to earthy Venus supports the need for quiet enjoyment of (solitary) activities that promote order and fulfill a functional purpose. Saturn can relate to the restful nature of Venus, since restfulness implies calmness and energy conservation (which appeals to Saturn). Saturn also helps the artistic side of Venus create well-structured forms of physical beauty (it's good for pottery, sculpting, weaving, stained glass, or jewelry-making—in fact, all crafts that require precise control of artistic technique). It offers us a needed dose of self-discipline and focus in order to help tangibly manifest our Venus expression. In addition, Saturn taps into the part of Venus that desires quality of form.

But Saturn can also be at odds with earth Venus in many ways. Venus seeks to have satisfying body pleasures. It can become too comfort-addicted and even lazy. Venus is motivated to act according to what feels good at the moment, while Saturn is able to put pleasure urges on hold, is work-driven, and doesn't like to feel idle or non-productive. So any Saturn/Venus contact puts some degree of constraint on our ability to enjoy things. Venus can be indulgent of the senses, but Saturn attempts to regulate how much and how often we get to indulge. We thus feel inwardly driven to curb our appetites and take a more moderate route. Squares and oppositions in particular can squelch self-gratification urges, making us feel guilty about pleasing ourselves and having a good time—but discriminate Saturn also keeps us from getting into unwholesome pleasure habits that can harm our body or drain our bank account.

Speaking of money, Saturn implies frugality and simplicity of need. Venus as a financial planet is thus steered towards a sensible management of funds. We seldom are extravagant in our tastes and instead look to buy items on sale; the better the sale, the more we feel empowered. Yet both Saturn and Venus seek quality as well, plus Saturn has an eye for durability. Saturn/Venus aspects are indicators of a desire to save more than spend. Saturn is always thinking about those "rainy days" and wants to conserve Venus' resources as a protective measure. Since Venus is a planet that does well with balanced expression, it is important that the Saturn urge doesn't become so powerful that we never want to part with our money or possessions, because then we could become tight-fisted and too insecure to enjoy what we own.

Careful investment of our finances—once we've done our homework and have researched our options—is an excellent way to channel Saturn/Venus. Saturn hates risks and Venus doesn't deal well with unpleasant outcomes. Both planets can be very security-conscious. Therefore, it's best to take a conservative approach that allows us to steadily invest over a long period. The regularity required here would prove satisfying to our cautious financial temperament. We never want to feel pushed or pressured in this area and instead prefer to go at our own (slower) pace. The commodities market would probably drive us batty with all its sudden, inexplicable fluctuations (that's more for Uranus/Venus or Jupiter/Venus). We cannot endure big risks or last-minute surprises. We probably have an above-average interest in how our funds are going to be managed. The details of monetary transactions are generally important to us. It's usually Saturn that wants to study details and learn terminology and general concepts—earth Venus just wants to take the least risky routes, plus know how much profit can be had and when. Saturn wants as much control over its financial dealings as possible. We could drive any broker crazy with our worries and uncertainties—we tend to want to do their job instead of putting trust in their expertise.

In general, expect Saturn/Venus aspects to denote level-headedness and the careful appraisal of buyable goods, putting focus on what is sound and sensible. Our value system leans towards the conservative and the socially sanctioned. We play it safe and try to make all the right moves concerning our ability to support our material needs. Yet, we also may have to grapple with self-worth issues (since Saturn tests our ability to feel deserving of the things we attract). Some of us wonder if we are truly deserving of the material comforts that come our way. We have to be careful not to be harsh and judgmental in our self-evaluation. The bottom line is that we need to appreciate ourselves more than we typically do and quit blocking our ability to be treated well (especially in the material realm).

Physical touch and closeness are important to earth Venus. Its motto could be "To Have and To Hold, Forever." However, Saturn tends to be anti-touch and is wary about too much closeness. It's not the sentimental planet that Venus is, and may have a hard time blending with the Venusian need for stable attachment. We may even feel we are not supposed to get too wrapped up with what we own, so that later on nothing can end up owning us on some level. Should our possessions become destroyed or taken away by force, we do not want to feel devastated. With Saturn's influence, we try not to give the things we own a lot of emotional value to begin with (which goes against a valid earth Venus need). This can result in not buying anything new but instead hanging on to outworn items or frequenting secondhand stores for cheaper goods.

Regarding materialism, there is another side to Saturn that could almost be mistaken for Leo: Saturn can purchase things that are commonly regarded as status symbols (I find this trait more common with Capricorn, however). Saturn/Venus operating this way means we are still price conscious, but not in terms of hunting for bargains. We are instead looking for what is expensive and highly prized, as if owning such items will offer us prestige, a sense of class, and the appearance of social sophistication. This is usually a strong attempt to overcompensate for a humble family background where making and spending money was a struggle. In the back of our minds, some of us vow that we will be poor no more. We will buy without regard to the cost factor. Still, I can't see Saturn comfortably purchasing expensive novelties (like guitar-shaped swimming pools). It would rather invest in a few Picassos than a pink Cadillac. Saturn typically is no fool when it comes to resale value.

TRANSIT

Saturn transits are reality-testing periods, offering us clarity and definition. They indicate where and how we meet duties or obligations requiring our serious attention. Here, we often need to question what we own and what we truly must have for our ongoing material support. We are urged to rid ourselves of excess baggage and any general over-accumulation. We trim away what is unneeded. This is a pruning period, when less ends up being more. Careful deliberation and sensible evaluation allow us to weigh the pros and cons of owning certain things at this point in our lives. With squares and oppositions, however, this is done with a sense of pressure and a sensitivity to advantageous timing. Saturn always attempts to remove whatever is unworkable or non-productive.

Money typically becomes a focal point during this transit. We either feel insufficiently compensated for our work and other efforts, or we realize we need to better organize ourselves financially and make wiser use of what we earn. Even if we are currently unemployed or under-employed and feeling fearful of increasing debts, building better material structures for ourselves becomes a realistic goal. Practical choices will need to be made that do not always permit our more idealistic objectives to be fulfilled now. Stagnation or procrastination, based on waiting unrealistically for the perfect moment to make required changes, is very unhealthy and will not be supported by taskmaster Saturn. We tend to feel stuck in certain roles, but our challenge is to do the ground work it takes to arrive at effective solutions. Nothing happens overnight with Saturn, but making that first committed step to improve our status is imperative. We have to apply ourselves more diligently and with greater focus.

If anything, our value system can now deepen. We learn to put the material things in proper perspective. Long-term security becomes important for us, as we learn to plan ahead for our future needs. Saturn abhors waste, and so this is likely to be a phase when we feel the urge to save what is truly valuable and not spend more than is necessary to acquire what is most needed. Saturn helps us fortify ourselves economically, but Venus wishes to make firm fiscal decisions without wavering. We will thus have to be single-minded about what we decide to do. Saturn emphasizes our sense of self-containment at this time. We stay on track by addressing our own immediate practical concerns, and striving to be self-sufficient and self-reliant. Other people are not to detour us with their own pressing needs, unless such needs also coincide with our own objectives.

Frivolous usage of time is not supported, but closet-cleaning and making essential repairs are. There may be work to be done around the home that should not be put off. We probably can't afford all this, but we can start the ball rolling on a small scale, fixing one thing at a time while funds are available. In fact, Saturn stress aspects almost demand that things be fixed or thrown out! Hard work and little play may describe this period, but all purposeful efforts to construct a sturdier material framework will be rewarded in the long run. Saturn always eventually reimburses our sincere efforts to overcome life obstacles. Again, savvy Saturn insists we shop around for the best prices and make sure we get expert help. But we lose when we try to cut too many corners costwise. We should only attempt the "do-it-ourselves" route if we unquestionably know what we are doing. It's no time for experimentation when the roof's leaking.

If we have been very tight-fisted financially or maybe too greedy in our material desires, a Saturn/Venus transit could suggest we suffer a loss or a setback that hits us in the pocketbook. A quincunx or an opposition could easily set this scenario into motion. If we overly identify with our Venus attachments and are unwilling to share, transiting Saturn plays out the heavy role of debt collector on some level. Maybe we do owe something to some authoritative structure (like the IRS) but have been refusing to cooperatively pay our debts. Saturn will put the brakes on that kind of fiscal irresponsibility. Maybe a newly purchased car gets stolen and is never seen again, yet we still have to make steep monthly payments on it because we were too cheap to properly insure it. Saturn seems to come down hard on those who could have afforded to do the right thing but did not.

In most instances, we probably will only have to let go of those material things that are on their last wobbly leg anyway.

We probably got a lot more mileage out of these things than anyone expected. If during this transit they should conk out on us and operate no more, we should show our gratitude for their years of loyal service—and then junk 'em and start doing some smart shopping for new replacements. This will require we part with some money and prepare to pay more than we did when we first got that old blender in 1974. But Saturn—planet of rust, dents, and permanent breakage—is urging us not to keep things already in bad shape hanging around for too long.

A Saturn/Venus transit could be a marvelous time for a major yard sale. Then we might even get paid for getting rid of items that have seen their better days, or that we rarely use much anymore. Saturn prefers an uncluttered environment where only the true essentials take up space (of course, earth Venus needs more than just the few functional basics—it is not a proponent of the minimalist school of interior design). We will have to deliberate a bit before deciding what we keep and what is instead to be put up for quick sale. But just allowing ourselves to transfer our long-held-onto goods to others (who could really use them) means we have fulfilled much of the Saturn end of the deal. If some of us are going to have a Saturn/Venus transit coming up in a few months or so, it would be a good thing to now be looking around at what we have (going from closet to attic, or snorkeling around the basement). We will be surprised how much stuff has accumulated over the years. Saturn now advises us to let such stuff go!

CHAPTER EIGHT

SATURN IN GEMINI

JUST THE FACTS, MA'AM

Points of contrast between Saturn and Gemini are plentiful. Saturn can endure in its concentration on details while restless Gemini is easily bored with minutiae and welcomes distractions. Gemini, being mercurial in nature, is eager for variety or at least any variation on a theme. Saturn is slow, steadfast, and intent on preserving the tried-and-true method of doing something, changing only when things prove unworkable. Saturn requires repetitive, predictable, controllable outcomes while Gemini thrives on moment-to-moment changes and is not particularly driven to organize matters in advance. Sociable Gemini needs liveliness and constant movement while somber Saturn desires long stretches of solitude, stillness, or silence in which to ponder and reflect on serious concerns. Also, Gemini's quick surface-level assessments of life do not correlate well with the thoroughness of understanding Saturn needs.

There are few common denominators found between planet and sign, yet Gemini's above-average adaptability may make contrasting themes less polarizing. One common meeting ground: Saturn and Gemini can be dispassionate in their observations of life. Both seek to clearly discern factual data and dismiss what appears to be illogical. Both show little interest in purely emotional approaches to anything, and they don't give much credence to imagination and intuition as being valid ways to gather knowledge. Both put a high value on what can be rationally observed and measured rather than theorized or invented.

Gemini's keen sense of logic and reason combined with Saturn's need for reality-affirming clarity allow us to pursue serious mental interests with much effort and persistence. This is atypical of most Gemini placements—Gemini alone would rather flit from topic to topic, just enough to satisfy its curiosity and learn something stimulating, without dwelling on any one thing for long periods of time. There is suggested here a skillful capacity to intelligently organize facts and figures, which can render an aptitude for mathematics, scientific pursuits, and the study of law or anything else that requires cool objectivity and emotional detachment. Life will discipline us to carefully structure the contents of our mind and concentrate on developing greater mental depth. This tends to be the least superficial, light-hearted Gemini placement.

TONGUE-TIED

Due to Saturn's thoughtful yet hesitant nature, verbal fluency and quickness of response don't come naturally to us and are normally not easy to develop. We may be acutely self-conscious of any deficiencies here. Some of us may tend to view ourselves as less bright than others as we learn to master our brain power and construct a sounder intellect. We seem to have to work at it a lot. Although we think much about serious subjects, we may be a man or woman of few words (at least in the early part of our lives).

We probably listen to language carefully and note the power written words and spoken thoughts have over people. Yet something inside seems to hold us back from mouthing off and directly saying what we think about things. (Of course, if we also have Mercury in a fire sign square Mars, we may not be all that quiet and reserved.) We typically find ourselves uncomfortable with small talk and prefer to engage in more serious conversations—as long as we are not the topic being discussed (Saturn can handle talking about the outer world but often feels unprepared when asked for details about its personal inner life. Saturn clams up when caught by surprise or avoids certain questions altogether).

Gemini desires diversity to keep it mentally satisfied, while Saturn emphasizes meaningful diversity. This planet also makes Gemini's short-lived attention span less of a problem. Thus, we are encouraged to seek out versatility of thought within fewer topics of interest, while still learning how to communicate what we know with appealing flair and expressiveness. Life is telling us to get focused in those areas where we realistically show much intellectual promise.

However, unlike the capacity for specialization shown by Saturn in Virgo, we tend to organize data in a manner that is less selective concerning what is ultimately practical, workable, or useful. Down-to-earth applications of knowledge are less important to Gemini. Virgo is more interested in the tangible results of accumulated information. Gemini collects the facts, but Virgo sorts them out meticulously and with a keen awareness of what is functional. So this Saturn must work harder to efficiently categorize all assembled ideas and concepts if they are to prove a true benefit to our education of life. By being challenged to do this continuously, and by adopting constructive attitudes towards learning and applying what we've learned, we can become "eternal student" types who feel it is our duty to feed our minds no matter what our age.

AFRAID TO ASK

Considering the self-blocking, inhibiting potential of Saturn, we may experience childhood frustration trying to get our thoughts out, or at least getting them to be heard and considered by others. It makes us feel a bit dumb. Yet outer appearances can be misleading, since our mental development and cognitive ability are usually quite mature for our tender age. Saturn in this sign seldom denies intelligence, but typically thwarts a confident demonstration of showing off what we know. Caution in relating our thoughts is evident (of course, we could become excellent listeners). Yet if fear rather than mere carefulness in speech becomes a motivating factor (and this is better shown by our natal Saturn aspects), much of Gemini's natural inclination to want to know and learn through random exploration within the immediate environment can initially be held back. We are afraid to be inquisitive and pick people's brains for information, which is more the typical Gemini style.

In our formative years, we may have been dominated by undereducated authority figures who instilled within us a fear of learning new things or a dread of asking questions about the many parts of life. Perhaps a parent proved difficult to talk to openly. Maybe we were raised in an environment of great mental inflexibility. We may also have been afraid we would give the wrong answers when asked questions. This could result in mental anxiety and self-discouragement regarding future attempts to educate ourselves. Exposure to open-mindedness is what we needed and perhaps did not get. In some fashion, our early upbringing stifled our inborn curiosity, failing to foster the right intellectual foundation we find ourselves needing as we grow up. We were surrounded by too many pivotal people who may have been tight-lipped for the most part (or, on the other hand, too chatty or shallow to help deepen our mind). So some of us learned self-preservation by remaining uncomfortably quiet, non-expressive, unanimated, and too scared to ask a "stupid" question.

EGG HEAD

Saturn in Gemini can also mean we may have had to struggle to compete with others and mentally perform our best in an early environment that presented us with almost impossible standards of intellectual achievement and perfection. Maybe one parent excelled in an academic or communications field or had strong, ambitious thoughts about the value of learning. Perhaps we had to face our own inner fears of intellectual inadequacy through the assertive mental strivings of a brilliant sibling as well as a parent (typically the father). Some degree of Saturnian resentment may have developed on our part. The learning frustrations typical of Saturn in Gemini could have been compounded by mental brooding. If the pressure to be smart became too much, we could have easily shown indifference towards our early educational demands, with bouts of discouragement thrown in.

Saturn can seek significance by remaining separate and distinct from others. With Saturn poorly managed, we may find ourselves resisting normal learning processes (as developed through early training in school). In short, we can act as under-achievers who use our assumed ineptness as a calculated (albeit unconscious) defense. We resist fitting into an intellectual mold prescribed by other seemingly capable family members. But if we are prone to use our Saturn in an assertive, striving manner, we typically feel throughout life that we have to continuously prove our brightness ourselves and our intellectual worth to the world. How do we do this? One way is to go back to school as much as possible and collect academic degrees. That's how some of us show society we have a mind and plan on using it. The rest of us will probably just read a lot and attend workshops or seminars in an effort to know as much as possible about whatever we consider important. We treat knowledge with reverence and view it as a power tool regarding our overall success. We feel it is almost our duty to turn out brainy.

THINKING BEFORE SPEAKING

While we often feel like late bloomers regarding our communication skills since we have to struggle long and hard to develop self-assurance, we are often highly aware of what we are thinking and saying. We aspire to communicate with careful precision. We feel quite accountable for the information we relate to others, and thus become anxious about its accuracy and how people receive it. Sometimes we would rather say nothing than make verbal errors or be accused of faulty logic. I wonder if Otto in *A Fish Called Wanda* was born with Saturn in Gemini: his often-repeated line in the movie was "Don't call me stupid!" Remember, with this position, stupid we are not! Insecure is more like it. Sensitivity to criticism of our thoughts is very strong—Saturn here implies we are thin-skinned until we mature and toughen up. We are afraid to make mistakes in how we communicate. On the other hand, we also can demand much coherence from others and are bothered with vagueness and sloppy thinking. Solid frameworks of thought are very appealing to us, especially concepts put forth by established authorities.

Our dread of appearing ignorant or misinformed may goad us to obtain a prestigious educational background, perhaps as a way to compensate for whatever we feel we mentally lack. Being mentally ambitious, we are able to work steadily at disciplining ourselves to fully utilize our mind. But we also need to be careful not to become intellectually dry and colorless due to a lack of integration with our imagination and/or feeling nature.

Proof Positive

This highly rational combination of planet and sign makes for a skeptic who only recognizes as valid those undisputed facts that have been filtered through the concrete mind. Saturn in Gemini may incline us to seek precise knowledge of the apparent workings of visible life phenomena. But without the balance of spiritual perception and abstract awareness we could be closed to other levels of reality that exist outside the limits of our narrowly defined boundaries of time and space. This is a position emphasizing linear thinking. It has an affinity for more scientific methods of proving things.

Unless other factors are denoted in our chart, we are not impressed by faith-oriented belief systems, no matter how potentially inspiring. Soaring idealism is not what we can readily relate to, since we can be a bit cynical, expressing a cold realism when in comes to assessing the human condition. It may be hard for some of us to conceive of an afterlife, for example. Where's the proof it even exists? Who has come back from the dead to give us a fact-finding report? Psychic channeling or spiritual seances just won't do for us. And so, since the soul cannot be measured or analyzed under the microscope, its existence for us is unsubstantiated. We may not be a total atheist, but may tend to put the exploration of the otherworldly dimension on hold or take an agnostic approach. We figure there is so much here on earth to keep our minds preoccupied that there's no time to speculate on unprovable intangibles.

MIND CONTROL

Saturn believes a mind is a terrible thing to waste. What we can expect from a well-managed Saturn in Gemini is a polished intellect working at its optimum. Exceptional mental achievement can result, depending on how well we control and discipline our mind. Multifaceted Gemini prevents Saturn from becoming too rut-bound or rigid in its approach to learning. Saturn serves as a protective screen, suggesting we need to be discerning regarding what data we take in—are we going to read the tabloids or the classics? We may find we have a practical kind of ingenuity, assisted by our ability to maturely analyze. Eventually, we can become experts at communicating the written and/or spoken word.

Astro-lebrities with Saturn in Gemini

Joni Mitchell	Sigmund Freud
Newt Gingrich	Nicolas Copernicus
Orson Welles	Paul McCartney
Dorothy Kilgallen	George Harrison
Bobby Fischer	Eleanor Roosevelt

SATURN IN THE THIRD HOUSE

DEEP IN THOUGHT

While Mercury is the planet that best describes our mind and what intellectually interests us, the Third House describes how we learn to adapt our mental equipment to transient conditions we meet up against in our personal day-to-day world. With Saturn in the Third House, we communicate with our immediate environment with a measure of thoughtful reflection. Our mental processes operate less effectively when presented in a spontaneous, impulsive, unplanned manner. We are better served by learning to be orderly and discriminating in our thinking. We are to carefully observe our surroundings and selectively retain useful data.

Life will teach us to assimilate what our senses perceive with an air of caution and a dose of patience. Due to the care with which we need to digest information, we may start off appearing to be slow, insecure learners. As children, we are sometimes told that we are dumb-dumbs who don't pay attention. Or, as adults, that we don't know beans about what we are saying, that our facts are all wrong. The word "slow" to us connotes being stupid, and stupid translates as worthless. This is the message we hear and fear whenever we are criticized for our ideas or even for how we try to teach ourselves to do things. It's an issue of being devalued intellectually. Such put-downs can be depressing.

Because knowledge-gathering is actually serious business and a lot of work for us, and because we often doubt our native intelligence, we can be afraid to make even innocent mistakes. For us, to err is not just human—it's humiliating. We may make too big a deal of how awful it is to say the wrong thing, show our ignorance, or simply appear misinformed. Our self-consciousness in these matters can create mental blocks that only further frustrate us. It would be great if some sensitive soul (preferably a parent figure) sat us down at an early age and told us that our mental pace only appears somewhat slower so that we may end up learning things more thoroughly and expertly. We should have been read the tale of the tortoise and the hare, where we learn that the slow but sure approach gets the job done. Another message we need to hear more often is that mistakes made are only stepping stones to true accomplishments. We can learn plenty from not always doing everything right the first time around. Try and try again, practice makes perfect, etc. Wherever Saturn is in our chart, it symbolizes our search for excellence. So maybe during report card time we could then feel satisfied with the thought that the "C" we receive in social studies is actually an "A" in the making!

Right Way, Wrong Way

Another reason for appearing to be a slow learner (aside from actual learning disabilities) may lie in our tendency to resist being told how to do those things others think we already should know but apparently do not. We especially resist when being drilled by irritated, unsympathetic authority figures, when it sounds more like scolding than instruction. It often does take more time for certain information to sink in. Perhaps we unconsciously reject learning such data because it is coming from people we deem cold, perfectionistic, or intimidating. Yet it is often our own unrecognized perfectionism that demands knowledge be presented in just the "right" way. We can become insecure and even defensive when it is not. That's when learning anything becomes a struggle and an unwelcome chore rather than the pleasant mental stimulation Third House knowledge-gathering can be. Perhaps we end up just like a parent who was unyielding, absolutist in thinking, or just plain negative and pessimistic (a parent we may still be critical of). Saturn in the Third House can be quite cranky and fault-finding when stressed out. Maybe we came into this incarnation already armed with an inflexible mindset and thus instinctively see things as plainly right or wrong, correct or incorrect. If so, we will need to learn about altering our mental rigidity by the time we reach our first Saturn Return—the time of psychological adulthood.

NOTHING FLAKY HERE

Ours is a mind that has a talent for organizing. We can give careful attention to detail, run things efficiently, put things in proper perspective, and in general come up with sound and workable results to problems. We are naturally task-oriented. We can put forth great mental effort in tackling those realistic projects well within our ability to manage and control. Our gift is knowing how to simplify data, weeding out all superfluous material. This is similar to a Sixth House Saturn, except we don't get as frazzled over contradictory material nor do we work as obsessively. Actually, for some of us, streamlining data becomes a challenge. Saturn in this house can ironically become quite long-winded, though not in the breezy manner of Jupiter. It becomes dry and pedantic, too fixated on the elaboration of minute details no matter how boring or unnecessary.

As Saturn's house position shows us where we set up well-structured boundaries, here it implies we can limit the scope of our intellectual focus to strictly conventional, orthodox approaches even in unorthodox fields of study. Saturn mentality lacks the spirit of invention and risk-taking experimentalism. Even the irrationality of the imagination may prove to be frightening. A lot of things can prove scary to us, or seem just plain crazy, so we may opt for safer routes of thinking. Such conservatism suggests we lean toward a scientific mode of thought rather than a mystical path. We are stimulated by that which has tangible, material application. We also could be the types afraid of losing our minds and going off the deep end, but our clear, sane mentality suggests that's not likely to happen.

NO TIME FOR CHIT-CHAT

Saturn in the Third House means we are very structured mentally and are best stimulated by well-defined concepts of a serious or even profound nature. We seek purposeful information such as self-help books or how-to manuals as opposed to gothic romances. There is little patience for small talk and trivial chatter. The topic we are either talking about with others, reading, or hearing has to have a point and has to be going somewhere important. Otherwise, you've lost our interest.

If you want to drive us crazy, ask us at the next "no-nukes" rally if we have been aware of the rising price of bananas lately in the supermarket. Don't be surprised if we glare at you. Our heads are too often heavy with weighty subjects. Need our mind always be so engrossed in life's serious concerns? Why must each thought or conversation be something meaningful enough for us to sink our teeth into? Perhaps someone in our family circle made us think early on that communication was never something to be treated lightly, or joyously. We probably were held accountable for whatever we said, and disciplined (maybe too stiffly) when we told untruths. Verbal attention-grabbing on our part was either ignored or stifled (even though a sibling with Jupiter in Leo in the Third House would often get away with it, since our folks at least thought he or she was entertaining). Being ignored, however, made us feel our thoughts were invalid, irrelevant, or unworthy of any serious response from others. Unless we had something really important to say, we learned to say nothing.

It's no wonder that our formative years were associated with an awkward sense of intellectual uncertainty. Later on, we appear reluctant to speak out to others with true confidence or candor. A fear of rejection may make it hard to articulate our thoughts, especially to authority figures. If we block ourselves even further, we may develop speech problems. But our most common speech "problem" is not verbalizing our real thoughts about ourselves and others, or the world as we experience it. By our own silence, we may convince people we really have nothing valuable to offer.

SMILEY FACE

Learning the art of gab, which works best when light and airy in content, can become almost a mind-expanding technique for us. Speaking can be a form of immediate mental or nervous release. After all, talkative Gemini rules the Third House in the natural wheel, not Capricorn. Those of you with Saturn in the Third House reading this should stop right here. Put down this book and attempt to do your broadest smile in front of a mirror. Do your mouth's muscles feel taut? Do you think your smile looks contrived or phony? Are you showing your teeth while smiling? Your gums? Probably not, since showing gums is peculiarly Sagittarian (think of horses laughing). The more uncomfortable you are with your smile, the more work it will take to overcome tensions in your verbal interaction. Being tight-lipped is sometimes a literal term. Plus people who smile easily seem to readily accept lightness (even foolishness) in communication. We need to turn any frown upside down.

MINDSTUCK

Overly impressed by what we deem to be rational, we can end up fixated on making the world fit our rather tight and unvarying conception of reality. Our range of perception then becomes too narrow and incomplete. While Saturn can denote an exacting, analytical mind that excels in clear, precise thinking, it also implies getting firmly mired in habitual mental ruts rather than testing out new ways of thinking. Do we find we only change our long-held opinions with great hesitation? Will only indisputable proof convince us that such opinions are no longer valid? Yes. Saturn is impressed only by hard evidence. But we need to avoid falling into the trap of rigid thinking. Viewing matters only in terms of either black or white tends to make the people we are trying to convince see all shades of red. We can seem stubbornly of a one-track mind. It's best we knock off the dogma and assess the facts with a greater reasonability.

We like to view ourselves as practical, grounded thinkers who do not dispense factual knowledge casually, and we don't like to feel we are being superficial in our observations. Remember, our security lies in our comprehensive understanding of facts and figures. Although we are better listeners than speakers, our patience can be taken advantage of by those people who think they are better speakers than listeners. They are thus likely to bore us—no wonder our smile is a bit stiff. Saturn basically likes information that is concise and to the point. It's a little like Mars in the Third House in this respect. It doesn't do well with verbal fluff and intellectual meanderings.

MOTOR MOUTH

Conversely, some Saturn in the Third House over-achievers can be quite talkative, almost in a manic, compulsive manner. It's hard to understand why Saturn sometimes acts like a high-strung Jupiter, but it does when we're in overdrive. If anything, Saturn is here to teach us about verbal mastery, so that others truly hear what we are saying. Chattiness could be a subtle device we use to distract others from probing into the core of our more intimate, private self. We don't let people get in a word edgewise, and that prevents them from penetrating our thoughts and maybe even reaching our deeper emotions.

Most of us do listen very well because we need to know all about the other person's mental structure (paying attention to his or her weaker points) before we even begin to reveal our own strengths. Our mind is good at creating mental strategies. We also believe in proper timing and rarely blurt out things before thinking them through. A certain circumspection is typically present. A few of us over-achievers can be blunt and strictly to the point in conversation, but usually this can be a position of tact and diplomacy, although not in the same manner as Venus in the Third House. Venus is sincerely and emotionally concerned with not offending others. Saturn is simply careful not to attract insults, arguments, or bad reviews. Fearing verbal backlash from others, Saturn opts instead to say the "right thing" for the moment, or sometimes wisely says nothing.

Smarty Pants

What is usually not emphasized about Saturn in the Third House is that it can be the signature of intellectual ambition. We can try extra hard to surpass others in our educational pursuits. When we have to, we can turn on great brain power in order to learn what we need to become knowledgeable experts in our chosen field of professional work. We can make excellent grades, even under pressure. Saturn is status-conscious and prestige-oriented. We may want to prove ourselves to be smarter and more accredited than others. Saturn-Mercury can also become so motivated. Perhaps an inner dread of being considered mentally inferior goads us to prove we are instead brilliant. We may feel driven to show off and prove to people from our past that their opinion of our "limited" intelligence was flat wrong. We may even go back to college at a later date to pick up another degree (or maybe our first). We need to feel we have risen above whatever learning handicaps held us back when growing up. When someone with this Saturn placement acts like they should have Mars or Jupiter in the Third House instead, suspect such over-compensation.

We over-achievers are no less vulnerable than are the taciturn self-inhibitors. Nor are we more comfortable with our intellect just because we eagerly and assertively demonstrate our knowledge and impress our audience. We might actually feel more secure and in control communicating *to* another rather than *with* that person. We may have become poor listeners—a defense symbolizing "I don't want to hear the complaints you may have about me, so you don't get to talk too much." Perhaps what we fear most is another's intellectual authority, that someone might know more than we do. We need to work on such insecurity. Otherwise, communication becomes competitive and less enjoyable.

Astro-lebrities with Saturn in the Third House

Hugh Hefner	Liza Minnelli
Sir Arthur Conan Doyle	Martin Luther
Christopher Reeve	Annie Lennox
Helena Blavatsky	Madalyn Murray O'Hair
Thomas Edison	Scott Hamilton

SATURN/AIR MERCURY ASPECTS

NATAL

The Gemini side of Mercury deals with our conscious mind's ability to quickly process the variety of external data impacting on us. It helps us sort things out coherently. This is a clear-headed Mercury that makes connections, intelligent associations, or logical links between two or more concepts or objects. It rapidly gathers information and enjoys facts simply for the immediate stimulation they provide. But Saturn seeks more than just quick stimulation. Saturn wants to store all relevant data so that it can be retrieved and re-examined at a later date when needed. Saturn (along with the Moon) probably has a lot to do with our memory process, at least from the organizational end of it. Saturn sets up the mind's complex file cabinet system from which we instantaneously look for and pull out specific catalogued information. Saturn demands reliability, and thus puts pressure on restless Mercury to slow down and to deeply and thoughtfully pay attention to the details, and to take in data in an orderly fashion.

We with Saturn/Mercury aspects usually need a quiet environment conducive to the proper absorption of knowledge (those grim Saturnian librarians who display their "No Talking—Ever!" signs are on to something). Saturn best operates without random distractions, and demands that Mercury tackle one thing at a time. The issue here is one of mental focus—something that air Mercury needs. As a result, some of us with these planets in aspect become good at concentrating our attention on whatever we wish for long periods. We pore over the material at hand and are able to attend to even the finer details (details that can later protect us when we are required to sign legal documents, for example). We don't want to overlook anything. Saturn/Mercury can be aspects of studiousness. We use our mind in mature ways. Life is teaching us the value and wisdom of being selective and discerning.

If this sounds more like a Virgo Mercury, it's only because Saturn and Virgo already see eye to eye on many issues. Perhaps Gemini Mercury would rather take breaks and not plod on so diligently, but taskmaster Saturn will provide inevitable stumbling blocks when we don't put our mind's attention fully into whatever we are doing. We will make mistakes, then have to backtrack and redo. In the long run, this becomes a big waste of time, and ironically, air Mercury will have created the scenario it initially wished to avoid—that of being slowed down by boring details. The quickness of a typical air Mercury process is here replaced by a more workable pace, allowing us to evaluate matters with greater thoroughness and patience. Saturn can be an effective problem-solver due to its ability to stick with something until a practical solution is found. It can analyze anything well.

Communication is a major theme for the Gemini facet of the Mercury experience. Saturn provides the need to make ideas concrete and well formed. We may work at being clear and sounding knowledgeable when we speak. If we don't know enough about a subject, we may opt to listen to others rather than dare to show our ignorance. This is normally not a mental risk-taking pattern for Mercury. We stick to what we know and play it safe when discussing things. At times, we may sound like an authority or one who has done his/her homework when dealing with those subjects that interest us. But if

our level of self-confidence is low, we may seldom voice any
opinion even when directly asked. At least, we do not articulate or elaborate on our thoughts; we simply provide the minimum needed to answer questions.

Some of us have developed ways to avoid dealing with
answering certain questions. It could be as simple as just
refusing to respond or as complex as answering with details
that serve to rationalize or justify our way of thinking.
Verbosity could become a way for us to take detours in conservation when we feel others are getting too personal with their
questions. Saturn at its best pushes for a moderate solution,
and for an honest and real approach. We need to work at
being less afraid we will be rejected or criticized for our
thoughts. We also need to recognize how sour-pussed we can
get with our negative thinking. We can be pessimistic, but
also touchy about hearing that we are so. Denial is not just a
Neptune issue.

If we don't like the way any conversation is going because
someone is getting too nosy or too forward, we need to learn to
just tell others we don't wish to discuss the matter any further,
and leave it at that. We don't need to provide details as to why
it makes us uncomfortable—at least when dealing with
strangers. But if it's a loved one and the relationship is truly
intimate in tone, clamming up and saying no more just won't
do. We can't afford to leave others in the dark about our deeper
thoughts. We can't put up that big "No Talking" sign just to
shield us from our own inadequacies. Saturn/Mercury (no matter the aspect in question) means we are here to iron out a lot
of mental wrinkles in this lifetime. Hiding behind defensive
poses or giving others the silent treatment ensures that we
will stay self-blocked and rigidly locked up in certain areas of
our mind. This is very unGemini behavior, and the Mercury
function suffers greatly as a result. So we should speak out
with conviction and take our chances. It is not our job to control what others think or say.

Travel is another Gemini theme. By freely going about
and exploring different environments, Gemini learns to be

adaptable and tolerant of changes. Traveling becomes quite educational. But Saturn only wishes to go places when there is good reason to, not for the adventure or thrill potential. In fact, Saturn does not acclimate itself easily when planted on unfamiliar terrain, so we may not be eager to explore new territory or get out of town just for a quick change of scenery. Conducting business when traveling may be acceptable, though. We then rationalize it's okay to be in strange locales, since we're busy being productive.

Maybe because of our unaddressed fears of being far from home, we unconsciously set up situations that can make traveling a real nuisance, fraught with delays, unscheduled detours, cheap accommodations, transportation breakdowns, etc. It may always feel like Mercury retrograde for us when we leave town, and our complaints can be numerous. Better just stay home with our miserable attitude rather than ruin the trip for others unfortunate enough to be our companions on the road! Saturn/Mercury means we can become "back-seat drivers" of the worst kind, being too safety-concerned and worried about the perils of being transported anywhere. It's just our luck that we karmically attract Jupiter-type drivers with Sagittarian intentions of having a good time while cruising along. At least *we* always keep both hands on the steering wheel at all times. Is everyone else buckled up?

I'm having a little fun teasing Saturn/Mercury. Being able to see life's humor can be an important antidote for these aspects, which often denote that we are too tense to relax and enjoy our playtime periods on Earth. We need quality "goof-off" time where we can take a vacation from being so task-driven and productivity-addicted, or where we can at least stop thinking of all the upcoming duties and chores we will have to tackle. Saturn always can come up with more and more work to do, but air Mercury needs to catch its breath and take impromptu breaks. It needs its lighter moments.

TRANSIT

Saturn transits to Mercury are usually more beneficial than we would suspect from reading older traditional texts written about them. We just have to be mindful that this is not the time for us to be mentally tackling everything our little heart desires. Only certain projects and tasks seem to get the nod of approval from Saturn, while others remain on hold indefinitely or are scratched off the list permanently. Mercury can be an indecisive planet, but Saturn at least tells us our choices are few. This could be a welcome relief for air Mercury, who could otherwise fall victim to a multitude of short-lived interests and a non-productive scattering of forces as a consequence.

Saturn/Mercury transits are excellent for the careful planning stages of anything. We are made to look at what we wish to accomplish from a very realistic view. Are we as prepared as we think we are? Have we looked at all the pros and cons? Do we have the staying power needed to take our project all the way? What has our past batting average been when previously attempting such matters? Should we become depressed or dejected even thinking about answering such questions, it's a sure sign we are not ready to take the big plunge—but it can't hurt to at least think about our potential here.

Before we can really get going at a workable pace, we first need to communicate our needs in a clear manner. What are we foremost wishing to accomplish? Do we have the means at hand to effectively do this? How do we best start? How much research might be needed? Transits to Mercury probably do drum up a lot more questions than answers, but Saturn says we have to begin by being sure-footed and aware of limitations that could conceivably loom on the horizon. Being forearmed with the protection realistic appraisal affords us helps ensure that our efforts will not be wasted. We need to measure our moves in terms of what can feasibly be accomplished. Time becomes very important to us, and we should use it skillfully and wisely.

Should we get our plans into motion only to run into a series of snags, Saturn is teaching us to be patient and to endure—as long as common sense tells us we are on the right track. Of course, air Mercury is not necessarily blessed with common sense, but it can be a quick learner with a willingness to try out a different plan when the initial one seems to be going nowhere. However, Saturn suggests we stick to the original script a bit longer before we abandon it for something new. We just need to analyze things and make sensible alterations when possible, then keep going. Doing nothing except stalling and waiting for a miracle doesn't seem to work for this transit. Saturn says we must always be doing something that can ensure solid, reliable results.

Letting valuable time slip by can push us further behind schedule with our objectives, and we could then start becoming very discouraged and uncertain about things. We are then tempted to drop out and abandon the project entirely, with much regret and guilt. Our thoughts can start to turn negative and self-critical, and we end up fretting over our future security. This is when Saturn/Mercury becomes no picnic, and problems that appear unfixable seem to beset us. We become short-sighted and very nervous about the possibility of undesirable outcomes.

In reality, Saturn is telling Mercury to snap out of it and get a firmer grip on reality. We are not in such dire straits as we think we are in most cases (although we need to look at all the concurrent transits operating at this time: transiting Pluto also squaring Mercury could indeed suggest our troubling anxieties are well justified). Just remember that Mercury is a clever planet and open to options. It symbolizes an internal part of us that simply won't let ourselves feel trapped or cornered for too long. We do need to apply greater brain power during this transit and much objectivity if we are to solve our dilemma. So all is not lost no matter how down we are feeling. We must gather more relevant information that can help keep us from feeling confused, and we should start talking about our issues to those who seem to be level-headed and pragmatic about life. We need their feedback so that we can begin to look at our situations from different perspectives.

It is better than being stuck in mental ruts that keep us end-lessly reviewing what led to our brick wall, regardless of whose fault. The blame game becomes an unattractive conse-quence of a mismanaged Saturn/Mercury transit.

Much of what probably happens to us during Saturn/Mercury transits seems to symbolize the Virgo facet of Mercury—cleaning up our act by ridding ourselves of our sloppy ways of thinking or behaving. But the Gemini factor can be suggested by our concerns about how we learn some-thing. We may feel we don't know enough about a subject that could help us with our career security (Saturn), and thus may be thinking long and hard about going back to school or taking training classes somewhere. It is usually a good time to take tests or qualifying exams. We will have to play the serious stu-dent and crack the books or attend all preparatory classes.

If fact, learning useful things in a controlled setup like a classroom is a great way to siphon off a lot of frustrated energy of transiting Saturn. We must find a proper channel to satisfy this planet's need for purposeful activity, because Saturn hates an idle mind. If going to workshops, seminars, or adult education courses is not within our budget, Saturn can still be satisfied when we buy a handful of (used?) paperbacks that can teach us what we need to know about ourselves and/or the work projects we may wish to undertake. Saturn loves those "do it yourself and save money" books and all that practical self-help material.

Real life will provide us with many different scenarios in which we can experience Saturn/Mercury principles combined. Mercury seems to rule a lot of things in our lives (cars, neigh-bors, writing tools, siblings, our mail, paperwork in general, etc.). Who knows how this transit will manifest? However, Saturn will typically focus on what has been neglected, or what is about to break down or malfunction if not attended to. Saturn spots the weak link in the chain and gives it a gentle pull just to get our attention. If we continue to ignore this, the pull becomes a forceful yank—and if still overlooked, that chain eventually falls apart beyond repair. We should think about our current affairs and figure out where we need to be sensitive to Saturn's warning tugs.

A well-handled Saturn/Mercury transit ushers in a time period when we do not feel aimless or at loose ends, and our sense of duty and commitment is not burdensome. Our life seems well organized and stabilized as we learn to approach realistic objectives with sensible expectations in mind. We can get things done, although at a slower pace than we prefer. Saturn supports a "one-step-at-a-time" attitude in its quest to instill healthy routines and help us get down to simpler basics. Necessity calls the shots now.

CHAPTER NINE

SATURN IN CANCER

THIN SKINNED

Both Saturn and Cancer emphasize the need to feel well insulated from external aggression by putting up a big wall of defense. Cancer describes the typical psychological shells we build to shield ourselves from personal attack and invasion. Saturn in Cancer suggests that such shells can be quite thick and impenetrable; certain facets of our emotional nature wear a suit of armor. Our uncertainties about being cared for can run deep and are enduring. Some of us seem to have an almost chronic case of touchiness. We obviously cannot handle criticism (or anger) well, and can assume we are being emotionally pistol-whipped by others even when we are not.

Saturn and Cancer also share a tendency toward traditional, conservative behavior and a reliance on the past for solutions. We exhibit a reluctance to take risks or gamble with our security. We emotionally respond to life in ways that help us feel safe and in control (especially if we are intense to begin with). We don't seem to want the vulnerable parts of our nature to spontaneously spill out and make a mess. Cautious and reserved in the demonstration of our intimate feelings, we are apt to incorrectly give off the impression that we are unemotional or even insensitive. As a result, people may think we are a bit too cool-headed and detached. Our softer side is kept from being exposed.

Some of us further encourage this image by rejecting our natural dependency needs in favor of overemphasized self-sufficiency. We might as well wear a big button that shouts "I Don't Need Any of You!" We could also disguise inner pain by appearing to lack depth of feelings, which is anything but the case. Saturn suggests we will learn the hard way to get tough with ourselves rather than feel like a walking target, put down by loved ones or by a harsh, uncaring world of strangers. An unconscious "sour grapes" attitude is often a root cause of much of our sense of alienation.

This can be one of the "crabbier" placements for Cancer. We need to work at not always being so pessimistic about the intentions of others toward us. Much of the above is more indicative of Saturn in bad shape, aspect-wise. Saturn/Mars, Saturn/Neptune, and Saturn/Pluto stress patterns can be particularly problematic.

CLAMMING UP

We absorb and react strongly to situations that support or jeopardize our safety needs, yet self-doubts tend to impede the smooth flow of open emotional exchange. We seem to intently study the responses of others, waiting for them to reveal their emotions. Rather than clam up, it would be better for us to display a dose of courage by daring to expose our true feelings. It is normally not easy for us to reach out and touch someone without anticipating rejection or even ridicule. With Saturn involved, we may find we have apprehensions involving closeness, attachment, and intimate commitment. Sometimes defensive Cancer further fortifies Saturn's urge to construct barriers to keep threatening psychological elements at bay. As a result, we may constantly be on guard against real or imagined rebuffs from others. Any anxieties along these lines are hard to eradicate, since they can stem from long-standing negative attitudes. Still, with Saturn in a cardinal sign, the best approach would be a direct and assertive one. We need to move out into life, externalizing our Saturn needs.

When mishandled, Saturn in Cancer suggests our inner psychological foundation is weakened due to an unwillingness to trust our instincts, an irrational fear of harm, and a lack of self-nurturing skills (sometimes manifesting in junk food addictions, yo-yo diets, or basic undernourishment). We may have a defeatist attitude regarding our ability to effectively bond with others. Why do some of us develop such symptoms? Cancer implies that we may have had to digest some harsh realities in our early family circumstances, often at a tender age when we were emotionally immature and vulnerable. Perhaps we failed to see real closeness and affection between our parents. The sympathetic tenderness of Cancer can be at odds with the cold realism of functional Saturn. Tearful Cancer wants an assuring hug while Saturn questions whether we really deserve one. Have we earned it?

Thus, we may have started off in life very hungry for emotional warmth. In our youth, we needed to feel touched and held a lot (and still do, even though we may squirm a little and receive hugs a bit stiffly). But if our parents failed to provide us with the nurturance needed in the exact manner required of us (and what parent always meets up with any child's precise expectations?) we probably retaliated by hardening our feelings in an attempt to cut them off or deaden the impact of our insecurity. This is when our expert shell-building talent takes over.

WOMB SERVICE

Saturn in Cancer denotes a lack of comforting security in our early home environment, usually due to emotional rather than material deprivation. Cancer is associated with parts of our image-storing faculty—our so-called memory bank, where long-lost impressions and buried imagery are alive but dormant until evoked (and brought back onto the big screen of consciousness for yet another showing). When combined with Saturn's pessimistic streak, Cancer implies we can harbor fearful childhood traumas that persist for years. As an adult, we may have trouble letting go of this stressful emotional baggage from our past. Learning how to therapeutically uproot and put the spotlight of objectivity onto such disturbing inner images becomes paramount at some point. Otherwise, they can suck out our vitality like a black hole and keep us from vibrantly being a part of the Now. We can function in a depressive state with little spontaneity and adventurousness.

We have often felt deprived of maternal affection and closeness. Our need to be lovingly mothered was blocked or denied in some manner due to circumstances we could not control. This can suggest that some of us may have developed an unresolved hunger for an almost womblike matrix protecting us from psychological hurts. But to continue to retreat to our psychological womb could also imply our failing to grow up and mature. Our ability to deal with adult interaction becomes diminished should we pointedly avoid life's emotional confrontations. If provoked, we still are likely to react emotionally in relationships like we did as a child, with similar frustrations. Either people give in to our needs, or we simply turn sullen and withdrawn—or even worse, indifferent. We just turn off our feelings. Ironically, while we fear being abandoned by those we depend on, we can end up emotionally abandoning them.

Cold-Blooded

By the way, turning cold is a defense mechanism all water signs are good at, not just Cancer. Traditional astrology has sketched for us a mellow picture in soft pastels of the water signs, depicting them as highly understanding, sympathetically responsive, sensitive to unspoken needs, empathetic to a fault, etc. However, real warmth does not come from the water element—it comes from the fire trinity. Think of it—water signs are represented by a host of cold-blooded creatures (with scales, shells, claws, pinchers, barbs, and other hard outer body parts—all cool to the touch and not very cuddly and huggable). That should give us a clue about another inner reality shared by Cancer, Scorpio, and Pisces: Water signs exhibit a capacity to retreat into their own self-absorbed world when hurt. There is an above-average ability to shut out the external environment (make it disappear) when they feel danger lurking.

Naturally, they cannot remain in such an isolated state forever. But when they do go deeply within and try to become emotionally invisible on the surface as their best defense, they become quite inaccessible and remote. The void of feeling they thus create can almost be tangibly felt by others. You are dead or non-existent to them for the moment, and they neither smile nor shed tears for you. You've been cut off or cut out in a surprisingly chilly manner. With Saturn in the water signs, this tendency is accentuated. The good news is that Cancer cannot bear to exist in this disconnected state for too long, and will come out of its shell to once again test the emotional waters in close relationships. Turtles are ruled by Cancer.

DIVING FOR PEARLS

I suspect a few of us with Saturn in Cancer have reached for the Kleenex after reading some of this dreary stuff, so it's time to focus on the positive attributes. Constructively, Saturn in Cancer provides us with a profound understanding of emotions—how they work, and the purpose for their built-in limitations. Saturn helps steady the mood fluctuations of Cancer. We learn to respect our emotional dimension, but also realize it is not the only valid way to assess reality. Feelings have their place, but so does sensible emotional control and common sense. This could mean we learn not to overreact to stressful issues and, if anything, find we can become a solid grounding force for others who are destabilized by their emotions. We get to play out a maternal energy that is very solid, soothing, and easily accessible. Saturn is a reliable planet, and others can depend on our ability to be effectively support-ive in our caregiving. We can help people trust that they have an inner foundation rooted in powerful instincts that they can draw from in times of need.

Since Saturn is a key to our career needs, in Cancer it sug-gests we can do well in professions involving close human interaction. We need to work with flesh-and-blood people issues that touch the heart and soul in some way. We may want to feel we are putting others under our wing and pro-tecting their needs, acting as a professional mom to many who depend on us. Because we understand feeling desperately needy, we often find our purpose in life by dealing with the socially needy. No matter what career we gravitate toward, we seek to feel at home with the objectives of that profession. They have to reach us on a gut level. If they do, we can give much of ourselves to that career.

Actually, we also need to integrate our Saturn urges with whatever is shown in the Tenth House and Sixth House to get the fuller picture. But our sense of security on the job is a Saturn issue, and with Cancer involved, we want to feel very involved and supportive in our role. Money and fame seem to mean less to us than working in an environment that offers us close bonding and warm connections with others who feel like an ideal family to us. In fact, we could opt to work at home in very familiar, secure surroundings.

STEADY ANCHOR

As Saturn in Cancer implies a potential for powerful security needs, we may find we can depend on our inner strength and rootedness to help us successfully overcome life's hurdles. We learn the value of giving our inner world its due attention, which in turn empowers our instinctual nature and even opens up the door to our "sixth sense" or intuition. This is important, because we often feel psychically blocked—but only because we have underused that extrasensory part of our consciousness.

Eventually, some of us may start to feel very connected to this dimension as we get older and find ourselves more secure within. We may find a little ESP can actually help us read people better and avoid disturbing misunderstandings. We must start by learning to trust our hunches. One little tip: Intuition cannot be controlled and manipulated the same way we handle our typical fears. We best let it flow wherever it wants to take us.

Emotional anchoring is as important to our well-being as material stability. We grow to realize that security is not something to be guarded, but something best shared openly with others we intimately connect with. This always requires a degree of risk, but also the promise of deeper rewards. Since emotional stinginess is one of Saturn in Cancer's more unattractive traits, we are often too preoccupied with our own ancient wounds to see how we make others feel rejected and neglected. We may be oblivious to how and when we don't let loved ones enter our inner world, or we invest little of ourselves in a relationship until we've put others through a security test to see the extent of their caring, supportive concern. We retreat into our shell while we demand others expose their soft underbellies to us again and again. We insist on their willingness to be openly vulnerable, yet we freeze when expected to do the same. This has to stop, and Saturn will find ways to make this point crystal clear.

However, we over-achievers go the opposite route and give, give, give, just to turn around and compulsively accommodate others some more. We could operate in a continuous state of overload in terms of unconditionally pouring ourselves out to people. For us, there is no holding back. We assume everyone needs our tender loving care. Unfortunately, what often results is emptiness and a sense of exhaustion as we realize we have attracted a lot of selfish takers who eventually abandon us once our well has run dry. And so, one Saturn in Cancer challenge centers on learning when to mother others in need vs. when to allow someone else to embrace our needs. We deserve the emotional food and physical closeness for which we have hungered for so long. We have a better chance of attracting that truly caring someone once we permit ourselves to believe that.

Astro-lebrities with Saturn in Cancer

Liza Minnelli	Queen Elizabeth I
Oscar Wilde	Napoleon
Michelangelo	Jackie Gleason
Marc Chagall	Dylan Thomas
Mia Farrow	Frank Sinatra

SATURN IN THE FOURTH HOUSE

HOME ALONE

In this house of psychological roots and subjective anchoring, Saturn suggests we may feel a deep lack of inner security due to our early family experience. It may not have been easy for us to digest the general atmosphere within the home during our formative years. Later, we may grow up making a concentrated effort to protect ourselves from whatever we regard as emotionally threatening. Saturn in the Fourth House can be an easily internalized placement. We can become quite adept at constructing defense mechanisms and other psychological barriers that insulate us from experiencing vulnerability in close human interactions, leaving us lonely and cut off from others at a root level of our being.

Some of us work hard to keep our real feelings from being exposed or even analyzed. Perhaps we fear that those we desire to attach ourselves to are capable of wounding us or—even worse—abandoning us in our moment of greatest need, so we may choose to remain impenetrable at the base of our inner foundation. How did we develop such a deep distrust of other people's ability to nurture and support us on emotional levels? Why all the hard-as-steel insulation? People may feel we are difficult to reach. Ever on the defense, we disagree that we are inaccessible. We probably just don't see ourselves like that, and it hurts when others do.

We may have viewed elements of our childhood years in the home as a source of discomfort, denial, pain, and general restriction. It probably made little difference, from a subjective viewpoint, whether ours was an environment of privileged affluence or abject poverty. Any sense of deprivation was more on an emotional level than a material one. We were paying close attention to how well our parents either responded to our needs or ignored them. Our upbringing and conditioning may have revealed patterns of rigidity, coldness, a lack of color, and varying degrees of enforced discipline and control.

Many of us took all this quite seriously, and seldom without anxiety. We may have been made to feel disliked and unwanted by at least one parent, whom we nevertheless tried to appease and gain respect from. What we basically wanted from that parent (and maybe from the rest of the family) was unconditional love and closeness—an affirmation that we were lovable for just being our imperfect selves, warts and all. We typically grew up feeling we never got that. The prerequisites for love and emotional nourishment centered on our obedience and model behavior. As few of us were flawless in word and deed, we may not have grown up feeling accepted. As adults, we may distance ourselves from our family at large rather than submit to their critical rejection. (Much of the above is also likely to be symbolized by a very harshly aspected Saturn: Saturn/Moon/Pluto conflicts in particular.)

MOTHER PROBLEM

This house puts us in touch with the maternal manifestations at the circumstantial level. We usually learn about our own caregiving capacity through interaction with our biological mother or early mother figure. With Saturn here, we want our maternal figure to be dependable and solid. We expect her to be predictable in her support. We can become preoccupied with this parent's ability to fulfill our need for safety. How well she does so can have quite an impact on how we express closeness and intimacy as adults. But astrology wouldn't put the sole blame on our mother if she did a poor job here. We are the ones born with Saturn in the Fourth House, and it is we who are projecting certain unappealing Saturn traits onto our mother. We may have trouble internally reclaiming these projections as we get older, but they will need to be reclaimed as part of our wholeness. Until then, our mother has to carry and act out much of Saturn's darker face.

In actuality, Mom could have been inconsistent or contradictory in her rearing of us, creating mixed messages. She could have been very protective of our welfare while also reluctant to be too warm and demonstrative with her feelings, as if driven more by parental duty than instinctive love. We tend to absorb this same inner complex, resulting in an ambivalence that typically doesn't sit well with the Saturn principle (which would rather opt for clearly defined expression). Maybe our mother was unable to show her love for us because daily survival needs were the number one priority, with little time for tender-hearted moments of maternal affection. Her opportunities to show care may have been limited for some tangible reason. Maybe her career needs were put before our baby needs. How this Saturn dilemma played out could have taken many paths.

It could also be that our mother was emotionally immature at the time, or simply wasn't very maternal at heart. Babies pick up on this quite vividly and can appear constantly cranky as a form of protest for getting the cold shoulder. In a few cases, our mom may not have physically been around long enough (due to abandonment, divorce, institutionalization, or death) to help us structure healthy security patterns during our formative years. Her absence created a void that may still need to be filled.

It is generally considered a social taboo, so we probably carry some weighty guilt about it, but some of us may grow up disliking or even hating our mother. Maybe we grow up realizing we function best by keeping a safe distance from our mom and her negative impact on us (often Moon/Saturn stress aspects are similar in theme here). We feel vulnerable around many of our family members, sensing they collectively know how to target our weak spots. But what we tend to dislike the most are the feelings of obligation and duty we may have towards them. Dependency issues unresolved in the past can be associated with an ongoing sense of doubt and frustration.

We may realize that our maternal relationship is neither healthy nor growth-inducing, especially if we do nothing about it but gripe and let resentment slowly build a nest of thorns. At the least, we sense a firm parental grip over certain aspects of our psyche—a power we cannot break away from completely without first learning the inner meaning of that power.

Saturn in the water houses is more apt to indicate "karmic" ties than when found in other house placements. With Saturn in the Fourth House we may feel quite bound to our mother (or the concept of mother), even if we don't like her personally or trust her motives and intentions. But by paying attention to what discomforts us about her, we may learn plenty about what we have trouble getting in touch with when others come into our life and attempt to mother and comfort us, or when they show that feared dark face and deny our needs by turning cold or leaving us.

DON'T LEAN ON ME

Some of us with Saturn in the Fourth House tend to block our ability to become emotionally dependent on another. We feel weakened by our own neediness. It is possible that we associate such dependency with loss, restriction, or even harsh criticism. Perhaps our early attempts at securing maternal warmth and affection were unsuccessful. We could misinterpret ourselves as unlovable because of it. Later, in our adult relationships, we may have little confidence in our ability to establish a sound emotional base. We could push others off who need to depend on us on some level. Yet we can deeply feel attached to others. Our degree of linkage can be enduring, but unfortunately we may associate such connection with powerlessness.

If we do not eventually examine ourselves and ask why we are so afraid to meaningfully connect with others, we could end up lonely and shut off from really intimate contact. This can be painfully felt near the closing years of our life (the Fourth House deals with our approach to "old age"). We need to carefully review our past, studying the nature of parental interaction—and especially that parent we strongly reacted to on the emotional level. Even if we lacked an adequate maternal figure altogether, we are still prone to fixate on the emptiness and hunger such a lack of nurturing could create.

Realize that Saturn in the Fourth House does not exclusively deny us warmth or sensitive responsiveness from others, but still we feel we must work hard to earn and secure such response. We may assume it will involve a struggle. We are as likely to doubt our own capacity to be caring of others (even of animals/plants/the home itself), but in truth, we are anything but uncaring and unconcerned at the roots of our being. One important life goal is for us to recognize this. We need to work at accepting dependency relationships and viewing them as redemptive and healing for us.

CLAN DESTINED

With a mismanaged Saturn, regardless of house, we often suffer because of our own unrecognized potential, underdeveloped strengths, or untapped capacity for excellence. Saturn in the Fourth House suggests we can convince ourselves that we are somehow emotionally inadequate. Maybe we inwardly doubt our ability to relate to people on a safe, connecting level. We think we do not bond easily.

Perhaps we take the "family" concept much too seriously. Inside us we crave having Ozzie and Harriet for parents but in reality got a less than ideal setup. Maybe we continue to over-analyze various family members (the Fourth House also describes the "family dynamic" as a whole) in terms of how they accept or reject us. Do they know we are sometimes full of hurt? Or that we are lonely or scared? Would they even care? Before we drown in self-pity, we need to recognize that our own standards of right/wrong or good/bad behavior for our family can be rigid and unyielding.

Our family unit probably did appear to us as conservative, orthodox, formality conscious, or bland and lacking in imagination. Everyone seemed to take the safe route of controlled interaction. Structured roles held the family together. But have we committed ourselves to forever seeing some family members in an inflexible manner? If they don't seem to ever change for the better, how much of that is due to our fixed attitudes and lasting impressions? We need to be careful we don't stifle their growth too.

COMING UP FOR AIR

Although our family typically didn't treat us like pampered babies (we certainly weren't spoiled rotten with attention), we may still grow up feeling as vulnerable as infants psychologically. Such emotional hypersensitivity either goes unrecognized by those we try to get close to for support, or is harshly reprimanded and devalued (we are brushed off as too clingy and suffocating). We are accused of always being hungry for unconditional assurance from our mate, our kids, even the dog; and can get very down and fearful when they start to back off and put up a stone wall of separation. Saturn can be tenacious and the Fourth House can be blind to its aggressive instincts to envelop others in its waves of feelings. We often are too subjectively wrapped up in our reactions to understand that breathing space is always needed in healthy relationships. We are subject to separation anxiety to begin with, but at some point in our development we need to consciously allow for independent functioning, especially in the home. The "empty nest blues" need not be our fate. It would be good to see how well we can live alone and unattached, if need be. Saturn will test our ability to be self-sufficient security-wise.

GIMME SHELTER

Economical difficulties in our family when we were young can make us sensitive to future deprivation. We may harbor doubts as adults about not being well provided for on the home front, fearing we won't have a decent roof over our heads. We over-achievers with Saturn in the Fourth House will make sure we have a well-protected home (or homes) that is ours to control (renting is less satisfying than owning for Saturn). But if we block our Saturn needs, our failure to properly self-nurture also expresses itself as a lack of support for our domestic security needs. We can end up living in places that are cramped, unattractive, worn out, or in constant need of repairs. It can get expensive to maintain such a place. Maybe we also gravitate towards unsafe housing, such as a dangerous neighborhood or living quarters that lack safety features such as deadbolt locks and peepholes. We may live someplace with cheap rent, but it may be drafty and a utilities guzzler due to poor insulation. We may even forget to lock our doors or safeguard our belongings in other ways (an out-of-touch Saturn behaves much like a careless Jupiter or Neptune). Whatever the case, we need to ask ourselves why we literally feel at home in such substandard dwellings. Don't we deserve a better nest, a safer shelter? Maybe even a real dining room?

Some of us over-achievers react to our anxious feelings of insecurity by doing our very best to build the most solid foundation we can afford. We insist on a sound and dependable home structure. We'd even like to have our own land to build our home from scratch. We also want to be grounded in natural surroundings. Our home must be our sturdy fortress, totally managed by us (Saturn is very much into protecting territorial rights). We typically desire fences, walls, heavy shrubbery defining boundaries, and other forms of clear demarcation. We may instead pick an isolated spot away from populated areas. However, we need to be sensible about how far we will go for the sake of ultimate protection. Why do we only feel safe when living in a home resembling Fort Knox?

Astro-lebrities with Saturn in The Fourth House

Marilyn Monroe	Nelson Rockefeller
Gloria Steinem	Albert Schweitzer
Mary Baker Eddy	John Travolta
Lauren Bacall	Judy Garland
Jessica Savitch	Ted Turner

SATURN/MOON ASPECTS

NATAL

Saturn and the Moon are both security-conscious and will respond to life with caution. Defensive by nature, their tendency is to protect and to insulate. We are in need of being very real with our emotions since we are sensitive and feel things deeply, but emotionality does not sit well with us when it leaves us feeling vulnerable and exposed to external attack. That's when Saturn tries to deaden the powerful gut reactions of the Moon and convince us that we shouldn't be reacting to something or somebody so strongly. Due to Saturn's ability to rationalize and justify anything, we often stop ourselves from getting too emotional with people or with situations that thwart our security needs. Saturn typically freezes an emotional response that would otherwise spill out, for example, as an irrational display of fear and panic. A frightened Moon knows darn well what it feels, but Saturn puts the brakes on any purely instinctual outpouring of feelings, especially intense ones. Saturn often adds an element of shame, suggesting that we harshly judge ourselves for reacting certain ways, even if such feelings are valid and appropriate. Our first impulse is to find fault with our reactions.

Saturn does not tolerate unpredictability well, and may fear that our emotions will be overwhelming and uncontrollable when left unchecked. So it tries to exert control, and we find ourselves not crying easily, not allowing ourselves to have a tantrum, and not succumbing to any other form of lunatic behavior. We sometimes seem too much in control of ourselves when we should instead be busting a gut over an incident that has justly disturbed us. We may also find ourselves enduring other people's childish outbursts and other dramatic scenes while we quietly stuff our feelings and continue to appear composed. Our instincts tell us that someone has to act like a functional adult—to be in charge at all times—and that someone is us. We feel it is our solemn duty to keep everything working together in life, shouldering all responsibilities, while keeping our personal needs way in the background and out of sight.

This could be evaluated favorably on the surface as maturity, or even misread as unsympathetic coldness. People may assume we don't cry easily or gnash our teeth in rage simply because we don't care enough to feel for whatever is happening to us or others. Saturn can make the Moon look convincingly detached and aloof. Life seems to be pushing our buttons and egging us on to break down our barriers, but we refuse to, especially in public. Still, we can't help but wonder how much more misery and frustration we are to endure. When is the dam finally going to burst? When will the floodgates open wide?

Actually, stressful aspects make this dilemma more vividly experienced. Saturn/Moon squares and oppositions seems to have a particular talent for shutting off emotions in order to carry on with mundane responsibilities and general self-preservation. Saturn can do a great job squelching feelings by using all sorts of fear and guilt mechanisms to make sure we don't fall apart at the seams. We may be calm on the surface, but underneath is a whole other emotional reality. Such tense aspects can bring people into our path who either try to inhibit the expression of our feelings and deny us our insecurities, or who are themselves so needy and dependent that we get scared and either terminate the relationship prematurely or play hardhearted Saturn and block their need to be close and intimate. As various times, we can identify with Saturn and project the Moon, or vice versa.

Usually, we are too cautious to begin with to get involved with anyone unless we've analyzed the situation and put the other person through a battery of Saturnian security tests (some of which can seem just plain mean). Only the strong and the patient survive and pass these exams. And often, once we are finally satisfied and ready to take the plunge, that individual gets cold feet (or gets smart), ends the union, or goes on to someone more accessible. We took too long to commit, and now we are left feeling abandoned and very uncertain of ourselves.

This abandonment theme (which is also strong with Moon/Neptune) probably started with our early family life. Here's how the dynamic often played out: We typically would see our mother as fit for the Moon/Saturn role, and it is she who usually gets our bad reviews (although sometimes it's our Dad, and often it's both parents). One big gripe is that we didn't get maternal support from Mom. She may have appeared unemotional or too strict to be truly nurturing of our tender needs. We believe she denied us closeness and warmth or we felt we couldn't open up to her. Maybe she was heavily work-oriented and failed to give us quality time at home. She could also have been a worrier with a pessimistic streak. Whatever her personality, we basically found ourselves critical of her as much as she might have been of us. Now, because of faulty bonding early in life, some of us may want to avoid our mother and be wary of her attempts to further influence our lives.

Of course, trines and sextiles and even a well-handled conjunction could indicate that our mother was supportive of us in practical ways (though still not too emotional) and sensible in her child-raising techniques. She's symbolized as a dependable person blessed with much stability and common sense, a welcome anchor in our lives when we need her to be, but not intrusive or a control freak. We learn from this relationship that emotional involvement and commitment do not have to mean we must micromanage every facet of a relationship to preserve it and ensure it works perfectly. Even when we are disappointed with how things occasionally turn out, we don't turn frosty and shut down parts of us vital to healthy intimate communication. A bitter Saturn, like a scorned Pluto, believes in punishing the guilty (those who disappoint us). But in this case, to do so by becoming frozen and untouchable can emotionally backfire on us.

Both Saturn and the Moon are preservation-oriented. They each have a reverence for ancestral history and for all cherished traditions from bygone days, with a special respect and appreciation for things of enduring value (old-fashioned virtues, antiques, and land itself). We don't take being uprooted easily, and can work hard to establish a solid home base that is quiet and orderly (although stress aspects can sometimes block Saturn, resulting in chronically messy, disorganized living quarters). The home structure itself can symbolize Saturn/Moon, with hedges, fences, shade trees, and walled-in backyards. We may favor settled, older neighborhoods.

Usually conscientious in the home, we work best when we set up maintenance routines. We often do all the dull but necessary jobs around the house, even picking up after everyone. We want to restore order. But we will need to resist the temptation to overburden ourselves by doing other people's chores and then complaining about it. Saturn/Moon can, in its own unemotional way, nag about doing any extra work it really should be leaving to someone else. At the same time, we tell ourselves we are not really that upset, just a little annoyed by not getting a lot of help or appreciation for our efforts. We need to honestly confront others with our grievances rather than start to build a wall of icy resentment. Learning to vent feelings in open and direct ways is always a challenge for Saturn/Moon people. We need to feel confident that we will be heard and taken seriously.

TRANSIT

Saturn natally tends to inhibit the open, confident expression of any planet it contacts, at least initially. We are pressured to go within and mull over the part of the psyche that planet represents for long stretches at a time. This may be frustrating and our limitations may seem never-ending, but Saturn also can lead us to a major experience of understanding and self-mastery. Saturn experience is always much easier on us when we are willing to work with this planet and stop trying to evade its pressing issues. And so, the slow unfoldment of potential is Saturn's way of ensuring a more mature blossoming and the bearing of ripened fruit. Saturn also insists on a sturdy root structure.

But transiting Saturn often tests the results of all that inner preparation. Saturn offers a reality check so we can clearly assess what we have already securely developed for ourselves through struggle and determination. At this point, we are to start using whatever the planet or house symbolizes more realistically. Saturn also highlights where we still need to do our homework due to weak, ineffectual structure, and compels us to concentrate fully on the issue shown by the transited planet or house.

Saturn transiting the Moon is often a time when we are feeling a need to pull back from our close involvements and review the reality of our relationships. We may not be happy with how things are flowing. We could be feeling stuck in a partnership that has no firm connective base (Venus rules love relationships, but the Moon deals with the security needs of such unions). Naturally, we desire continuous emotional fulfillment and assured security, but Saturn implies this is not to be had if any union in question is unworkable or is too damaged to be repaired. Saturn could mercifully try to end a situation that has been hard on our feelings, or unsafe on some level. That doesn't mean always ending the actual relationship, but simply eliminating its malfunctioning parts. Saturn, being forever pragmatic, doesn't drastically terminate things in the extremist fashion of volatile Uranus or passionate Pluto.

Trines and sextiles could mean we that have something salvageable here if all parties involved are willing to do the necessary rebuilding work. Some of us, however, are without a partner, and so we are to internally work on ourselves steadily and consciously. In fact, such supportive aspects can help us restore a semblance of order to many parts of our life that had been shattered by enforced change (maybe due to Uranian challenges). Saturn trines seek sane solutions and push for everything to fall back into place. Saturn sextiles are more willing to accept the alterations all changes imply, making the best of strained situations at times. A main theme of either aspect is the need to replace outworn security symbols with new improved ones that better fit our current development. Well-managed Saturn/Moon can also fortify what has been working consistently for us regarding our emotional stability.

The Moon is a part of us that sometimes clings to people and things far too long. Its instinct is to not let go, even if its attachments prove heavy and burdensome. Transiting Saturn appreciates the Moon's need to hold onto the familiar, but will not condone mindless attachments that are more the product of habit than true need. Saturn will spot the weakest element of this unsatisfactory situation and start the unraveling process, perhaps slowly at first. If ignored, it persists until our structure is riddled with big gaping holes that cannot support solid form. We are forced to be weaned away from what we assumed was feeding us emotional energy, but in reality was only draining us, or keeping us in a childlike state of insecurity.

The good news is that Saturn will try to opt for sensible solutions, because it is driven to problem-solve. Whatever our predicament, we have an extra measure of resolve to clarify our needs and find practical ways to work around difficulties. With the Moon as the target of this transit, we will need greater objectivity in order to see our emotional framework clearly. We will have to address our trouble spots, which typically involve psychological baggage we've been carrying around since early childhood. Saturn helps us better focus and concentrate on chronic issues that usually tie in with abandonment, separation, loneliness, inhibition of feelings, etc. There is no overnight fix when Saturn is involved, but defining our problems is the first step in dealing with them.

We need to articulate our emotional fears and uncertainties, and this requires much courage and honesty. Saturn supports an attempt to feel things as they really are, even if we initially become depressed and saddened by doing so. It is likely that elements of our past will need to be laid to rest.

This is a good time to look at our parents or our family issues in general and reflect on where we can make our ties more solid and durable. We should not be so quick to shut down and pull away from any responsibilities, even if we are having a tough Saturn/Moon contact. Patience and confidence will help us weather any testing conditions, whether strictly emotional or economical. We are probably more concerned than usual about having a roof over our heads and being able to materially sustain ourselves, since the survival instinct is stronger at this time. We probably will find true security comes from plodding on and making cautious moves based on the desire for optimum timing rather than unfounded fear. Much really depends on our natal Moon's aspects—and especially its natal sign.

The natal sign of the Moon determines the overall mood of Saturn's transit. Look for common denominators between that sign and Saturn to see where and how reinforcing factors may interact. Obviously, Moon in Scorpio can get very deep and introspective with a Saturn transit, and much too serious about consequences. But a Gemini Moon might scratch its head in puzzlement and wonder what to do with some of this strangely heavy energy. Gemini already has a harder time focusing for long periods, and what Saturn wants us to concentrate on may not be fun stuff for Gemini. At least this adaptable air sign won't intensely overdramatize the elements of loss or separation that can characterize this transit. Gemini might even feel more grounded with its instincts.

If we have undergone a successful Saturn transit to our Moon, we feel emotionally sturdier and more able to cope with whatever life throws at us. Of course, as our reward for developing such inner strength, life then eases up a bit and offers us a period of stability when our routines and our intimate relationships bring a degree of contentment. We trust our environment more and feel safe in our day-to-day interactions. Our disposition is more worldly at this time in that we willingly tackle projects and tasks at hand with a sensible concern for building durable material frameworks. We can be very much our own best parent, giving ourselves tender loving care when needed, but also educating ourselves about the security of imposing certain reasonable limits when advantageous.

Squares and oppositions suggest we have dearly earned any fruitful Saturn/Moon passage, not always with a lot of external help. We may need time to rest and recuperate if the maturation process has been exhausting in its demands. Still, the one common thread shared by all these transits is that we can start to feel more at home with ourselves, knowing we have laid down a dependable foundation from within that will provide real support for a long time to come.

CHAPTER TEN

SATURN IN LEO

HEAVYWEIGHT CHAMP

Leo's desire for personal recognition, glory, and adulation reinforces Saturn's drive to scale the heights of social success. The
executive prowess of authoritative Leo—rather than its joyous,
fun-loving side—is more readily evoked by no-nonsense
Saturn. Although Leo can represent the power of personal love,
Saturn in this fixed sign leans more towards the love of personal power. Saturn's ambitions are magnified and vitalized by
Leo. We are proud of our drive to accomplish, though not
always openly so. We can concentrate our tremendous
willpower toward all desired objectives with much deliberate
focus. Leo can add a sense of flair to Saturn's managerial abilities. However, due to the royal nature of this commanding sign,
we may feel it is our sole responsibility to dictate the actions of
others according to what we believe is the greatest good.

However noble our motivation, such an approach can
appear heavy-handed and domineering to others. We can feel
frustrated and even resentful when our aims are questioned,
interfered with, or simply met with resistance. Leo's egocentric
drive to exercise centralized control can become too inflexible

119

with Saturn involved. In fact, Saturn in any fixed sign can be uncompromisingly rigid and absolute (even in Aquarius, which is co-ruled by Saturn).

Dignified, praise-seeking Leo coordinates well with Saturn's need to be respected and honored. Leo's more stately (rather than sunny) nature is underscored by formality-conscious Saturn. This is perhaps the least radiant, beaming, playful placement for Leo (with the exception of Pluto in Leo). We may feel awkwardly self-conscious and unwilling to fully let go of ourselves long enough to experience the spirited exuberance that is an essential part of Leo's inner make-up. We are very conscious of the impact we make on others, for better or worse. Saturn and Leo like being securely in the winner's circle, although Saturn downplays such a desire while Leo is reluctant to pay all the necessary dues it takes to get there. But sometimes, by sheer force of will, we win the gold medal.

CAREFULLY CRAFTED TALENT

Cautiously expressive, sometimes doubtful, and often uncertain, Saturn is less than confident about the worth of its Leo creativity, and less easily satisfied with the products of its inspiration. We with Saturn in Leo are not denied talents or special skills, but what is typically indicated here is a high degree of frustration, inhibition, or hesitancy in showing off our creative power. Leo loves to shine in a bright and bold manner, yet somber Saturn by nature would rather send in the clouds.

As a result, we may have a problem feeling comfortable with what we create and display. We might demand of ourselves a state of perfection that may be beyond our realistic capacity. Even when close to success, we often manage to impose restrictions on the vital flow of our ego-driven juices. We can suffer performance anxiety in a very un-Leolike manner. Critical of the quality of our output, we take all personal deficiencies in this area too much to heart. Any sense of lack (Saturn) becomes tied to our ego needs (Leo) and resonates at the very core of our being. Should our insecurity be strong enough, we may not even attempt to test out our talents for fear of failure or personal humiliation. In this case, we need to be careful not to resent or become envious of the seemingly superior abilities of others. Negative Leo cannot stand to be in the shadows while someone else is receiving the full spotlight; positive Leo is magnanimous in letting others deservingly shine.

When well managed, Saturn in Leo suggests we show much patience and discipline when developing our creative gifts. We are able to work long and hard to achieve the level of mastery we aim for, as Saturn seeks to excel and be as polished as possible in whatever it dedicates its time and energy to. In this instance, we do not take our talents for granted. We structure their expression with great care and attention to detail. We abhor anything slipshod to the point of being considered fixated.

SERIOUS PLAY

Leo is associated with our ability to enjoy ourselves through all forms of pleasure pursuits, recreations, amusements, games, and speculative activities involving elements of risk and chance. Leo urges us to adventurously participate in these life interests in a wholehearted manner, and with a high degree of spiritedness and optimism. We are to learn the art of playfulness and the wisdom of joyous self-extension, and to value gambling with life rather than always insisting on taking safe routes.

All this sounds great for pure Leo energy, but creates anxiety for the Saturn part of our psyche. This can be Leo's least adventurous placement. When Leo filters through Saturn, we find ourselves less comfortable with leisure, probably due to the functional urges of this work-oriented planet. If anything, satisfaction and enjoyment are derived more from purposeful involvement in specialized activities demanding great responsibilities, or those offering prestige and recognition. Even though Saturn will claim that the work is its own reward and disdains all the glory, Leo really wants to be held in high esteem—and this is where we can be in a state of inner conflict. We take our pleasures seriously and gravitate toward worthy pursuits allowing us full control, but we need to be careful not to be sore losers. We know it's not the winning that counts as much as how we play, yet we are not easily convinced that losing shouldn't be all that big a deal. It is for us.

SORROW THROUGH LOVE?

A traditional, deterministic-sounding warning associated with Saturn in Leo is "sorrow through matters of the heart." That means trouble with love and romance. Why should this manifest as such for some of us? Bad luck? It would appear so on the surface—but realize that Leo rules our capacity to demonstrate the strength of our love ability with much warmth and ardor. Saturn, discouraging intimacy and its vulnerabilities, cools off the romantic expression of passionate Leo. The result can be emotional stiffness or an inhibition of affectionate display. We can be disinclined to show our love due to our fears of inadequacy, rejection, and possible humiliation. This could manifest in a few instances as actual medical heart problems. The symptoms are real, but the source may have something to do with not feeling loved or being able to openly show how much we can love. We need to learn to relax, take a chance, and let our loving feelings for others radiate freely and spontaneously. (Esoteric astrologers would suggest we suffer from a blocked or congested heart chakra—our special vortex of energy located in our chest area.)

With this placement, we can be less than generous with ourselves and less willing to cater to our own emotional needs. We may even be intimidated by the consequences of too much sensual indulgence, including sex. Thus, we can be hesitant in giving ourselves completely to others we find attractive and desirable—at least with the degree of wholeheartedness Leo is capable of. Given enough time and maturity, Saturn will teach us the value of realistically confronting our emotional doubts and fears so that more fulfilling love attitudes are developed. If we seek a deeper, more lasting love union to appease the inner emptiness we often experience, we will first need to take an honest look at our own blocked sense of self-love and self-respect. Perhaps through unconditional self-acceptance, we are better able to eventually open up and give our heart to another with confidence and faith that it will be cherished rather than trampled on. Saturn in Leo can indicate the potential to build the inner strength and courage needed to enable us to experience a deeper intimacy in our most significant relationships. There need be no more sorrow through loving and being loved.

SUPERIORITY COMPLEX

Unlike Saturn in Aries, this fixed Saturn placement implies we have a well-defined sense of personal identity, apparent since early childhood. Sometimes our self-image is too rigidly defined. We over-achievers normally feel no struggle to become someone meaningful to ourselves. We know we are special in some way, almost as if put on the planet to fulfill some distinct destiny (Saturn can be a fate-sensitive planet and Leo can feel like a favored child of the gods). However, if anything, we may have difficulty feeling recognized as important in the eyes of others, yet Leo's ego growth requires that it receive full attention from an adoring audience by playing the hero who gets all the thunderous applause.

Being a sign of the subjective-interpersonal Second Quadrant, Leo is less self-contained than Aries, and more dependent on external responses from the environment for its sense of self. Saturn in Leo denotes our vulnerability to both real and assumed threats to our self-esteem. We can take offense at the slightest hint of insult or negative insinuation. Our gut-level urge is to respond with a defensive air of superiority in an attempt to belittle our opposition. We try to thwart others by making them feel insignificant. Those of us who are very self-inhibited can turn cool and distant on the surface, while seething with rage within.

Obviously, this position is less representative of the nobility and majesty of Leo. Judgmental Saturn suggests we can display a carping, critical, petty attitude in a dramatic manner when affronted. Fiery Leo can also blow things out of proportion when upset—everything is big stuff for Leo. Normally, this magnanimous sign overlooks slights due to its indomitable sense of self-regard, but defensive Saturn suggests we can react strongly to character assaults. Self-pride can be used as a defense mechanism. Arrogance and haughtiness are two of Saturn in Leo's most unattractive traits. Such unwarranted displays of self-importance may masquerade a weak ego foundation riddled with deep self-doubt. If we feel driven to attain a position of great importance and dignity, we will need to put the brakes on our own ego projections.

I LEAD, YOU FOLLOW

Both Saturn and Leo find leadership roles very appealing, yet if Saturn attempts to apply uncompromising control tactics due to fears of being overpowered, it evokes the bossy streak in Leo. We need to learn how to rise to powerful positions without resorting to dictatorial behavior. It might be too easy for us, when under stress and pressure, to adopt the unpopular role of the autocrat. Although comfortable in positions of central management, we may create an intimidating sense of distance due to our demanding nature. We could end up feeling isolated on the emotional level from people who nevertheless must serve our needs.

Constructively, Saturn in Leo tones down some of the excesses of this potentially flamboyant fire sign. This can be the most self-restrained Leo placement of them all. But we need to make sure not to deny Leo its hearty appetite for living. Vanity and conceit are seldom our problems unless we are overcompensating for feelings of mediocrity. We are rarely susceptible to flattery or lavish praise. If anything, we may become too self-consciously humble, unable to accept compliments from others easily—though we'd feel hurt and dejected if nobody paid us homage when we felt it was due. We intensely need attention, but we also want to control the amount. Life is teaching us to stop trying to control the world's response to us. We will be respected and admired for our true worth once we finally trust our creative instincts.

SORROW THROUGH CHILDREN?

Another traditional Saturn in Leo admonition is "sorrow through children." Why this fateful warning? For one thing, Leo signifies the psychological child within, regardless of our actual age. Leo depicts the "forever young" aspect of our psyche—the irrepressible, joy-filled abandon of innocent and carefree youth. With Saturn here, early conditioning may have prevented us from being children in the true sense. The expression of typical juvenile traits may have been stifled. Perhaps we felt an undue pressure to act with mature self-control at an uncommonly early age. Programmed to fear behaving childishly, we learned to win favor and praise (Leo values) by emulating adult-like behavior. Yet in attempting to do so, the development of healthy childlike qualities may have been detrimentally neglected or devalued by ourselves and our parents.

Later on, when dealing with our own offspring, we may expect or demand that kids function in the same controlled, adult-like manner, showing a low tolerance for frivolous, silly behavior—exactly what many young children are good at. We may also view child-rearing as an unwelcome burden or tedious responsibility, done more out of duty than love. Yet, perhaps compelled by guilt, we make sure we give our children expert supervision, which the kids can find oppressive at times. Maybe we instinctively fear and resent children for being too unstructured in spirit, and thus unpredictable. This alone could threaten our own insecure need to control. We may resort to being unyieldingly disciplinarian in our demands and expectations. Should we become tyrannical or too judgmental, some of our children can grow up defying our iron-fisted authority (and society's as well). They could very well end up becoming a source of "sorrow" and disappointment for us later.

Astro-lebrities with Saturn in Leo

Arnold Schwarzenegger	Elton John
Billy Graham	Steven Spielberg
Indira Gandhi	Theodore Roosevelt
Leonard Bernstein	Jessica Lange
Thomas Jefferson	Liberace

SATURN IN THE FIFTH HOUSE

STIFLED

At some point during our formative years, our sense of self-esteem may have been bruised. Somebody important to us (Daddy, or even Mommy playing Daddy?) may have sat on our spirit long enough to make us feel puny, unworthy, or painfully insignificant. One result of this is the formation of a fragile ego. We doubt our creative talents and/or question our right to openly and expressively display our "star power" to the world. Some of us who self-inhibit can suffer an inferiority complex that stirs much inner turmoil and frustration. A few of us who over-compensate are constantly attempting to prove ourselves superior to the rest of humanity. We work hard at risk-taking in those areas where we feel most competent, but do we really believe in our own glory?

The problem here is complex and multi-layered. Part of us has a strong yen to be regarded as special and significant, in spite of feeling shunned by at least one confidence-destroying, kill-joy parent during childhood. We will rarely if ever get praise from that parent in this lifetime. We need to accept this and take pride in ourselves anyway. Equally potent is a worry that we may actually turn out to be humdrum "ordinary people"—merely another bland member of the statistical norm.

We seem to have a dread of being labeled mediocre (even "notorious" would be a more acceptable label). To top it off, we may also feel anxious that others might discover we harbor swell-headed opinions about ourselves as well as hang-ups about being a no-talent devoid of any real sparkle. Are we just ugly ducklings, or truly beautiful swans in the making?

FEAR OF FLYING

While we do not necessarily fear flying in the literal sense, we may have a hard time giving ourselves permission to creatively soar. We need to know what our audience's reaction to our act will be—do they really, really like us?—even before we even agree to perform. We want guarantees of approval and favorable reviews ahead of time, which is impossible. Spontaneous risk-taking scares us, and that's too bad because such fear goes against all the natural promptings of the Fifth House, Leo and the Sun. But being able to take bold chances with life can also have its allure—we marvel at those totally self-possessed people who do "bold" so well in the world and get away with it to boot.

Principle Five has little to do with premeditation or calculated response. It has lots to do with going out on a limb for the sake of joyous ego-extension and a heartfelt willingness to robustly participate in life. This principle symbolizes a warm, passion-filled demonstration of honored selfhood. The Fifth House highlights anything that facilitates the child-spirit within us to happily emerge and enjoy its impact on the world. This house encourages us to take emotional gambles and adventures of the heart. However, little of this sounds like Saturn, our key to more staid adult-like behavior. Our problem thus becomes a reluctance to act out our vital need for aliveness without the promise of total ego-security and the safety of social acceptance. Saturn at all times seeks to walk on solid, safe ground, but the Fifth House suggests life is a party and much fun can be had by letting our hair down, even if others have a problem with that. Why sweat over the sourpuss attitudes of a few of life's party poopers? We need to spread our colorful wings and take to the skies in faith that the winds will carry us far and wide.

AREN'T WE HAVING A GOOD TIME?

Unfortunately, we take a circumspect approach to those same social affairs others have little trouble throwing themselves into with festive self-release, like the people we see screaming and whooping it up in TV wrestling audiences. We feel uncomfortable in large public arenas designed for mass enjoyment, including dance clubs and other pleasure spots where happy folk congregate. While others let loose and cha-cha at the "Mingle-Singles" bash, we instead quietly sip our drink (we have a self-imposed two-drink limit), cross our legs, and periodically check our watch. Maybe someone fascinating will come sit by us, but it's okay if nobody does because it's almost time to go home anyway! Or perhaps we over-achievers work at becoming the life of the annual office Christmas party. Even then, we are still conscious of time passing, especially when things are going flat and we've run out of comic material. Whatever the scenario, many of us have an annoying habit of putting a damper on fun, usually when the socializing starts to become a bit loud, wild, or rowdy.

We typically have a tough time divorcing our self-consciousness (Saturn) from most Fifth House activities long enough to experience the joy of true recreation. Typically, we are not having such a good time—at least as long as we suspect our performance level is being constantly observed, evaluated, and critically judged by those we hope would simply love and admire us instead. Saturn is ambitious, though, and will not shrink from testing its strengths, so many of us will feel compelled to do our best and attempt to outshine all others, even if it takes a lifetime (and it often does).

If we cannot come out on top (or at least convince ourselves we cannot), some of us may not bother to even play the game. If we play but do poorly, we tend to withdraw and sulk, feeling ego-wounded for a long period of time. Saturn in the Fifth House can aptly be the signature of a "sore loser." Hearing that about ourselves usually makes us feel worse. Perhaps that's because, deep down inside, we assume it is our responsibility to always keep up a happy face. Some of us feel guilty if we're not always radiating, but Saturn reminds us that the show must go on anyway.

WHY ISN'T IT ROMANTIC?

What about romance? Courting-and-sparking is a strong Fifth House theme. This life sector tells us plenty about our style of "coming on" to others. It tells us how we behave when we feel sexual chemistry at work. Saturn here suggests we have the endurance to infuse our love life with a great deal of passionate energy as a result of focusing our desires. We want to be satisfied and seriously so—once in love with the right person. We have lots of inner control and are willing to wait it out until the real thing comes along. Meanwhile, we fret over the vulnerability of potential rejection by someone we find appealing. We don't send our own signals out across a crowded room with much confidence. We'd rather that our subject of attraction make an unambiguous beeline towards us—but not too aggressively. Saturn likes the slow build.

Astrologers would agree that Saturn in the Fifth House defines a realistic attitude about love, but since Saturn is also a symbol of perfectionism—demanding quality and excellence—we could actually be more unrealistic about our romantic expectations than we realize. We desire qualities that are nearly impossible for any one partner to fulfill. Just because we are serious in intent does not always mean we are also reasonable. By insisting on such high standards, we could actually be avoiding commitment, since few people are going to successfully become intimate with us. As we allow fewer and fewer people to have a sweeping Fifth House emotional impact on us, we remain autonomous, in control—and all alone on a Saturday night.

Choosing to pursue love and romance this way entails hard work. We assume that maintaining a love affair requires a great deal of time and energy. It's a demanding job. This can make us feel trapped, thinking that love will distract from other important objectives. We cause additional problems by making the whole issue more anxiety-producing than need be. A central challenge here is not getting love but freely giving love to another. Saturn will test our ability to offer love with courage, self-assurance, and no regrets. With Saturn in the Fifth House we sometimes wonder if we are actually warm and lovable people to begin with. We may harbor deep insecurities about our capacity to share ourselves body and soul with our significant others, no matter what our Seventh House says.

Insecurity may also explain why we try to supervise our love affairs as we would our children. Maybe we see our lovers as children at heart who need parental guidance. If we do not trust life to orchestrate our romances, perhaps it is because we fear life will handle the unpredictable parts badly. Although our approach is one of cautious self-interest, we need to period-ically risk making fools of ourselves and to take a few awesome chances due to address the constant demands of our heart. By doing so, we can become vividly aware of the joys of such an emotional adventure. Let's face it: when was the last time our inhibitions best served our heartfelt needs? Never!

CHILD'S PLAY

Many older astrological texts go on and on about how Saturn in the Fifth House denies us offspring, or at least brings us a heap of burdens through our raising of them. What are we to do with such information? Avoid human parenting altogether and buy an attention-demanding cockatoo instead? Some of us have indeed taken such a route, raising pets as our substitute kids. Yet a little honest self-examination might help us under-stand why we have a hard time when it comes to children.

Many of us have not had satisfactory childhoods ourselves, since we often had to squelch our own childlike instincts in order to gain adult approval and more control over facets of our young life. We needed adult acceptance for our development of self-respect, which didn't and still doesn't always come from within. But as a result, we later grow up realizing we know little about being a kid—a goofy, silly, messy, rambunctious little kid. Thus, psychologically, we are indeed denied children by first rejecting the voice of our own child within.

What we typically seem to like least about children is their unnerving ability to express themselves through a purely instinctual mode that, at times, is uncontrollable, beyond reason, and raw with open emotion. For them, loud laughter easily rings out and sobbing tears heavily flow. Perhaps it's our concept of what it is to be adult that needs to be reviewed, because we could have picked up some negative messages along the way. Our early role models (generally our parents) were apt to be adults who were stiff or regimented on some level. While orderly in habit, they might have been repressed in their emotions, and generally unwilling or unable to be light and playful with us. We later assume real adulthood means always being self-controlled and reserved in expression. Not surprisingly, this is often exactly the kind of adult we become.

But what about our own offspring? Can we allow them their sometimes immature reactions, their occasional bouts of forgetfulness, or their pesky, prankish ways? Usually not. We never got away with such misbehavior, so why should they? Unfortunately, such a sour grapes attitude can make us quite capable of not only stifling childish behavior, but also the marvelous imagination typically possessed by youth. We will need to be careful not to interfere with our children's natural inclinations to play-act just because it makes us feel uptight. The structures we provide need to allow for ample room to keep all creative juices flowing, including our own (mismanaged Saturn tends to dry things up too prematurely—in this case, from sour grapes to withered prunes).

Another issue is that of knowing when to let go of our children's lives. We tend to want to wait until they've at least made it safely into their fifties! We think it is our duty to mold their life pattern, making it as mistake-proof as possible. If and when they later reject our tireless efforts (especially us over-achievers), we end up feeling very let down and dejected. Or we may feel bitter and resentful, seeing our kids as ungrateful and opportunistic at our expense (we've done so much for them, we lament). Our children are not here to live out our unrealized dreams any more than we can perfectly fulfill their ambitions. If this is mutually understood early on in the parent-child relationship, there should be no reason to fear they will turn cold and indifferent when they leave home. They will happily and lovingly come back. Meanwhile, Saturn's wisdom tells us we need to grow up and become like children ourselves as we age! Once emotionally secure in our child-spirit, we at last might master the art of play.

No Luck at Bingo

What about Saturn in the Fifth House and the traditional warning against gambling? Why do we seem to have so little luck in games of chance? Why do we end up thinking raffles, lotteries, contests, or winning prizes are for someone else? Probably because gambling is a clear form of risk-taking and "iffy" speculation. We rarely allow ourselves to gamble on emotional levels, so why do it on financial ones? With Saturn as a key to our conscience, we might feel we won't attract windfalls because deep down inside we believe we haven't earned easy rewards. But as long as we assume this, we will remain losers in this area. Slot machines simply won't cooperate for us. We also approach most other matters of speculation and investment with caution and suspicion. Even in games of skill—as in sports—we assume the gods will favor the other player we're competing against for the shiny trophy or the big fat winner's check.

We can change much of this by first analyzing why we choose to lose, or why we only permit ourselves to win after much struggle and sweat—and even then appear to be uncomfortable winners. Saturn is often hung up on the work ethic, rejecting the "something for nothing" philosophy. Yet the Fifth House house believes activities should be so pleasurable and entertaining that we forget we are even exerting ourselves, and thus appear to be getting more than we are putting out. With Saturn in the Fifth House, we just need to raise our own stakes and gamble more on feeling well-deserving of some of life's overflow. Once we start giving ourselves first-class treatment, we'll find ourselves on a winning streak. Bingo!

Astro-lebrities with Saturn in the Fifth House

Mae West	Sir Winston Churchill
Bill Gates	John F. Kennedy, Jr.
Bob Dylan	Shelley Winters
Helen Keller	Wolfgang Amadeus Mozart
Shirley MacLaine	Henry Kissinger

SATURN/SUN ASPECTS

NATAL

The Sun and Saturn have more in common than astrology has formerly recognized. Tradition has it that self-restrained, calculating Saturn is antithetical to the spontaneous, combustive, self-expressive Sun. So what traits do they share? For starters, both like to be in the driver's seat, securing control and central management over any project or objective. They are each inclined to gravitate toward positions of authority where they can exercise the power to supervise others and delegate responsibilities (perhaps the Sun more than Saturn, who has a harder time letting go of doing all the tedious work itself). Each is ambitious and will strive for social advancement when properly motivated.

Saturn may appear less ego-absorbed and attention-grabbing than the Sun as it patiently and steadily climbs the ladder of success. But it still can work long and hard to improve its status and ensure a permanent foothold in a desired power role. The Sun merely is more up front about glory-seeking, more innocently honest about its true motives. Regardless, both planets exhibit a need for upward social mobility, especially when they aspect one another. Each wishes to make a definite impact on the environment—one that commands respect and positive notice from others. They describe a drive to stabilize the prestigious positions they achieve. However, Saturn's sense of ambition is more conditioned by society's imposed limits and is based on the approval of the community at large. The Sun's sense of ambition springs forth from an inner core of well-being, and is based on subjective self-approval. The Sun always radiates from within rather than depending on an outside power source.

When well managed, Saturn/Sun aspects imply we will work to elevate our status in the world. We at least want to make something of ourselves and lead a purposeful life (even if our chosen path is an unconventional, anti-establishment one or crime-related; stress aspects here can sometimes suggest problems working with mainstream society's rules, regulations, and laws). In general, we want others to take who we are and what we do quite seriously and respectfully. Many of us are self-directed, though others require a strong sense of outside direction and clarity of focus to succeed in our endeavors. Life this time around is telling us that we cannot afford to become too aimless or ambiguous in our approach, no matter what other factors are shown in our chart. A thoughtful concentration of our will, a conscious sense of responsibility, and a practical application of our talents all help us get to where we want to go.

Saturn/Sun aspects also reinforce within us a need to feel distinct from everyone else. These aspects emphasize our sense of individuality and separateness. With squares, oppositions, and even the conjunction, that sense of separateness can prove problematic and socially uncomfortable. We are apt to erect barricades around us that thwart the cooperation of others who otherwise could assist our ambitions. Some of us may be quite reluctant to surrender our isolated selfhood. We resist pressures to conform to the mass consciousness (but from a different perspective than would Uranus). The conjunction in particular shows a tendency to tightly retain a well-structured sense of self (unless Neptune is also involved in the pattern).

Any Saturn/Sun contact can stimulate the desire to achieve and accomplish something of significance on both societal and personal levels. We are urged to not only feel important and influential, but insist on being busy in activity worthy of our efforts. Sextiles and trines are more inclined to find meaningful social involvement without resorting to aloofness or the distancing act typical of the tensional aspects. What is required of Saturn/Sun is that we pursue our primary life goals with organized planning and steadfast application. We function better when actively productive, focusing our attention on what is of central importance in the present. We want our life to provide us with steady work, systematic routine, material stability, and concrete manifestations of our inner objectives, and we are not adverse to making the required effort to achieve this.

On the downside, both planets have an authoritarian streak, desiring to wield executive power and take charge of others. Both pull back from the influence of external authority, favoring autonomy. Self-governing is emphasized, and so we have a hard time being followers. In a herd of sheep, we'd rather find ourselves being the border collie keeping things operating smoothly and in order. But being the shepherd would even be a better role for us here. The point is that we are reluctant to bend to the will of others in control. We'd rather be the boss than have a boss.

Learning to adjust to and accept the terms of established authority becomes a constant life theme for us (something astrologers normally would think of as more a Uranus/Sun or Uranus/anything issue. This can be explained by the fact that both Uranus and Saturn rule Aquarius, the "rebel with a

cause"). The more we willfully defy supervision, the more dictatorial and ego-stifling our projected authority symbols can
become. Mismanaged Saturn/Sun means we have a power/con-
trol dilemma to deal with. Constructively, when operating
within appropriate boundaries, we supervise things in a masterful way, with Saturn leaning more toward the necessary
sense of responsibility and duty, and the Sun simply feeling
capable and deserving to be in the center of things. Otherwise,
we can behave in ways that are overbearing and alienating.

This planetary combo also suggests a strong sense of inner
conviction and trustworthiness. We want to be regarded as
dependable, substantial people who can safely be entrusted
with important duties. Both planets are fascinated with
strength and endurance. The Sun is symbolic of the Hercules
"hero" archetype, while Saturn can be viewed as Atlas carrying the weight of the world on his capable shoulders. Saturn's
sense of determination and steadiness is easily understood in
this context, but the Sun's steadfastness and ability to concentrate becomes more comprehensible once we realize this
"planet" is actually a fixed star, representative of inner con-
stancy and stability. The Sun is our symbol of centeredness,
backed by our willpower.

Saturn may evoke the leadership potential of the Sun, but
the Sun does not carry a theme of childlike spontaneity when
interacting with Saturn. Dignity and pride become major
issues for both planets. How we are treated in public seems to
be a big deal for us (being adored is not as important as being
respected and honored). We are sensitive to attacks on our
integrity and our reputation (although don't expect Sun sextile Saturn, for example, to be devastated by bad press; it's
certainly not as vulnerable to social judgment as is Sun opposing Saturn). Still, we take ourselves and our carefully packaged image very seriously and want the world to recognize
that we are solid in who we are, and anything but flaky. We
also are frustrated with our own high standards at times—we
simply expect too much of ourselves. We need to learn how to
relax and cope with life's unexpected changes to our plans.

TRANSIT

The transit of Saturn to our Sun (especially the conjunction) has been needlessly dreaded by traditional astrology. That's not to suggest it's hassle-free. Much depends on how we have raised our sense of self-esteem and honored our integrity thus far in our inner development. Our ego structure and the harnessing of will are issues that come to the fore at this time. Of course, our Sun's house placement is typically the center of action here, but also see what additional data about our situation can be gained from wherever Leo is on a cusp or intercepted. This transit is typically a time of sober but sensible self-evaluation, where we have a chance to weigh our growth from life's previous challenges against those areas where we still need to come to grips with certain realities about ourselves.

Saturn is trying to help us define what's really operating at the inner core of our being. Are we on solid footing with ourselves? Is our primary path at this life juncture clear and well thought out? Saturn asks, have we paid our dues and now are deserving of a successful unfoldment of our ambitions? Do we even have ambitions? Obviously, our answer to many of these questions will be different if transiting Saturn is squaring our Sun versus trining it, but that just indicates a different take on the same themes. Saturn is still Saturn and the Sun is always the Sun. Maybe the dialogue will change, but not the roles.

Certain facets of our life are slowing their pace, and our overall operating consciousness (the Sun) is feeling the pressure to settle down and focus on essential priorities. Saturn by transit will weed out whatever is unnecessary, and here we may have invested our ego-drives in a few areas that are going nowhere for us (energy-consuming as they might be). Usually this is in the career or professional zone. We could feel stuck in an uninspiring situation with little promise but a lot of here-and-now drudgery and hard work. This is particularly so with the stress aspects (including the quincunx). We may feel we have no choice but to plod on while building inner resentment.

This is not the kind of life we originally had envisioned for ourselves (the Sun, being positive in attitude, thinks big). But a harsher reality seems to be calling the shots.

If uncompromising reality now has the upper hand, we need to start getting real with ourselves. In this case, Saturn requests that we ask ourselves what we can and cannot legitimately and reasonably do to satisfy our needs. What are our limits? Where can we push ourselves until life forces us to go no further? Maybe we are being "put in our place" or in a position where we can achieve solid results, but nothing like this will occur for us if we have a bad attitude about inner and outer authority. Some of us will clash with the boss and get the ax. Others can break a few clearly laid-out societal rules and get in trouble with the law. Maybe we have been lax in following certain legal procedures and now have invited closer scrutiny from The System (local, state, and federal).

Whatever the case, Saturn aspecting the Sun does not want us to shirk our responsibilities, pass the buck, or blame someone else for our shortcomings. After all, these are *our* shortcomings and we've taken a long time to create them! We must instead own up to them and do what it takes to restore our sense of duty along with a more secure and respected place in the world. We cannot expect quick fixes for such long-standing, self-created predicaments. Saturn does not believe in magic. Forget winning the lottery as our ticket out of this mess. Miracles will not bail us out, but organizing our lives by tackling matters one day at a time can work wonders. Passivity only breeds self-contempt.

We also need to realize we probably don't have the usual amount of physical energy available to us at this time (the Sun rules vitality; energy-conserving Saturn reduces the flow), so it is important that we apply our forces purposefully and with constructive intent. We don't have to expect to mope around feeling devitalized and yawning a lot—but if we do, this could be a good time to consider how we have been fueling our bodies over the years. Have we opted for cheaper, adulterated junk-food gas instead of the fortified higher octane nutritional stuff? Health could be a concern for those of us who have been chronically neglectful of proper self-maintenance. Saturn asks, Why try to build a mighty empire when you're already too sick or drained to run it? It's a waste of time and energy. We may need to build ourselves up with better nourishment and adequate exercise before we take on any new, demanding projects.

If we honestly appraise our situation, we will agree that we may have some loose ends to wrap up and maybe a few material issues to resolve before we can launch into an exciting future of fresh enterprise. But if we are in good shape already and have conscientiously attended to all our obligations, Saturn contacting our Sun could signal a time of the careful initiation of practical ventures that do not require fast results, because this transit favors a slower development process. We will have to be willing to pace ourselves more realistically, and our patience will be put to the test. Being diligent helps. A few of us will gratefully be able to let go of an old cycle of commitment that no longer is growth-inducing (whether it be a career or a relationship). We get to examine our options, and then are ready to make a sound decision (I think the sextile is excellent for this, but real life shows that many people feel pressingly urged to be decisive when met with the conjunction, square, or opposition).

Not every responsibility has to be dumped on our shoulders, especially with transiting Saturn trining our Sun. People in authority can assist us if we are willing to let go of the reins. Practical networking with level-headed individuals should be welcomed. People we attract can play out the Saturn role of wise counselor, helping us sort out our Solar needs more effectively. But we need to be flexible, considering that we may hear a few suggestions that we're likely to resist at first (our autonomy issue can be a stumbling block). This is a period in our lives when we either can't do it all alone or we don't have all the correct answers, and so we need to let Saturn bring us expert advice in any manner necessity chooses. The ultimate purpose of such involvement would be to build a sturdier framework on which to hang our worth-while goals. Pushing such valuable help away would only prove counter-productive in the long run.

In general, Saturn transits to our Sun become a time to simplify our lives by uncluttering elements of our current experience and focusing on those fundamental concepts that define who we are on our own terms, not just society's. This is a good time to hang out with ourselves rather than get lost in a crowd or escape into other people's complicated worlds (better our own company now than the wrong company). Some degree of quietness or solitude is needed so that we can listen to our heart more attentively. Escaping into a hectic hustle-and-bus-tle world of high-pressured wheeling and dealing is not what will do the trick. We must have greater self-focus. We need to hold back from mindlessly achieving power and position, and take some time off to reflect on our authentic self.

What if we are instead in a depressed slump, feeling like a major failure because our life is in tatters? Saturn then becomes our guardian angel in disguise, mercifully putting a stop to the misery we've had to endure by being blind to our own power to direct our lives successfully. Saturn is giving us a wake-up call, letting us know that now we can revitalize our ego/will power slowly and sanely. We can take measures to reglue our broken parts where necessary, but also throw out the trash and face up squarely to what must be done to survive this moment—then move on feeling stronger about our lives.

CHAPTER ELEVEN

SATURN IN VIRGO

BEAT THE CLOCK

Here we find Saturn operating in a highly meticulous manner, as Virgo is a patient sign attending to reality's small but necessary parts. A serious, discerning look at the world under the microscope is the life approach suggested by this Saturn placement. Saturn likes organization and Virgo must have order. Virgo needs technical explanations while Saturn is impressed by sound logic. The efficient nature of time-conscious Saturn is strongly accented by the industriousness of punctual Virgo. Saturn and Virgo can be perfectionistic and detailed. They have a mutual dislike of waste, excess, disarray, and idleness. They hear the clock ticking away and realize there is still much to be done in the course of a day. For this pair there's hardly a moment to rest, unless that means taking a break by focusing on a different attention-demanding task.

If not careful, we can get so wound up with our need to be productive that we can lapse into moments of feeling like a well-programmed robot with a specialized circuitry system that makes us endlessly toil away the hours. Why bother sleeping? Who needs to waste time eating? Maybe it's not that bad for most of us, but still we would feel better if there were more than twenty-four hours in the day to catch up on our very pressing chores and duties, and maybe a little time left over for a few select hobbies.

GET OUT THE SLIDE RULE

Saturn's expert ability to assess reality on any level is taken to even greater degrees of accuracy when placed in this fastidious sign. The critical faculties of observant, reasoning Virgo easily complement Saturn's own analytical, scientific bent. When well handled, this placement indicates we may have an above-average capacity for clear, unbiased understanding of everyday matters at hand. Both Saturn and Virgo seek out well-presented factual data. We may have a fondness for precision and will go to great pains to make sure something is designed, assembled, constructed, or organized just right (whether a bookshelf or a sentence). We need everything to have its own place, space, and function. Saturn's great fear here is not being clearly understood or being accused of making stupid mistakes, so Virgo is pressured to work overtime at explaining things or following procedures carefully, not leaving much to imagination or chance.

As there is a technical appreciation for how things work or why anything functions as it does, a stronger-than-average interest in science, medicine, and all high-tech fields is possible. But for most of us who do not want to wither away in research laboratories (wearing our spotless white coats while taking detailed notes on the altered behavior of rats on drugs), Saturn in Virgo simply means we want to know what the serviceperson is planning to do and why when coming over to fix our air conditioner. When the mechanic jiggles a few electrical wires under the hood and tells us the bad news, we want to make sure it's really an expert diagnosis. We learn that we have to give people breathing space and not watch everything like a hawk, since that kind of scrutiny can make others edgy and annoyed—but to not be in the know can make us nervous.

This can especially be so when we are at the doctor's office and are not being given technical explanations for why our small intestine is having its little spasm-like sensations. Surely there must be a term for it we can look up later in our medical encyclopedia! We don't want to be treated like dummies and are capable of handling big, fancy words. We don't necessarily need to sound like rocket scientists, but would feel better just having a little practical, working knowledge. All this can become useful information at a later date when we decide to take a chance and fix a few things ourselves. Thank goodness we always save our manuals!

ANOTHER FINE MESS

So far, Saturn in Virgo sounds too perfect for words—as well as very dull, a little nerdy, and probably pretty uptight about things that screw up or turn out sloppy. It's true that both Saturn and Virgo emphasize neatness and having everything lined up correctly. However, a few of us self-inhibitors can be amazingly untidy and disorganized, both mentally and situationally. Astrologers would suspect parental strictness and inflexibility regarding cleanliness and orderliness (maybe to the point of neurosis). Simple things became complicated chores because of Mom or Dad's authoritative insistence that either we "learn to do things right, or don't bother doing them at all!" Somehow, that last option sounded good to a few of us. Saturn squashed Virgo, and an unexpected form of procrastination resulted.

We may have rationalized, "Why bother then to do my best, since I can rarely do anything right to satisfy the picky people around here? I just won't make any real effort if it's only to disappoint everybody and I end up getting criticized anyway." This might not be quite the dynamic at play, but it seems like part of what could be behind our superslob act. What we need to realize is that messiness and carelessness mean we take longer finding items or doing things important to us, and that can be a tremendous waste of time. We need to work at setting up little efficiency routines and unclutter our mind's aisles of useless junk. We can be excellent at finding solutions when we put our heads on straight and stop being so self-critical. We can learn to do things much better than we suspect.

Executive Doubts

There are some areas where Saturn and Virgo do not easily blend. Virgo tends to be humble and subservient. Its sometimes meek, servile nature enables it to adjust to low-ranking (and low-paying) positions without much complaint (perhaps due to its Pisces polarity, Virgo prefers operating in the less obvious background rather than in the forefront of affairs). Saturn is apt to want to rise slowly to levels of power and authority in order to secure a position of superior rank and elevated status (although not in the blatantly assertive manner of Capricorn). Saturn does not have a gung-ho go-getter mentality, but it does seek out situations allowing for control and central management. The question is: are we going to be the master or play the servant (Virgo)? A psychological conflict of interests is evident.

Thus, many of us with Saturn in Virgo do not feel comfortable with the supervisory roles typical of Saturn (unless perhaps we are in over-achiever mode and our Saturn happens to fall in the Fifth or Tenth House). Virgo lacks the aggressive, initiative force that Saturn would require in this context. It's not a particularly self-confident sign to begin with and is prone to too much self-questioning. Virgo won't allow for human error. Its analysis of itself tends to be harsh. Saturn, on the other hand, is more at home in signs that have less trouble taking immediate control of circumstances. Compared to Virgo, Saturn has more of a "take-charge" ability, which is what is needed in most leadership roles. Interesting enough, Prince Charles has Saturn in Virgo. It remains to be seen how he will adjust to the role of future King of England (if his Saturn in Scorpio mum would first let go of her jealously guarded royal seat before her death).

Both planet and sign do not handle risk factors very well, but at least Saturn does the stiff upper lip routine and hangs in there once committed. Virgo, however, is apt to worry that risks lead to errors in judgment, and thus hesitates in taking any action. Power gained strictly through a commanding worldly persona or a dynamic social position is less important to many of us. We may secretly be thankful we usually don't have to function on that level anyway, since we lack true executive ability. Maybe we could volunteer to lead the annual neighborhood clean-up drive over the weekend, since it's a good thing to do—and anyway, just how much darn executive power does it take to get everyone to gather up their plastic bags, put on their protective latex gloves, and start picking up junk along then roadside?

JOB WELL DONE

We are able to quietly, dedicatedly concentrate our abilities on upgrading the quality of our personal work and services. We strive to master (Saturn) our skills and perfect techniques, presenting them in a polished, professional manner. We have much respect for work (and not only our own) that shows a lot of forethought and preparation. Saturn in Virgo means we apply ourselves with great seriousness and consistent effort until the task at hand is completed. Saturn's capacity for depth, operating through alert, exacting Virgo, indicates a talent for handling technical complexities with carefulness, thoroughness, and organizational intelligence. We can develop a reputation for being a stickler for details and may painstakingly attend to the minor issues of any job or project. Some of us are reluctant to allow others to assist us in our work process, since we desire full control (if you want anything done right...). This obviously can symbolize a real workaholic position for Saturn—even more emphatically than most Virgo placements. But with hard-driving Saturn involved, overwork could be our way of compensating for periodic feelings of inferiority and social inadequacy (two negative Virgo attitudes). In addition, Virgo's worrisomeness mingled with Saturn's guilt mechanisms can make this a strained position. Some of us seldom feel comfortable enough to relax and enjoy ourselves unless involved in demanding work or intensive studies. Maybe we feel less uptight or critical about ourselves when kept busy. Saturn pressures us to make every minute count for something worthwhile.

GOTTA GET IT RIGHT

Perhaps the most conscientious Saturn placement, Saturn in Virgo fixates on being correct. We can become readily peeved by all sorts of relatively incidental flaws and mistakes. Being picky to a fault, a few of us can become stern critics with authoritarian undertones. We can be too severe in our own self-analysis plus uncompromisingly critical of the weaknesses of others. We wonder why others are oblivious to those annoying little things that bother us so much. Because we have a tough time accepting things and people as they are, we may reason that it is our solemn duty to reorganize everything into more "workable" forms. But by attempting this, we unwittingly waste time and energy fussing with trying to readjust life's endless inconsequentials. Perhaps behind all this perfectionism is an underlying dread or rejection of anything chaotic, disruptive, or uncontrollable. Unfortunately for us, real life is not as neat and tidy as we think it should be. We'll have to discipline ourselves to let life's less important things slide from time to time, without getting all bent out of shape. Although well suited for tedious, methodical work, we can make simple tasks feel more like drudgery due to our anxious concern over non-essentials, which can eventually produce irritability and nervous strain. Saturn and the process of maturity will teach us to be discriminate in this area. When well managed, Saturn acts like a filtering system, helping Virgo become even more selective.

HEALTH KICK?

Since Virgo rules health matters and all therapeutic measures geared toward proper body/mind self-maintenance, we learn the necessity of moderation (usually in our diet) if we are to avoid serious, even chronic health problems. We tend to either show much self-discipline and restraint along these lines, or else great resistance and self-neglect. The real goal to shoot for is a sensible balance (organic vitamins in the morning, and a scoop of Rocky Road ice cream at night—but not wolfing down half the container in one sitting).

On a psychological level, illness can manifest when we are dissatisfied with the quality (or lack thereof) of our work or working conditions but are too fearful or insecure to make the required adjustments. We could get symptomatic when we are forced out of a job or unemployed over too long a period (mental depression and sluggishness can set in). In any case, we are to learn to abide by the laws governing optimum physical functioning. Too much sedentary mind work at the expense of vitalizing our bodies through exercise is also to be avoided. Health consciousness, once valued, becomes more than a kick or a fad. It becomes an attitude we adopt for the rest of our lives. We learn to honor staying fit.

CLOSET VICTORIAN

Virgo's emotionally reserved nature combined with Saturn's sober disposition requires that we learn to lighten up our ponderous approach to whatever house Saturn occupies. We may have an unrecognized fear of social criticism and condemnation, and can be defensive about having our personal shortcomings pointed out (even though we've been reviewing them ourselves for years). We take our own errors of conduct and action quite seriously and are too intimidated by the possibility of negative consequences. We tend to appear prim and proper (while in public), or at least humble and unassuming. Some of us may be too hung up on what is traditionally deemed appropriate behavior (and not just our own). On the surface we may appear prudent or even prudish. We refrain from acting like animals and letting passions rule us (that includes anger). But behind the scenes, if other parts of the chart give support (i.e., Mars/Pluto or Venus/Uranus aspects) we might be more lusty

and uninhibited than anyone would suspect. Even in our sen-
suousness, we keep ourselves in check, detaching mentally
when we suspect we are getting in over our heads. We need to
feel in control (which is typical of Saturn, but further rationalized by cerebral, purity-conscious Virgo). It must have been
Saturn in Virgo who first coined the phrase "safe sex."

Astro-lebrities with Saturn in Virgo

Prince Charles	Federico Fellini
Sir Thomas Moore	Pope John Paul II
John Calvin	Bonnie Raitt
Meryl Streep	Claude Debussy
Leona Helmsley	Johann Sebastian Bach

SATURN IN THE SIXTH HOUSE

STRONG WORK ETHIC

Saturn in the Sixth House suggests we are to learn how to
render dutiful service to others without feeling like slaves or
work machines run amok. We want to be productive, but
Saturn here means we do best when we learn to be discriminating, selective, and conscious of our daily routines. Are such
careful, detailed actions always necessary? Are we tackling
our tasks the hard way when efficient shortcuts would work
better? To remain unconscious suggests we can concentrate
too much time and effort on monotonous tasks that can drain
us or leave us feeling like we'll never ever get to go to the ball,
whether due to our lazy wicked stepsisters or otherwise. This
position implies for us the danger of playing "doormat" and
"dishrag," two roles unworthy of us and our above-average
organizational talents. Work is always serious business and
something we need to structure with great thoughtfulness
and care, but we are not here to straighten out any and every
mess others try to toss our way. We have to know what is
really our job and what is someone else's problem.

We tend to execute our daily chores methodically. Some of us feel we must follow the exact directions or step-by-step instructions when doing a task. We want to do things the right way the first time around to prevent ending up frustrated with shoddy results. Saturn in the Sixth House gives great patience and endurance, helping us work long and hard. We simply must recognize whether or not any job at hand is worth our one-pointed focus and attention. Exacting and conscientious, we can attend to every pertinent detail and achieve excellent outcomes, but if we habitually gravitate towards menial work because we underestimate our abilities, we are apt to resent such labor—or we could approach it with a degree of ineptitude as an indirect statement of our boredom or disgust. Since our sense of commitment to useful activity can be strong, we are here to make the finest use of our practical skills.

PICTURE PERFECT

Many of us are quite perfectionistic in our expectations, since both Saturn and the Sixth House are sensitive to flaws and are driven to make needed corrections. This can motivate us to master techniques in our chosen field, specializing in those areas where we feel assured we can control and manage conditions most successfully. Our tendency is to always be busy improving our work performance, analyzing our past mistakes (sometimes too thoroughly), and evaluating what we need to do to avoid future errors. We moderates are able to objectively view our failures as stepping stones to more solid ground. We know how to handle the need to be perfect because we don't let it become too compulsive an urge. All flaws and defects are put in proper perspective. This fits well, because the Sixth is a house that really appreciates moderation.

But if it lacks moderation, the search for perfection in everything has a darker side, and this is a face of Saturn a few of us know well. We self-inhibitors can convince ourselves that we cannot do anything right, that we are all (broken) thumbs, and maybe not so bright to begin with. We feel insecure handling tasks with too many details or technical data (learning to calculate a birthchart by hand could have seemed an imposing challenge for the astrologers among us). We also may fear that our manual coordination is off and we cannot use tools or mechanical instruments well. Some of us will stick to pecking away at our old typewriter and leave those complicated, scary computers to somebody else. Whatever our fears and excuses, we inwardly avoid challenging problem-solving and solution-finding. We convince ourselves that a lot of things are just too difficult to master. We feel sure we will do a poor job, inviting the criticism and judgment of others, which only reinforces our inner feelings of being useless and inept. When thus mishandled, Saturn in the Sixth House implies competence-destroying attitudes that misshape our image of our real capabilities. Failures are always humiliating for us, not educational. No stepping stones for us here, just treacherous quicksand.

Sick Leave

One way we cope with the above negative inner conditioning is to pick only those safe jobs that offer little challenge or risk-taking. The working environment itself could be a plain, no-frills set-up with few amenities. We get by sticking to our established routines while doing our job quietly and consistently. We don't want to stand out too much in our small office but would rather blend into the cheap furnishings. Another "technique" is to constantly change our employment before greater performance demands are made of us, or before the boss offers us an elevated position. We fear such a raise in status can lead to our eventual failure to live up to someone else's expectations of perfection. Saturn/Mars stress aspects also behave like this, bailing out just before being given a promotion to a key position. It's quite self-defeating. We could also get ourselves fired by wasting time, being idle, taking too long to get organized, coming in late to work too often, and even giving the boss or co-workers the cold shoulder.

One more way to indirectly deal with all this is to get too sick to go to work. Being under the weather often is how some of us deal with the negative side of perfectionism without feeling too guilty. We reason that after all, if it wasn't for these darn symptoms, we'd be back in the office working as hard as anyone else. Maybe we rationalize we're the victim of working in a "sick" building with all sorts of hidden toxins that are weakening our immune system. Instead of self-reflecting, we are more prone to seek an outside source to blame. However, being ill a lot offers us a perfect excuse for why we aren't being more productive or caught up with our workload yet.

Having a bad case of the flu is certain to get more sympathy than if we merely stood up at our desk, announced we hated our job and our do-nothing co-workers, and then suddenly demanded a four-day vacation with pay. If we typically get sick during peak business periods when everyone is required to be more productive, that should tell us something. We who chose to use illness as a way to avoid life's many necessary tasks and duties can become better at it as we get older. That's when we start to manifest more chronic and serious symptoms while resentfully remaining in dead-end jobs.

Working Overtime

We over-achievers can turn into classic workaholics. Our most pressing problem is learning how and when to stop working. We are so good at labor and believe in the work ethic so strongly that it takes all the discipline we can muster to ease up from our stimulating states of daily "busyness." It's difficult for us to learn to relax when off duty so that we can enjoy free time with ourselves and others. Mars in the Sixth House can have this problem too, especially in fixed signs. Small wonder, since Saturn over-achievers can take a Mars-like approach to all forms of Saturn expression as a way of over-compensating.

We believe that hard work is (or at least should be) the way to the top. The quality of work for us Saturn in the Sixth House go-getters means much more than our fancy business titles (prestigious titles, a string of letters after our name, and credentials in glassed frames are really Tenth House issues). We will work plenty, but not in any way that undercuts our abilities or our status. We loathe doing other people's work: why, we reason, should they get paid for work we do? Saturn in the Sixth House can be shrewd and savvy about self-preservation when it comes to work (especially Saturn in Scorpio or Capricorn: Ross Perot has Saturn in Capricorn in the Sixth House, although practically at the cusp of his Seventh House. He certainly doesn't appear to be someone who can be easily taken advantage of on the job). We tend to understand office politics and use that knowledge strategically.

Psychologists and astrologers alike suspect that chronic workaholics are not as enamored of their jobs or work per se as they appear. It's not so much devotion to the important tasks at hand as a fear of facing vulnerabilities in intimate relationships. Interestingly enough, the Sixth House is actually the Twelfth from the Seventh in the system of derivative houses: Place the Seventh House cusp at the nine-o-clock position where it becomes a symbolic ASC, and then see that the Sixth House falls where we expect to find the Twelfth House cusp in a chart. A traditional theme of Twelfthness is self-undoing on some level. By pouring ourselves into our all-consuming professional roles in an almost fixated manner, some of us workaholics are assured little quality time or energy to develop mature emotional relationships. We avoid those life confrontations we feel least able to cope with, and justify this by pointing to our demanding schedule, our travel itinerary, or simply our "crazy hours."

We over-achievers may balk at this apparent psycho-babble, but it does contain a grain of truth we need to face. We can't just live and breathe for work alone and expect our close relationships to magically thrive in our absence. Not even our pets (also ruled by the Sixth House) like it, unless we work at home. We may provide well for others materially, but that's about it. We need to put away that beeper, unplug the answering machine for a weekend, stop browsing through our appointment book, and instead sit down with our dear loved ones and do some really productive interrelating.

ALTERING THE PROGRAM

Typically, our natal Saturn house represents problems that take hold as a result of our early difficult dealings with authority in the home. In the Sixth House, we may have been vulnerable to statements made by at least one parent who held psychological power over us—statements that seemed critical and fault-finding. Bickering and petty arguments within the household most likely made a deep impression on us. Although siblings with Saturn elsewhere (say, Saturn in Sagittarius in the Eleventh House) probably were less affected by all this, such discord bothered us. The message that sank in was that we operate in a world based solely on what is correct vs. what is wrong (and being wrong is always a bad thing). No gray zones or ambiguities are allowed. No tolerance for "almost" getting something right. We may unconsciously assume that the world can also be a very hard place in which to exist if we don't know what we are doing, and that nobody is willing to give us any breaks we haven't already earned by not making mistakes or false moves. Only those without flaws get lucky, we surmise.

We can thus grow up fearing that hard-nosed reality will prevent us from ever getting away with taking the easy way out. We reason that only through toil and labor can we count on some degree of security and protection. The parent behind all this was the one who was hard to please, the one we always heard complaining or nagging about something, the authority figure we had a difficult time feeling relaxed around. We didn't know how to appease this person who might have picked on us for no apparent reason. We could have also had a parent who was always sick, who we had to attend to and serve. The childhood manifestations of our parental fixation can be numerous.

But the bottom line remains the same: We may have been programmed to always be useful, competent, and inured to the emotional stress factors that break most people down. We are not to be lazy, indulgent, or willing to give into weakness: no tears allowed. "Cope-ability" means capability. We figure that hard work and putting our noses to the grindstone will eventually pay off, while shortcuts to success are invalid. Only losers whine and whiners lose. With such tapes running through our head, we will need to discover therapeutic techniques that can help bolster our self-worth and allow us to become more fluid in our attitudes. We are flesh and blood, not industrial machinery.

HONOR THY CO-WORKER

Maybe we are not machines, but neither are the folks whose fate is to share working space with us. Our utilitarian approach to much of life may be okay for us, but can seem harsh and unfeeling to others. We come on crisp and professional, but much too business focused and somewhat socially aloof. For us, our essential purpose for being on the job is to serve. We have work to do, and we are willing to handle the tough, dull, or sometimes dirty tasks no one else wants to touch. It's the work we center ourselves on, not the personnel. Emotion and socializing are merely counter-productive distractions. But is this service with a smile? Rarely. While inwardly brooding about how little thanks we get for our services, we also give the outer impression by our demeanor that we don't need much praise and attention. We shun having a big fuss made over our accomplishments. We downplay those things we've done well, but get annoyed when others downplay our efforts too.

Our working partners thus have little idea how badly we want and need their recognition and praise. Since we don't make that need clear, others may seldom give us pats on the back and compliment us. When they try to, our cool and emotionally flat response can make them feel awkward (especially if our Saturn forms stress aspects to our Moon or Venus). Our inhibiting sense of reserve can also keep us from appearing as attractive to our superiors as our more charismatic co-workers (whom we can grow to resent). Unless we can work alone and avoid this scenario altogether, we have to deal with this issue in real terms. Although we give off signals that the work itself is more stimulating than the office relationships around us, we will need to appreciate the concept of being a team player (a theme that gets even stronger with Saturn in the Eleventh House). Part of that means being more personable and leaving our frowns at home tucked away in our little black worry box. The work experience for all involved can be made more pleasant if we realize that it's a team effort, and a little human touch doesn't hurt. Effectively handled, this Saturn suggests that people at work admire our orderly approach and our calm, reasoning temperament. We have a solid quality about us that is comforting. We can become the steady anchor for many others on the job.

Astro-lebrities with Saturn in the Sixth House

Johannes Kepler	Julie Andrews
Jonas Salk	Ted Danson
Humphrey Bogart	Gloria Vanderbilt
Anne Frank	Mario Cuomo
Grant Lewi	Ethel Barrymore

SATURN/EARTH MERCURY ASPECTS

NATAL

The Gemini facet of Mercury is quick at gathering knowledge and learning a wide variety of things that do not necessarily coordinate We find it studying Buddhist writings one day, and reading all about the mating habits of penguins the next. There is a thrill to feeding the mind something fresh and new for this part of the Mercury experience, and as a result we are less ignorant and boring. We also have the option to pass on this information to others for their feedback or at least their education. Air Mercury doesn't have to possess the knowledge it obtains, nor does it necessarily feel a commitment to do anything with it. Knowledge is valued for its own sake and often nothing more. This Mercury can be content with entertaining purely abstract thought.

But it's the Virgo side of Mercury that is more concerned with where information is going, how well it's organized, and how it can be realistically used. This is the practical mind at work, gifted with common sense (not just the logic and reasoning abilities both Mercurys possess). While air Mercury enjoys the mental stimulation, earth Mercury knows that certain data hold the long-term power to influence thought and needs to be used responsibly. Where will these facts we are learning or teaching others lead us? How might they best be used in the real world? Most importantly, are they accurate and reliable, or are they just the product of hearsay, mere speculation, or outright misinformation? Together, these two sides of Mercury are vital to a well-tuned mind working at optimum levels. Thus along with reading the following, it's important to read or reread what was said about Saturn aspecting Mercury from the Gemini perspective. We are using the traits of both sides of Mercury all the time, with varying results.

We with Saturn/Mercury aspects take facts seriously and are careful about their sources. This is a skeptical approach to fact-finding whereby information has to pass our rigorous test of approval before it is accepted and assimilated (especially when involving the square). While knowledge is valued for its useful application, how it is packaged is also important to us, since earth Mercury is more form-conscious than air Mercury. We want books to be readable (the print can't be too small) and handwriting to be legible. Some of us are attentive to grammatical structure and the correct usage of words. Any Saturn/Mercury aspect therefore has the potential to be good at proofreading, editing, doing page layout for publications, and whatever else it takes to turn out excellent hard copy. The stress aspects can even sometimes excel in this, due to their pressing need to do things correctly.

Saturn/Mercury is unlikely to state as fact any information it hasn't researched or received from an authoritative source. There is a sense of discretion about how information is conveyed, as Saturn reinforces earth Mercury's need to filter data selectively. We are not necessarily quiet or uncommunicative (that's more a Saturn/air Mercury issue). In fact, we could be very much interested in instructing others about relevant information in a detailed manner. If we have done our homework on a subject, we may feel it is our duty (Saturn) to explain it thoroughly and clearly, which implies a lot of focused communicating.

In any case, we rarely engage in small talk or aimless chatter. Seldom do we relate what we know in humorous or entertaining ways. There is the risk of sounding too dry, too technical, and too detailed. People may not wish to hang on our every word because we lack verbal flair.

Earth Mercury has little of the lightness of air Mercury, and this is made more evident by its aspect to Saturn. We tend to worry more with earth Mercury, probably because we are sensitive to consequences. We believe in the letter of the law and feel less secure assuming things. We want the rules clearly spelled out. Our problem-solving skills can be very strong, as is the need to find security through workable solutions. When we cannot come up with answers to mounting problems, we can fret and/or get nervously anxious. There is more of a mind/body connection with earth Mercury, and negative thinking is prone to manifest as health symptoms (maybe the signs of Saturn and Mercury can give clues as to what parts of the body are affected). Usually the nervous system is a target for stress, and Saturn can be associated with stiffness, hardening, blockage, coldness, and the underfunctioning of something—as in all those "hypo" medical conditions.

A constructive way to use Saturn/Mercury in this context is to study medicine, nutrition, exercise, or healing techniques in general in order to learn the laws (Saturn) underlying the preservation of our health and physical fitness. There is a lot available to study in this area, and we can make a life-long study distinguishing established facts from unsubstantiated theory. But since the mind can turn towards the problematic potential of anything, and also since Saturn can be pessimistic, some of us must use our common sense and a little detachment so we do not become hypochondriacs or worrywarts. As patients, we brace ourselves for the bad news before ever entertaining optimistic outcomes. We tell our doctors to give it to us straight and pull no punches. We can handle the medical jargon but must also be armed with the facts. When Dr. Feelgood does comply, what we hear may typically confirm our worst fears. Whether we take the news soberly and then work on a plan of cure or recovery, or become dejected or very scared of what may lie ahead for us depends on our Mercury sign (typically, Mercury in Cancer, Pisces, or Virgo can get very worked up with anxiety).

In real life, we are probably always blending the qualities of Mercury from both its air and earth perspective. They don't appear to operate in two separate camps. Don't expect to be able to look at a friend's chart and quickly answer the question "Does Frederica have an air Mercury or an earth Mercury?" Astrology has no universally valid formulas for establishing these distinctions, but perhaps Mercury in the Sixth House would favor the Virgo side, while Mercury in the Third House is more Gemini in tone. It is important just to know that with Mercury, as with Venus, we are always dealing with two sides of a coin. Both facets of the Mercury experience are needed for a well-rounded development of the Mercury principle.

Too much air Mercury (especially when not aspecting Saturn or Pluto) can make for a happily superficial mind. We can become shallow, dilettante intellectuals, content to dabble with thoughts. Perhaps we intellectually "play the field," claiming that all ideas are relative and none are absolute, and the facts today may not be the facts tomorrow, as more data are compiled. But at least by keeping a flexible, open mind we can learn what not to get too hung up about. Life can be forever interesting for air Mercury, and this approach to mental development keeps us young inside our heads and highly adaptable—but real depth and profound understanding are not part of this package.

On the other hand, too much earth Mercury (especially in aspect to Saturn or Pluto) can make for a somber, no-nonsense intellect that carefully observes, measures, analyzes, probes, and dissects information in order to uncover what is exclusively factual, often at the expense of the ability to casually communicate or have fun with the learning process. We are prone towards inflexibility in thought and can get lost in detail, missing the overview. We never simply toy with ideas—we develop complex strategies of thought.

TRANSIT

Saturn transiting Mercury puts attention on our need to become more mentally focused in the here-and-now world. We are to sort out the details of our lives with greater clarity. A purely functional approach to coping with everyday issues is emphasized, with Saturn adding an extra dose of level-headedness. This period can be a reality-testing time for our ideas and developing plans. If they are sound to begin with and well prepared, we are offered secure outlets leading to their successful implementation. Hard mental work and steady concentration are normally typical of Saturn/Mercury transits, plus a willingness to wait for just the right timing. Meanwhile, we can review our options and through a process of elimination arrive at what is most workable for us. This is definitely a transit telling us to put on our thinking cap and patiently sift through the details to spot faulty logic or possible flaws in our strategy. Much of what is being analyzed can deal with our work or career decisions.

Delays and postponements of our plans are common, even with sextiles and trines, but wise Saturn knows that rushing into matters prematurely would result in failure or uncertainty at this moment. Life demands that we move forward at a deliberate but cautious pace, taking one sure-footed step at a time. Besides, if we make all the careful moves required now, a much better timetable is set up for us later and everything seems to finally fall into place—and earth Mercury likes things that properly fit into place. But if Mercury is in a fire sign, Saturn may have a harder time convincing us that "slow" is better than fast, or that "later" makes more sense than now. As usual, we need to look at the whole chart before we come up with too many quick conclusions. Still, Saturn will always be Saturn, and that means it doesn't rush the growth process of anything. "No mind is ready before its time..." could be a Saturn/Mercury motto.

The Virgo side of Mercury is concerned with the security of routines whereby our mind runs along familiar tracks of experience. This is not Mercury in its more restless, distractible expression. Saturn supports any steady application of time and energy. Thus some of us, in trying to ensure consistency in our lives, may have become rut-bound in our thoughts and actions (especially with fixed Mercurys). We may find that our lack of adaptability can get us stuck in the mud. We feel we are at an impasse in certain critical areas (oppositions and squares are most prone to cause such stagnation). Much of this may have been brought on by our refusal in past cycles to alter our viewpoints or breathe new life into daily routines, and now things are feeling a bit stale, even suffocating.

Transiting Saturn in this case implies that our sense of being blocked gets stronger, often to the point that we either feel miserable about things or are forced to undergo a self-review. Needless to say, our attitude about a lot of our current life issues can be sour. Examining how we got to this mental state of affairs is a must if we are ever to get out of such a heavy funk. Professional therapy might help us get back to working order should we sink deeper into despair or fear, but we certainly are not losing our minds, which may be one of our secret fears. If anything, we are too much caught up in the realism of the world we live in, with its increasing pressures and predicaments. We may see no way out. But being able to talk about all this emotionally—even angrily—to someone who will listen and not judge us can make a real difference.

Saturn in this case means our responsibility is to define our issues and vent our feelings unambiguously and without thinking we are failures, weaklings, or just plain messed up and beyond repair. We simply need authoritative permission to try new healing solutions to old problems.

Saturn's transiting sextiles and trines (and the quincunx when well handled) usually don't bring up the pressing life issues so far described. We may find this a helpful period where we can organize a few things in our life and catch up on personal matters we haven't had the time or inclination to tackle in the past. It's a good time to eliminate what is no longer needed (there's lots of paperwork hanging around that probably needs to be reviewed and then saved or dumped). Are there any old books we'll never read again that could find a better home in a used book store? It is a good time to check our shelves and closets to see what we can rid ourselves of. This is similar to what was said about the Saturn/Venus transit (earth Venus), especially if what we are willing to part with has less emotional value. A cheap mystery paperback is easier to let go of than our old pair of denim bell bottoms (with those custom-made embroidered patches) hanging in the corner of a closet and taking us back to the more innocent "salad days" of our youth. Whenever we have mixed feelings about letting go of items due to sentimentality, what we thus own is under the domain of earth Venus (plus the Moon). Mercury has more of a take-it-or-leave-it reaction to stuff that is here today, gone tomorrow.

Our ability to be objective and clear-headed is typically stronger, which helps in getting things done. Maybe with the less tensional aspects we can look at ourselves in a sensible manner. Earth Mercury believes that a mind is a terrible thing to waste, and Saturn believes time is a terrible thing to waste. Thus with Saturn transiting Mercury, some of us will attempt to live out our days more efficiently. There is little desire for leisure and more comfort with the daily grind. We are usually very reliable and will deliver what we promise, but we had better keep our promises to a minimum and not attempt to overload ourselves. Our working habits add to the overall impression that this is a well-organized period for us, but not necessarily a sociable one. We are trying to unclutter whatever is unnecessary, and we may sense that too many social obligations can derail us regarding tasks we are eager to see completed. It can be a wonderful period for finishing up projects that were begun a while back but got sidetracked. We can wrap up loose ends and address whatever has been needing our attention.

It is good to reread what I've said about Saturn/Mercury from the Gemini perspective, as many of those themes will probably also be at work with this Saturn transit. Together, they should provide a fuller picture of what we can expect from Saturn as well as how our Mercury can benefit from this contact. We may look back at our Saturn/Mercury periods and realize that we got a lot of things done and maybe even learned a few useful techniques and practical skills in the process—something to write home about indeed!

CHAPTER TWELVE

SATURN IN LIBRA

FAIR AND SQUARE

Libra's sense of fair-mindedness combines well with Saturn's concern for ultimate justice, making this a naturally judicial placement. Both have an association with law and social order. In their purer form, both are able to operate in an impartial, unbiased manner. Saturn represents the workings of law in its most abstract sense, through the cosmic system of checks and balances called karma. The abstract quality of Libra's sense of justice is well depicted by its symbol, the Scales. This symbol is unique in that it is the only inanimate symbol in the entire Zodiac, suggesting its principles are not associated with basic animal or human nature, as are the remaining eleven signs. Saturn and Libra also have formality as a common denominator. Saturn is concerned with proper conduct and appropriate behavior. Libra is very much associated with proper protocol, civilized manners, and all the social graces. Both wish to act in accordance with what is acceptable in society and worthy of approval in the eyes of others.

However, due to Saturn's judgmental nature, we tend to be too stern at times in our evaluation of those who fail to follow set rules of conduct. We may feel intolerant of others who break even those minor precepts we ourselves feel obligated to abide by. Our judgments are based on principles we adhere to, and are not easily dissuaded by sentiment or unpopularity. This is a Saturn that needs to know how to blend law with mercy so that absolute law doesn't run roughshod over the imperfect human element.

As a point of contrast, Saturn does tend to consider the practical realities of any situation while Libra reflects on its more refined, ideal potential, so some of us will carefully and fairly look at the many sides of anything before reaching a firm conclusion. At that point, Saturn will alleviate the typical bouts of indecisiveness Libra is famous for. We will consider the ideal, but also realize it must be brought down to earth and made workable.

FACE TO FACE

The ambitious, striving side of Saturn is evoked by its interplay with the competitive, strategy-oriented facet of Libra. We have the determination to overcome (at least mentally) all challenges presented by others. This is one of the least accommodating Libra placements (along with Pluto or Uranus). Our will is not as easily directed by the assertion of others, and we do not give in or back down merely to create a false or temporary sense of harmony. Saturn holds its ground and doesn't budge without good reason. Competitiveness, however, seldom stimulates us to resort to ruthless, underhanded tactics. Cardinal Libra will openly consider and respect the rights of others, even when engaged in direct confrontation. A basic theme of Saturn in Libra is the development of a responsible, level-headed sense of cooperation.

Compromise, when necessary, must be both realistic and suitable for the needs of all parties involved. We are not benefited by resorting to the "peace at any price" approach Libra placements are typically tempted to adopt. Dutiful, conscientious Saturn pressures us to establish a firm balance of expression in any union with due consideration for our rights as well as those of others, reiterating the sense of fair play Libra strives for. Saturn helps preserve our identity in any one-on-one relationship, rather than weaken or lose it through the demands of others. It emphasizes our self-preservation needs in partnerships due to its strong sense of separate identity. It won't bow down to domination from others without resistance or resentment.

MAKING UP MY MIND

Saturn operating through Libra puts limits on this sign's capacity to waver and vacillate endlessly before reaching definite conclusions or taking decisive action. Due to a need for organization and a clear-cut definition of any situation, Saturn demands concrete resolutions no matter how uncomfortable. Even if things are going badly, Saturn will want closure. Libra can prolong the finalizing of any experience by entertaining too many viewpoints or options while remaining indecisive (especially in emotional relationships), but Saturn will not allow us to leave matters up in the air while we switch sides repeatedly. Saturn tries to dictate a direct course of action based on a firmly made decision. Although both appear at times to be too preoccupied with the consequences of action, Saturn's inner strength and fortitude enable us to eventually make necessary choices and then brace ourselves for the results.

Usually, strategic plans of action are well conceived and aided by the combination of Saturn's cool logic and Libra's excellent sense of objectivity. Libra intelligently evaluates and deliberates before acting, assessing the pros and cons of any issue, which helps with decision-making. Pragmatic Saturn tries to come up with sensible ways to incorporate all facets of any experience before discarding any factor for the sake of another (something Libra alone would do). If the situation demands an "either-or" resolution, we can expect to choose whatever is the most practical, applicable, and fair in the long run—particularly so in our intimate unions.

SERIOUSLY SIGNIFICANT OTHERS

In close one-to-one relationships (Libra), we are motivated to get involved according to the nature of our safety urges and commitment needs. Relationships must psychologically provide us with a secure anchor with which we can feel well grounded and insulated from outer threat. That could be a heavy burden to place on someone. The outgoing, open-handed nature of gregarious Libra is kept somewhat in check by the cautious and often untrusting nature of Saturn. Therefore, it is not easy to identify the manner in which our potential sense of self-limitation will operate in partnerships, since Saturn is capable of great subtlety.

With Saturn in Libra, the sign of "other-awareness," self-restrictive concepts may at least be partially objectified through (or projected on) our chosen partner(s) as well as the overall structure of any relationship. Our actual unions tend to disclose our own inner relationship with the Saturn principle. While a well-managed Saturn wants to clarify, simplify, solidify, and elucidate its purpose for involvement, a mismanaged Saturn shields its vulnerability through obscurity, camouflage, and complication of its hard-to-articulate intent. Normally, we tend to adopt an avoidance approach in relationships in our early years, more so if Saturn has several natal squares and oppositions. We can shun the development of deep ties with others as we grow older. Saturn's aspects suggest more about such non-involvement by indicating which other parts of our psyche are affected.

This avoidance of direct association with peers may not be that obvious on the surface. It can be masterfully concealed, partly because of Libra's adept ability to show an agreeable surface demeanor operating alongside Saturn's reluctance to show vulnerability. Conservative Saturn combined with harmony-seeking Libra normally make us less inclined to go against the grain of any established social mode to begin with (unless we have a Saturn/Uranus or Saturn/Pluto conflict aspect). The appearance of being easygoing could be our best strategic defense against attracting personal criticism or severe judgment from people (although we are probably anything but easygoing and casual with people, at least on our inner levels). We thus are able to fit in with others up to a point and interact without apparent conflict. The trick is not to slip up and show any outstanding or highly individualized traits that could put others off. But the more we do this, the more we end up developing a middle-of-the-road temperament that plays it much too safe.

For a few of us, peer avoidance can take on a more extreme form of expression. We develop a loner quality as a response to a lack of popularity or common acceptance from others, and our withdrawn behavior further perpetuates the standoffish attitudes of others. Typically, though, much other support for this manifestation needs to be shown in the birth chart (such as Saturn/Neptune or Saturn/Venus in conflict aspects).

WALLFLOWER

We may experience a period in our lives when we feel remote and unattached in those social situations in which open and free association would be regarded as normal and pleasurable (a little like Saturn in the Fifth House). For us, assertive expressiveness in the company of others may at times feel awkward and somewhat embarrassing. Even if Saturn is basically operating without undue conflict, we can be reserved in nature and formal with others. We can keep people at arm's length with politeness and proper manners. As civilized as that may appear, it certainly can prevent chumminess. Extreme cases can behave as if surrounded by a thick wall of unapproachability, seeming too aloof to allow for either casual sociability or deep intimacy.

As we reach adulthood, we may either make great personal strides in developing a well-structured social identity, allowing us to share ourselves more fully with others, or we could further withdraw from active participation with people on the personal level and deny our need for human interaction altogether. Better yet, we could strike a balance and mediate both urges (Libra), coordinating them in a complementary fashion—in other words, attending to the needs of any inter-personal relationship, but also knowing when and how to allows ourselves the solitude required for deeper self-relating. We thus learn to purposefully adjust the Libra scales of equi-librium. This lesson could become crucial by the time of our first Saturn Return, if not sooner.

Tall, Dark, and...Older

Saturn in Libra should not necessarily imply that we are seeking out partnerships with people older and more settled than ourselves, even though it often does mean this. Perhaps as we are approaching the long-awaited Aquarian Age, our search for a surrogate mother or father figure instead of a true equal as a mate becomes less appealing or necessary. It is typically not the person's chronological age that is attractive to us, but what that difference in age might represent—such as maturity, experience, and wisdom. Some of us do seem to have a single-minded ideal of what we will accept in a partner (although physical appearance is not as important as it would be for most other Libra placements), but such specific ideals typically exclude many people, and can reduce our chances of establishing a relationship.

If an age gap is always present in our choices, a study of our chart can help us dig into the possible psychological moti-vations. Perhaps we choose older partners because we associ-ate age with maturity, maturity with competency, competency with protection, and protection with not having to take full responsibility of the many practical elements of our own life. Do we wish to have another individual manage and direct our affairs because we feel less capable and organized in this area? Would we later use that person as a scapegoat for our own inadequacies when serious problems arise in the union?

If partners are instead consistently younger, are some of us inwardly associating youth with inexperience, inexperience with immaturity, and immaturity with less power for our partners to wield in the relationship? (How, we rationalize, can they call the shots when they are just so darn inexperienced about life?) Are we not seeking an unequal partnership so that we can have the upper hand in controlling things? Our ability to teach our younger partner the basic ropes of life can indeed give us a satisfying sense of authority in which we can play out a parental role, but a proper maturation of both individuals is what Saturn seeks. If we always insist on being the responsible provider and policy maker in these relationships, we'll eventually feel deprived and let down when *we* need to be supported and provided for. We'd find we aren't able to rely on a partner who is so well trained in playing the needier role. We probably would do better with someone as self-sufficient and independent as we are.

WEDDING BLUES?

Contrary to the traditional interpretation, marriage is not necessarily delayed or postponed due to lack of interest with this placement. Saturn in Libra does want the formal contract provided by a legalized marriage with its binding status. If we do marry a little later than most, it's probably our choice not to take the big plunge until we feel more well defined and more in control of ourselves. We are choosy about who is proper marriage material for us. A longer-than-usual engagement may be indicated. We put our prospective mate through a reality test, which gives us ample time to spot flaws and weaknesses in character.

It's advisable not to rush into an early marriage because we need to first know how we feel about sharing our identity with another in such an intimate manner. How do we address the give-and-take issue? A partner could demand a lot of time and attention, and we need to make sure we do not resent that aspect of interaction, finding it intrusive. Those of us who have put off marital commitment need to analyze how we feel about autonomy and space; this is not just a Uranus or Jupiter theme. Saturn in Libra can feel claustrophobic when trying to function within the wrong unions to begin with, very much like Saturn in the Seventh House.

By giving ourselves time to review our attitudes and mature a bit more, we may be fit for marriage at a later period (perhaps even after our first Saturn Return). But first we will have to overcome some blocks we've set up regarding the "perfect" partner. Our standards might be too rigid and self-defeating in the long run.

Astro-lebrities with Saturn in Libra

Jane Austen	Judy Garland
Sting	Doris Day
Charles Bronson	Carol Channing
Isabella Rossellini	Richard Strauss
Steve Allen	Oliver Cromwell

SATURN IN THE SEVENTH HOUSE

SOLEMN VOW

Saturn in this house of peer partnerships means we tend to be insecure about our ability to relate to others on an equal footing. It's no wonder that the prospect of marriage is given much deliberate, careful attention. We're afraid to suffer the consequences of not choosing the right person, though this is not always a conscious fear. We take partnership very seriously and are intolerant of any failures or disappointments in this area. We want our primary relationships to bring us a lasting sense of security, which can be more meaningful to us than something as intangible as mere "happiness." We want something solid and self-evident that we can count on—but there are often obstacles in the path. First of all, many of us are not certain that we will ever have fulfilling partnerships. We fear we will fail our significant others in some basic way, or that they will disappoint us, so we proceed with caution regarding marital commitment and sharing our lives in long-term involvements.

Self-honesty and careful analysis will help us to deal with our doubts so we can work on developing more encouraging attitudes. While we cannot control and plan every step in order to prevent unexpected challenges regarding matrimony, cultivating a sense of reasonable expectation will help us to develop a realistic perspective. Until then, our inner fears and worries can make us project all sorts of unattractive Saturn deficiencies onto our partner. Such perceived traits of our significant other then appear to stifle our expression, inhibit our emotions, and keep us at a cool distance. What concerns us very much is the dread of deep commitment to people who might box us in and keep us in a constant state of vulnerability. It thus becomes easier to break off a developing relationship that is getting heavier rather than to confront the real issues.

Someday we will have to own up to the fact that we give our counterparts a lot of authoritative power over us, whether overt or subtle. We can turn them into our managers or agents of oppression rather than simply becoming equals. We want them, at least unconsciously, to run the show for us and do much of the organized structuring a marriage may call for. These people must have their act together and be highly capable in our eyes. It is often observed that Saturn in the Seventh House means we seek a parent (typically a daddy figure) in our marriage who can also act like a business manager (the Seventh House also deals with live-in lovers and close friends, in whom this Saturn dynamic can also be observed).

BIG DADDY

In traditional astrology, Saturn/Capricorn/Tenth House symbolizes a father figure, someone who we depend on for our outer direction, our social status, and our ego-structuring. This is somebody we expect to help us focus our energies realistically and materially. A partner of either sex can become our surrogate father figure. Age is not always a factor either, even though having a Seventh House Saturn suggests that we gravitate towards older individuals, assuming they have more experience dealing with the real world and handling authority. We figure their apparent maturity allows them to cope with the world more successfully than we do, and that can be comforting to us. But again, they can be younger people who act older and wiser than their years, or it could be we who insist on playing Big Daddy, regardless of our partner's gender.

Seeking out a paternal figure in any relationship conducive to a merging of equals can still be a positive thing, as long as we learn to switch the parental role ever so often (switching roles every so often good advice for any Seventh House planet). This is not something we realize very early on in our relationship experiences, though. We typically fixate this father-image need onto our partner who then must perform according to our subjective assumptions of correct parental behavior. With Saturn here, we can be very sensitive to anything that appears less than perfect. We must feel ultra-safe. Our partner is not allowed to get away with too many shortcomings. This can be quite a burden to place on somebody's shoulders, and could feel suffocating to them.

A typical scenario is a childhood where we felt we didn't have a close enough relationship to our own father while growing up. That doesn't mean we have had rotten fathers who couldn't care less about our existence. Such cold abandonment is sometimes the case, but it is not the only reason we grow up seeking our father in our partnerships in order to tend to unfinished business. Even if our relationship was good and fulfilling, it may also have been incomplete; for example, when we love a father very much who dies early on in our development, or who divorces Mom and then moves far away to live a completely separate new life, only visiting us occasionally, if at all.

I Married for Karma

So what if karmic debt is behind it all? That just means our relationships specifically demand well-defined resolutions in this lifetime, or they will become even more fated and insistent in future incarnations. However, we shouldn't get too upset when metaphysical astrologers speculate on how unloving and mean we were in past lives, or how we did a masterful job using people selfishly and then disposing of them like Kleenex! Our present situation may not necessarily be punishment for being a real stinker in those bygone days during the Dark Ages. Regardless of what we did or didn't do way back then, it becomes obvious that our ability to realistically address our partnership needs is being put to the acid test here and now. If our one-on-one unions are indeed karmic, then we best approach them consciously and thoughtfully. Most of us with this position seem to be slow to initially open up to those who strongly pull us toward them. We wonder why we feel moved by and drawn to such people, while we also feign disinterest at first. Saturn in general doesn't enjoy feeling compelled by anything—that's more Pluto.

We may be convinced that anybody who is important enough to us that we would consider marrying them must be at least honest, consistent, enduring, successful, ambitious, level-headed and morally decent. And responsible. And trustworthy. It seems our check-off list can go on forever, which is the main problem with Saturn in the Seventh House. We want to wed someone who is hassle-free, and who presents us only with what we think we can handle, with no surprises or shocks awaiting us. We want the whole situation to be predictable and thus controllable.

It may be hard to swallow, but we want power in our relationship. We want the upper hand. We make sure in marriage that we get to hold the reins tightly by attracting someone who is almost incapable of rebellion. Perhaps shades of karma past. Regardless, we feel more secure when we have a guarantee that things won't get out of hand in our union, and that regularity is assured. We often are masters at passive power plays; maybe working with a therapist can help make such issues clear to us.

Married Too Young

Astrological tradition gives marriage before age twenty-nine or thirty—in other words, before we've had a chance to experience our first Saturn Return—a "thumbs down" for people with Saturn in the Seventh House. Such early marriages typically last about seven years before they either fall apart or turn into something totally alien to their original intention. Whether involving matrimony or not, our Seventh House can be a one-on-one battle zone. Some nasty Saturnian games can be played out here (cold war, for instance), not just mating calls.

A more typical scenario is where we get the idea that marrying early is one sure way to escape from long-term parental pressures and restrictions. We just want out from under the yoke of our family, so our daring act of rebellion is to get married and enjoy our instant independence. Or we could be tempted to allow practical considerations, rather than real emotional love, to help us make our decision to wed (Saturn in the Eighth House can carry this theme as well). We rationalize that two can live more cheaply than one. We would deem it an irrelevant coincidence that our partner's family is loaded. Of course, Saturn can use wealth just as easily as it does poverty to teach us in the school of hard knocks. If we married too young, before we got to really know ourselves, we could feel trapped and owned while surrounded by luxury and privilege—something that wouldn't have happened if we had waited and grown up some more before going down the aisle.

We may also marry for the wrong reasons, which Saturn will never condone. The deeper and more satisfying aspects of a marriage elude us, and we eventually begin to feel confined and stifled by the arrangement. Normally, the more we want to be free from our marriage, the more clinging our Saturnian partner becomes (or vice versa). Since we hate to abandon ship, a trial separation could make us feel less guilty or ashamed of how things have turned out. Legal separation might give us an opportunity to sort things out and rectify conflicting feelings before we are forced to take that final step.

THE DREAD OF DIVORCE

We are anti-divorce at heart. We find the idea very distressing that one day we may be forced to actually do it. For many of us, getting married was tough enough, but not being able to stay bonded can be devastating. Besides, we typically resent having to go through the humiliation and aggravation of divorce proceedings, especially if an uncooperative partner wants to drag it out and make a public spectacle of the whole thing. It makes us feel quite exposed in a most uncomfortable manner. Sometimes it's simply wiser to listen to our attorney, who then acts as our new parent figure for the moment.

But once we have made up our minds to go through with a full-fledged legal ending to our suffering, that's it! We have no wishy-washy feelings about making such a decision, especially if we are the one filing for the divorce. Maybe we kept up our side of the bargain but our partner failed to. Maybe we are being restricted to the point of suffocation. We typically feel we got burned in this marriage somehow, but perhaps now we can be free again to find a new partner for more of the right reasons (rather than because of unexamined fears and insecurities).

So why aren't some of us smiling? Because we are terrified. We already are haunted by the crumbling of marriage number one, which we mistranslate as all our fault and our failure. Yet as down as we can be at this critical point, we probably are not going to jump into another legal union out of desperation or infatuation. Remember, Saturn means we get wiser as we get older. We will probably shop around more carefully next time (if we even want there to be a next time).

First, though, we have to reclaim those Saturn traits we unconsciously projected onto our partner. We need to realize that we reject people a lot more than we were aware of, basically because we typically reject ourselves as being a suitable partner. A step in the right direction is learning to tap into our own inner strengths and become more self-reliant. We need to incorporate many of the characteristics we find appealing in people we attract, but to manifest them our way.

TALES OF THE UNWED

Saturn in the Seventh House implies that if we are too cautious in approaching relationships, we may permanently scare ourselves out of matrimony. Severe self-inhibiting may be behind our solitary state. We can come up with all sorts of reasons we have delayed marriage or have been denied companionship by forces beyond our control. However, our Saturn house is seldom an area really beyond our control. The fateful tone it carries has much to do with our resistance to make required changes, and that is something controllable.

So what's the real story? Usually it's an unrecognized but deep-seated sense of unworthiness. We may subconsciously assume that no one attractive would stoop so low as to value us. Karmically speaking, there is probably nothing in the Akashic records that demands we are to be alone forever against our own choosing. It is only ours to decide to go that route. So let's not feel like a victim of cold, cruel fate. Living alone for some of us is simply psychologically easier, but doing so may also be a cop out.

It is usually better to share our lives with our Saturnian someone than to wing it solo. If choosing not to marry is really a conscious decision, based on careful evaluation of the pros and cons and backed up by self-awareness, we can then live single without repercussions. Yet if we are merely looking for an escape hatch in order to prevent confronting certain realities about ourselves, being uninvolved keeps us in a state of feeling incomplete. Saturn here is telling us we may lack clear focus in the art of intimate relating. Marriage may not be a necessity for us, but knowing why we don't want such commitment is.

BUSINESS IS BUSINESS, PARDNER

Our business partnerships may work out better than our marital ones because they require less emotional content and intimacy. We still can be very reserved in our expression, though, which may not be good for conducting business. Our partner(s) may also be hard to reach at times, usually due to being tight-lipped or inarticulate. We also take our business losses too much to heart, with a tendency to blame our cohorts for ineffi-ciency. Partners have to be competent and grounded with an inner settledness if we are to take them seriously. We expect them to be shrewd analysts who can spot those things we inno-cently overlook. We only want savvy people on our side. We want to be treated with respect and dignity, we will do the same for the right business associate. All parties involved can be uptight about being analyzed, yet without constructive crit-icism, our partnerships can become static and nonproductive. We need to feel safe opening up and communicating our thoughts without fear of another's rejection or resentment, and we need to be careful of our parental projections.

Astro-lebrities with Saturn in the Seventh House

Queen Elizabeth I
Edgar Cayce
Whoopi Goldberg
Thomas Jefferson
Louis Pasteur

Diana Ross
Woody Allen
Norman Mailer
Warren Beatty
Jacques Cousteau

SATURN/AIR VENUS ASPECTS

NATAL

Air Venus' domain is relationships. The Libra perspective promotes other-awareness and the value of cooperative give-and-take. Here, Venus is less self-absorbed, less focused on personal pleasure and creature comforts, and more sensitive to the desires of others. Our enjoyment comes from another's satisfaction, as well as his or her urge to give to us. This side of Venus is also more idealistic and abstract. We can be as much in love with the concept of love as with our actual part-ner. Earth Venus gives us information about our material values, while air Venus better defines what we value in another's character. Our Venus sign thus gives us clues about those traits and qualities we find very appealing and attractive. There is also, as with earth Venus, an ability to appreciate physical beauty as well, but with an added touch of refinement and sophisticated taste.

It appears that much of this Venus' expression is learned through culture and social conditioning. Earth Venus is more earthy and instinctual in what it finds desirable, and seeks to possess what it likes, but air Venus takes a mental approach to the cultivation of its desires. Manners, courtesies, and social graces, which are aesthetics normally defined by our cultural surroundings rather than something inborn, are linked with this Venus. This is a main distinction I make between these two Venus principles: earth Venus expression is more tied to our instincts while air Venus expression represents responses learned by observing the social interaction of others.

I call Saturn "cosmic glue" due to its phenomenal binding power. Natal Saturn in aspect to air Venus suggests we want to feel firmly attached in our partnerships and can be very loyal. This combination of planets pushes for solid, workable unions in which the parties involved have a lot in common and are dedicated to the same goals. We study relationships even at a very early age, paying attention to what makes them harmonious or contentious. But Saturn/Venus is also suggestive of deep insecurities about losing control of the relationship, or having someone either push us away and operate too independently, or simply leave us high and dry. Stress aspects are especially vulnerable to feelings of being cut off or cut out of a committed relationship due to an insensitive, cold, detached partner. We begin to realize that we have put in more effort to commit and stabilize the union than has our lover or spouse. In our desire for predictability, we have given the union little room to breathe.

Early childhood conditioning may have made us feel we had to control our own expression of love and affection. With sextiles and trines, this could have merely made us interact in a mature fashion, and our obedient temperament could have been well received by surrounding adults. We grow up cautious, but not fearful of our capacity to love and be loved. Our approach is level-headed and clear-eyed, not self-deprecating or unreasonably perfectionistic. As a result, we trust our ability to learn from the relationship mistakes of others, and from their success stories as well. This helps us hone in on attracting people whose inner qualities are complementary to our own, and we will take our time developing ourselves while we keep a watchful eye on our potential for a solid, grounded partnership. Saturn/Venus is in relationships for the long haul, well aware of the needed work it may take to keep a partnership thriving. We have the degree of emotional stamina required to deal with a union's ups and downs, provided we have attracted someone who is also willing to realistically hang on in there and tackle challenging issues as they develop.

As with all Saturn/Venus aspects, we do not easily get swept off our feet by romance and passion. We are too practical for that. Instead, we will quietly observe a potential mate under a wide variety of life situations to assess whether or not he or she is someone we could feasibly spend a long, long time getting to know better in a devoted, monogamous union. We are very much aware that both parties involved have to make a sincere effort for this to happen—yet still some of us behave like it's basically our job to keep a union afloat.

With squares and oppositions, practicality can give way to skepticism regarding love and attraction. We can be plagued by crippling self-doubts about our ability to be lovable and desirable to others. With the square, our self-worth can be low or at least poorly defined; we tend to package ourselves to others in unattractive ways. The source of the dilemma is often self-created, even though its origins may have come from early family situations. Since we do not see ourselves in a favorable light, we might convince others through our behavior and actions that we are indeed unworthy of their attention and affection.

With the opposition, we are more prone to attract people who thwart our attempts to get close and intimate. If we "do" our Venus, others play out the Saturn end (and sometimes badly so). We thus get a strong sense of highly conditional love in such relationships. Whatever internal Venus/Saturn issues we are dealing with, oppositions are prone to be worked out through our involvement with people we interact with. For example, the Venus/Saturn square could make us assume "nobody really wants me here at this party. I can feel it. Maybe I should tell the host I have a splitting headache and quietly leave." But with the opposition, we could be in quite a party mood until we overhear a few ungracious types mutter "What is she doing here? Who invited her? And do you see what she's wearing? With that figure?..." It seems we get rejected by others before we even get a chance to reject ourselves. With the opposition, feeling awkward in social situations is common.

The stress aspects between these planets can explain why we feel miserably out of place in many people-oriented situations, but we must work through them if we are to ever understand what the Saturn principle is trying to tell us about ourselves. These aspects are not given to us as punishment, although it may sometimes seem so. If a lot of people don't easily warm up to us, it could be Saturn's way of filtering out the undesirable types who evaluate others based on superficial standards. We may not possess their shallow requirements, but we should be glad we don't. What we need in our relationships are individuals who fall in love with who we really are inside. Much of what I've said so far especially applies to self-inhibitors.

However, some of us over-achievers will try to beat our detractors at their own game by outdoing them. We try to overcome any Saturn/Venus deficiencies by looking or dressing better than anyone else, or by attracting all the right material props (i.e., a big house in the best neighborhood and luxury car in the garage) that should tell others we are very important, very well off, and deserving of very special social treatment. Here's another instance where Saturn over-compensates and starts acting like Jupiter. We find ourselves with a competitive ambition to be as highly desirable to others as we can. We can be fastidiously well groomed with impeccable taste. We are supremely status-conscious and are only interested in suitors who have money, power, and big prospects.

This extreme manifestation of Saturn/Venus is not common, but it does occur. Instead, if our tastes are not so glamorous, we may still knock ourselves out working at the gym just to have the well-toned bodies that will turn heads. However we do it, our motivation is to create whatever impression or image it takes to get society to admire us, envy us, or just take us seriously.

TRANSIT

Saturn aspecting our Venus, especially by conjunction, square, and opposition, is a time to test out the reality of a love affair, a marriage, a business partnership, a close friendship, and any other one-on-one relationship. Is this a union of mutual consideration and cooperation? Are we getting back the sense of support we give to another? Is this relationship on solid ground or on its last leg? Saturn suggests this may be a time to attend to whatever or whomever is in need of repair. We are to try to fix something broken if possible. Is our relationship salvageable, and do we understand why it got damaged in the first place? Saturn has no trouble encouraging us to fortify whatever is already strong and positive about any relationship, but it does want to put the brakes on whatever is careening out of control. Saturn tries to get rid of whatever we have outgrown and can no longer fit into. In this context, that can be another person and/or a lifestyle associated with that person.

Students of astrology tend to feel uncomfortable seeing the "Grim Reaper" hanging around the planet that represents love and marriage. We sense we will meet up with limitations that hit us on the emotional level. We fear our heart will feel pain somehow. We anticipate feeling lonely and without the comfort of a loved one. All this may be true. Saturn can attempt to throw us back on our own internal resources (since that's how inner strength is developed) and demand of us the bare bones of self-sufficiency. This is a time of no thrills, no frills. Our love life and its emotional realities need a sober review. Our marriage and where it's going needs to be put under the microscope. Our business partnerships are up for an objective evaluation. We need to know what is real in these areas and what is not. Thus, Saturn throws a cold splash of water in our face and insists we wake up and start operating more alertly and with greater accountability.

One thing we cannot afford to do during this transit is to take anybody for granted who is part of our emotional life. We may need to be more open in the manifestation of our Venus, because Saturn wants any planet it contacts to make itself real and well formed. In this case, instead of inhibiting our feelings, we may need to articulate them by showing open affection and other direct expressions of our love. Of course, this will take courage on our part since we still can be rejected or pushed away, but we will never know our own depths of feeling until we make our intentions clear and direct.

Of course, with the opposition, a delicate balancing act is required since we are to manifest Venus with more conviction while having to prepare ourselves for a Saturnian reaction that may feel contrary to our desires and expectations. That doesn't necessarily mean we will be disappointed, but the potential is there. If this becomes the case, we will give it our very best and patiently wait for a constructive response. If our Saturn partner doesn't meet us halfway, and even turns colder or becomes harder to reach, that's our sign that the relationship is too far gone to be revived. Why would we want to raise the dead at this point anyway? It hurts to realize this, but it would make more sense to bring this union to an end. Learn from it, but move on.

Venus alone will urge us to do whatever it takes to keep love alive, even if we have to manipulate ourselves and others, or jump through hoops, or make heartfelt promises to be more forgiving and understanding. But Saturn is calling the shots now, and Saturn will not let any shams or futile fantasies continue. If we are in a horrid, loveless union, Saturn transiting

Venus means we must separate if we are to emotionally survive. Actually, my interpretation may sound too dramatic for
the typical Saturn scenario. Perhaps in real life, we simply
stop caring, turn cold, and call it quits. It could feel like a
practical, cut-and-dried matter, and one we have been quietly
contemplating for a long time before life gave us a good reason
to actually do something about it.

On the other hand, transiting Saturn contacting Venus
can be an excellent time for some of us to manifest a love relationship. (Saturn in the Seventh House is also good for solidi-
fying a relationship and even getting married, although many
traditional texts would say the opposite.) If we have been
alone for too long, we can use this period to structure our relationship needs better and come up with some well-defined
reasons we want a partnership now. Our clarity here can
assist us in attracting someone who can help fulfill our needs.
At all times, patience is needed and the realization that
proper timing holds the key to the right kind of attraction for
us. We are not going to benefit ourselves at all if we approach
this issue with a sense of desperation or urgency based on fear
of loneliness.

We also need to apply some common sense, especially if
Saturn is making a challenging aspect to our Venus. This
means we need to carefully pick people who are totally accessible and safe. The safe bets have steady jobs, are not
attached to others, have money in the bank (that's a sign of
fiscal responsibility, which will be important to us later when
the Taurus facet of Venus starts to kick in), and are not in
trouble with the law (better think twice about doing a love
connection with that prison pen pal). If we are not in love
with those kind of folks, but instead are falling for wonderful
free-spirited souls who are spiritual and have lots of compassion—yet are temporarily unemployed—we are still barking
up the wrong tree.

Saturn is telling us to get real and get going with what it
takes to form a reliable love bond. If we can't find a suitable
person, we are to continue to enjoy our own company until

someone truly worthy of us comes along. Our poet-mystic "new friend" who may be good at pointing out our inner beauty should remain just that at the moment—a good friend, because his/her temperament does not fit our here-and-now Saturn needs for growth. Some of us will find that hard to believe, and will want to (almost defiantly) seek out very un-Saturnian partners regardless—but this is a recipe for heartache and confusion.

Sometimes, Saturn can mean the wrong person may stick to us stubbornly and not accept our proposal to go our separate ways. I'm not implying a stalker (that's more Plutonian), but simply someone who doesn't want to hear "no" and who will do whatever it takes to woo us back. A guilt trip can be laid on us because of this, and perhaps out of a weird sense of duty (or a lack of other proposals), we may continue the union. This is not a good idea. We will wake up one day and say "that's it!" and then terminate this ill-fitting relationship in no uncertain terms, but the whole thing can feel awkward and uncomfortable, with lingering bad feelings. So why get this sorry affair started to begin with? If we are born with Neptune/Moon or Neptune/Venus hard aspects, we really need to reread these last few paragraphs, since we can color our relationships in ways that seldom allow us to touch the firm ground of reality Saturn worships.

SATURN
IN SCORPIO

IRON FIST

Scorpio is a tough-as-nails placement for this planet. The intensity of Scorpio combined with the steely determination of hard-nosed Saturn may help us overcome many of life's major obstacles. We can face up to and overcome traumatic difficulties that would devastate or obliterate others with less indomitable wills. We can be forceful and fearless in our persistence. Our sense of our own depth of reserved power can allow us to confront life's problems with much courage.

Fixed Scorpio doesn't give up on any challenge that has captured its interest, while Saturn adds the stamina and endurance needed to fully pursue what we investigate. This Saturn acts like a bloodhound intently focused on the trail and fixated on ferreting out all that is hidden. Likewise, we can sniff out less obvious elements in our environment.

But the compulsion to control and manage people and what they own (their resources on all levels) is very strong. We can rule and dictate with an iron fist, and some of us can play dirty when trying to call the shots. Both Saturn and Scorpio have to be careful that they don't succumb to a "the end justifies the means" philosophy. Our need to overpower and conquer can be much more important than the ethics of how we play the game.

Many of us will probably attract critical life situations pressuring us to test our tremendous inner strength and hard-to-match durability. Scorpio's ability to recharge its vital forces, even after exhaustive energy expenditure, works well with Saturn's ability to continue with something until reaching a conclusion. In fact, Saturn helps Scorpio better modulate its energy so that it's not misused in extremist ways, because Saturn is always pushing for moderation of expression But this measured approach doesn't appeal to a few of us overachievers, who will push the limits of human capacity—ours and others—to the nth degree. We can become very hard taskmasters, almost incapable of giving in to weaknesses and vulnerabilities. Nobody gets to see the tiny cracks in our fortress walls: we make sure they see the intimidating mesh of barbed wire instead.

EMOTIONAL BLOCKADE

Scorpio can be an intensely emotional sign, but you wouldn't often know it by observing its surface expression. Though its cool and unexpressive exterior implies aloofness and detachment, that is far from the truth; it just shows how really secretive and unrevealing this sign can be. But Saturn also appears unmoved by emotion, and to look at this pragmatic planet you *would* know it. Together, planet and sign can have trouble demonstrating feelings. The potential to keep emotionality under lock and key is very great. Saturn may even impede the regenerative flow of Scorpio, further evoking the repressive side of this reserved sign. There can be a damming up of more psychological material than can be feasibly transmuted. Deep blockages and fixations can be born of this.

Although Saturn seeks to set safe limits on Scorpio's otherwise insatiable desire nature, the result can be an unhealthy storing up of forces that periodically will have an eruptive and sometimes uncontrollable release—exactly what Saturn was trying to avoid. Thus, putting the Saturn-style clamps on our desires can ultimately backfire. We may have had parental conditioning in our early formative years that unduly restrained our ability to show raw emotionality, meaning outbursts of tears, temper tantrums, or even unbridled exuberance—things normal to the childhood growth process. Someone may have made us stuff all these passionate expressions deep down, setting us up for a lifelong pattern of turbulent self-denial and an obsession with mastering powerful feelings. Yet we also find ourselves battling the urge to volcanically unleash a wide gamut of unsavory feelings and seething hostilities. Former British Prime Minister Margaret Thatcher (whose nickname while in office was "The Iron Lady") was born with Saturn in Scorpio, and this underground seething quality, hinted at in her eyes and her taut facial expressions, was often unmistakably conveyed whenever she was compelled to deem something as "appalling." There is a book written about her by Bruce Arnold with the telling title *Margaret Thatcher: A Study in Power*.[1] Perhaps this placement means we are here to study our own power drives and learn how to responsibly apply them.

THOSE DICTATORIAL WAYS

Saturn, while not bossy in the typical manner of Leo, still wants to be in charge of whatever it can control. Saturn will naturally gravitate toward the supervision of a project or a person. Scorpio is notorious for not submitting to another's control, whether real or imagined. But due to its hard-to-fathom insecurities, this sign can turn the tables and try to get the upper hand on others. It will even engage in preemptive strikes in order to outmaneuver the "enemy." Planet and sign need to recognize their tendency to dominate and overtake by attacking the weaknesses of somebody or something.

Saturn's urge is to fix or eliminate any defect that impedes proper functioning, but its tactics can be heavy-handed.

Scorpio is the one with the hidden agenda involving total takeovers, feeling driven to overwhelm the object of its attention. When mishandled, we can become too imposing in how we reach out and grab what we want. Once it's ours, even if we obtained it the wrong way, we do not let go without a fierce fight. Our need to control and manage can be all-consuming. This can be a ruthless Saturn.

Yet, who in the world is even allowed to attempt to dominate us? Nobody. There is probably a deep, internal sense of isolation when we operate in this defense mode. We keep people at such an arm's length, emotionally speaking, that others are shut off from helping or influencing us for our own good. Even if we really could use their input, we deny them access to us. Dictators universally are lonely people, cut off from the security of human trust and the comforts of warm intimacy. People under a dictator's rule are not actually seen as people, but as objects to be manipulated, often for ulterior motives. This is one of the prime dangers of having Saturn in Scorpio. Instead of the discipline of mastering ourselves, we attempt to discipline and master others against their will.

LETTING DOWN OUR GUARD

As Saturn's reserved nature is compounded by Scorpio's circumspect temperament, we may seek self-preservation through the construction of an icy insulation when we are feeling threatened or violated. Our ego-guard goes up whenever we sense a confrontation. We do not want to be made powerless by authoritative or menacing forces. Saturn's need for respect fortified by Scorpio's hidden pride gives an aura of cold dignity. Our frostiness keeps strangers and other "invaders" at a safe distance. We probably over-analyze everything and read too much between the lines, suggesting that even innocent gestures on the part of others can be negatively misinterpreted. Just like the joke of the two psychiatrists passing each other on the street, where one cheerfully says "Good morning!" and the other one thinks "I wonder what he meant by that?" we may always be looking for darker motives in people. This is a Scorpio position that is paranoid about the intentions of life itself—and this is often a projection of our own inner manipulativeness.

One source of this basic distrust of others may come from the emotional tone of our early family experience. Perhaps a parent (father or father figure), in the guise of merely being strict and disciplinarian, may have actually been cruel and abusively punishing. Maybe abject neglect taught us at a tender age that people cannot be counted on for support and comfort, and that we have to teach ourselves cunning survival skills to cope with a potentially harmful and uncaring world. Saturn in all the water signs carries this theme in varying degrees, but in Scorpio we can turn this into a life-or-death drama. We will survive by not letting ourselves be done in by the oppressive forces swooping down on us.

Accordingly, a whole lifetime awaits us in which we learn to break down the barriers, brick by brick, to allow old wounds to heal. Our karma, if you will, is almost forcing us to undergo a deep metamorphic phase of soul redemption in order to balance out the awesome power we may have wielded in past lives. Must we wait for this life to bring us to our knees and strip us of all power before we see the light, and before we learn to forgive ourselves and allow others to forgive us for all our totalitarian ways? Dictators have been known to die tragically. Even if we expire quietly in our sleep and in our own bed, an unexamined life would qualify as a human tragedy. We are to do some serious self-reflection, consciously make amends, and then get on with our much-needed emotional inner work to avoid coming to such a sad and futile end.

KEEPING SECRETS

It is practically impossible to pry things out of us when we are not ready to expose what we know or feel. Both Saturn and Scorpio can be very tight-lipped and silent when necessary—but we also are the ones others trust to safeguard their uncomfortable secrets. This position can be excellent for some of us who might be inclined to become professional therapists, psychiatrists, or counselors who deal with the private or painful disclosures of people at critical crossroads in their lives. For example, Saturn in Scorpio could handle suicide hotlines, comfort victims who retreat to shelters for the battered, or work at an AIDS crisis center, and even do volunteer service in hospices. We probably can stomach the more gut-wrenching life experiences than the average person. We have the required detachment to grit our teeth, roll up our sleeves, and do the dirty work that must be done without complaint or revulsion, much like a surgeon in a trauma unit or a homicide detective assigned to a gruesome criminal case. Violent death, physical decay, severe trauma, unspeakable assault—all such gripping human experiences are meet with a rare, unflinching strength that can prove comforting to those in desperate or dire need.

Elisabeth Kübler-Ross, well known and respected for her enlightening work on the process of dying, was not only born with Saturn in Scorpio, but Saturn also in the Eighth House. She serves as an excellent example of Saturn in Scorpio's courage in action and power to offer tremendous healing for the soul.[2] We may be the keeper of many secrets and hidden feelings others can barely articulate without shame or dread, but regardless of our natal aspects to Saturn, it is our solemn duty to help others renew their own sense of inner power. Saturn in Scorpio can be strongly restorative when used in its highest and most unselfish expression. Getting to this level is no easy task, considering how self-preoccupied we typically are, but it can be a truly self-empowering goal to aspire toward.

CONTROLLING THE PURSE STRINGS

Money can be a source of power in our materialistic culture, and Saturn in Scorpio thus feels naturally drawn to handling and controlling finances. Saturn's sense of responsibility and

Scorpio's fiscal know-how combine well to suggest a natural ability as a treasurer or financial strategist. We can turn the pursuit of profit and amassing of wealth into a serious study. We over-achievers can be too interested in money, and not just ours. Whether in marriage or business, Saturn in Scorpio has to be careful not to take over other people's financial affairs or other resources in a heavy-handed, coercive, or manipulative manner. Having a tight financial grip on people can make us feel very essential to their economic survival. This can cause deep resentment and even hatred, as others feel we are too controlling of what is technically theirs to own and spend.

If we really feel that protecting money and other valued funds is so important to our own security, why not turn our focused interest into a career option? Being a full-time broker, financial planner, tax attorney, or even a part-time CPA could be acceptable vocational outlets for us. Then we would be paid to have access to people's financial setups and to assist them in controlling and utilizing their resources

But we self-inhibitors are tempted to prey on others for our financial survival, because negative Scorpio can usurp, expend, and exhaust resources, although not always consciously. If we don't manifest with Scorpio's independent resourcefulness, we may gravitate toward involvement with those who can attract powerful assets. Legal financial affairs are prone to be troublesome for us, either due to our attempt to defy the law (tax evasion) or our tendency to avoid financial reality (bankruptcy). Money handling is tied in with our maturation process. Things may get better for us as we get older.

SAFE SEX

For some of us, safe sex means no sex. This is a good placement for undergoing periods of celibacy and abstinence. But while some consciously abstain due to fear of contracting deadly sexually transmitted diseases, a deeper reason could be feelings of sexual inadequacy. We may be too performance-sensitive to relax and enjoy sexual release unless we are in control, pushing another person's erotic buttons. This is more work than play, at least in the serious way we do it.

Over-achievers seek to become experts in sexual pleasuring and may be obsessed with practicing a lot to get it right. Self-inhibitors may feel plagued by varying degrees of sexual dysfunction, typically tied to a denial of our own gratification. We need to stop trying to micromanage the whole experience and surrender to our body's natural responses, even if this is easier said than done. Our sexuality can improve with age and with the right kind of intimate experience. Lovingness applied to ourselves and our trusted partner has to fit into the picture.

Astro-lebrities with Saturn in Scorpio

Elisabeth Kübler-Ross
Martin Luther
Johnny Carson
Marilyn Monroe
Richard Burton

J. Edgar Hoover
Charlton Heston
Queen Elizabeth II
Marlon Brando
Goethe

SATURN IN THE EIGHTH HOUSE

DIGGING DEEP

Unless Saturn is also in Scorpio, there doesn't have to be anything too emotionally gut-wrenching about having Saturn in the Eighth House. Scorpio uses its own kind of powerful fuel to drive Saturn's engine—but in Gemini, for instance, it might be a different story altogether. Thus, the sign involved will give needed clues as to what motivates this Saturn to operate. However, Eighth House matters all deal with circumstances that are typically experienced behind closed doors, away from public scrutiny, so secretiveness and privacy can still be the Scorpio-like issues intrinsic to this house. We find ourselves drawn to serious life situations that are ponderous, complex, and sometimes mysterious. Saturn here suggests we have an urge to control or master those things that have enormous power implications for us, whether within the layers of our own psyches or outside of ourselves in a world of high-stakes survival games, whether involving business, finances, passionate conquests, or intimate but stormy relationships.

If we are to get a grip on these things (and we often feel driven to), we will need to do the inner work required to help us periodically face life's mightier challenges. This can be a position for Saturn where the struggle to overcome imposing hurdles is more evident. The Eighth House is a crisis zone in our chart where we are compelled to tap into our dormant psychological resources and bring out our hidden strengths under pressure. Nothing is treated superficially in this area, so we must be willing to dig deep in order to uncover our buried inner treasure. The problem, however, is that some of us are scared of what we will find. Could what we unearth become overwhelming for us?

Squares and oppositions involving Saturn in the Eighth House imply that we first must deal with an internal resistance to knowing about the depths life can take us to. With these aspects to Saturn, an unwarranted fear of being overtaken by the darker elements of the Unknown can keep us from going too far below the surface of ordinary consciousness. Even something as ho-hum as recognizing the existence of ESP can be frightening for those of us wary about anything we can't register with our physical senses. Psychic phenomena and altered states of consciousness become too unnerving to even consider as possible. In fact, psychological concepts like the "shadow," the "id," or the "unconscious self" might also be met with skepticism. Even the existence of multiple personalities would be too ludicrous for a doubting Saturn in the Eighth House to accept as legitimate.

Yet a few of us braver souls are willing to enter the sometimes bizarre world of the mind's interior and our psyche's underground chambers. (Trines and sextiles here suggest we find Eighth House areas more inviting and intriguing than threatening and anxiety-producing.) We can serve as a skillful tour guide, helping to reorient lost and troubled souls wandering through their own minefields of unexpressed turbulence and rage. Saturn here can be the signature of a very adept therapist (Sigmund Freud was born with Saturn in the Eighth House), a true psychic counselor, a fearless shaman, or even a highly effective astrologer willing to do in-depth, long-term work with clients via the archetypes in birthchart.

DEATH CARD

But even the bravest of us eventually have to meet up with a longtime enemy of earthbound consciousness—Death. How would Saturn deal with the concept of total annihilation of that lucid waking state people on this planet practically worship?

Anyone who has had a few Tarot readings or has bought a deck of these cards to attempt to give his/her own personal readings has probably seen the thirteenth card of the Major Arcana pop up. Death is here portrayed as a conquering warrior or as a maniacal scythe-wielder, with terrified people on their knees nearby or hacked human body parts strewn about the ground. In either case, Death's image as a grinning skeleton come alive symbolizes the nightmare Saturn in the Eighth House could have about the death process (by the way, nightmares are an Eighth House form of psychological release, acting as natural safety valves for the expression of unaddressed fears and toxic anger). Saturn rules the skeleton itself—the part of us that remains in the grave wearing its obscene smile of apparent victory over our dream of immortality. Many of us with this position think about life and death in a profound manner—maybe because we suffer the losses of those people to whom we have had very strong but insecure attachments. Maybe they've physically left us in painful, fateful ways that have troubled our soul.

It's no wonder that the death or enforced departure of others leaves a bad taste in our mouth and a degree of bitterness. Maybe we assume we can conquer death by refusing to even think about it, or by pushing it behind us as far and as long as we can, at least until the next sorrowful incident when it rears its ugly head once more. Death can obviously be depressing for some of us who have barely allowed ourselves to be part of the exuberance of living. It seems unfair that Time marches on and kills off our allotted vital life force slowly during our lifespan. We may resent this because we feel we've gotten off to a late start getting the hang of living out the potential of all our other houses. Why have it all robbed from us just when we are getting better at managing our inner and outer existence? It is natural for an Eighth House Saturn to want to stop the whole process of aging and its all too deadly consequences.

But once our tears dry and we realize that reality is going to continue to be what it is, we have the option of dealing with death and dying in a no-nonsense manner. We can look it in the eye unflinchingly. We do not deny death its power, but we also do not grieve more than we must. Metaphysics would suggest that the "death" of the spirit begins the moment we are born to this level of physical reality. As the kicking new-born baby vigorously gasps for air and cries its angry-sounding cry, the spirit within has become entombed during its new physical incarnation. Saturn in the Eighth House could benefit from considering this birth/death paradox—dying on one level of awareness while simultaneously being reborn on another. Since Saturn appreciates continuity, we may feel more secure when accepting the existence of an afterlife.

HEROIC MEASURES

Some of us may find we already have a level-headedness about death, trauma, and dire emergencies that allows us to function unemotionally and efficiently during times of disaster or chaos. Yes, the plane may be going down, but we have eighty screaming, unfocused people to quickly organize and safely prepare for ground contact! Even during such intense scenarios requiring split-second thinking, Saturn suggests we draw from something deep within to help us remain calm, reasonably collected, and focused, with a level of authoritative command that gets the job done. Some of us may even make a career out of crisis management such as working in firefighting, on bomb squads, with paramedic units, in trauma clinics, or rendering critical services in wartime operations.

SEX & SIN

Saturn in the Eighth House can mingle sexual arousal with fear, with "dirtiness," or even with evil in some cases. The highly structured form of morality Saturn subscribes to is pitted against the bottomless well of primal sexuality pulsating in the depths in the Eighth House. Prudish Saturn does not want to admit to itself or the outside world that we possibly could be as lusty as goats in heat. Many Eighth House impulses could be labeled as "animalistic" urges: not just sex, but also our lust for blood when our fangs come out and we're filled with venomous rage. Of course, not even animals act as badly as we do when we are pretending we're not animals!

The less religious among us may not be as plagued by harsh moral judgments regarding sexual interest, but we still live in a culture that can be condemning of certain behaviors, and sex becomes a sure-fire target for the conservative elements of society to attack. Some of us may refrain from showing anything about ourselves that could be deemed sexy. We keep our erotic leanings under wraps, while on the outside we rationalize that we are simply very private people. If Saturn is undergoing stress aspects, the truth could be that we are merely hung up about a lot of things associated with sexuality. Saturn would suggest that we have a hard time warming up to intimacy, both physical and emotional. We may have difficulty surrendering to our own or someone else's sexual energy, and thus we can dampen the fires of passion. Impotence and frigidity have been noted with this Saturn (but look to the Fifth House for further clues).

We over-achievers can almost put too much focus on mastering sex. We work hard to perfect our or our partner's sexual performance and can end up feeling like "sexperts." But the less confident and self-valued we feel, the more we obsessively demand sexual stimulation to compensate for our feelings of inadequacy. No wonder this whole area of sex became an enthralling fixation for Dr. Freud—and since his Eighth House Saturn was in Gemini, of course he wanted to talk about it!

Actually, sex as in "the sex act" and what we like to enjoy here can be more a Fifth House issue. The Eighth House is the realm of our development of a sexual identity, whether we ever get to act it out physically or not. Even when celibate, we are still sexual beings capable of great sensual pleasure.

The Buck Stops Here

One often-mentioned interpretation of an Eighth House Saturn is that we can attract a mate or business partner who tends to have a lot of financial problems. That partner doesn't manage his or her funds very well, or may have a self-worth issue to work on that can manifest as poverty. Whatever the case, Saturn hits that person in the pocketbook, and we are prone to want to enter the picture and restructure this shaky situation. Our partner is usually dependent on us to provide the material security needed.

Some of us appreciate the boundaries required in all healthy one-on-one relationships and will only step in to assist when directly asked. We do what we can, with no strings attached, and bow out when our partner is able to be self-sufficient. Expect sextiles and trines to Saturn to urge us to know our own limits more clearly in these matters—we realize we cannot take full responsibility for another person's fiscal dilemma. When well handled, Saturn always knows its limits and can abide by them.

But a mismanaged Saturn in the Eighth House creates a problematic relationship, for not only is money management a source of frustration, but power struggles can relate to the handling of shared resources. In this case, we may demand to

198 • CHAPTER THIRTEEN

take over the organization of all joint financial and property affairs. We cannot allow for any mistakes or incompetence. If our partner is not able to attend to matters here, or is unwilling to, we feel obligated to intervene and take full control. But once we do this, it becomes hard to trust our partner enough later and let go of the reins, and this can keep our significant other in a state of immaturity or ignorance regarding money matters, both legal and personal. We pay all the bills, do all the taxes, sign all the insurance policies, take out the bank loans when needed, and probably even draw up a will spelling out in detail how our assets are to be divvied up after we...(gulp)...die. Our consuming concern is for complete financial protection.

While this sounds all good and noble of us, at issue is how we orchestrate such financial planning. Saturn in the Eighth House can be a control freak. Our compulsion is to keep track of where money goes and especially how it may be wasted on non-essentials. We can keep partnership funds as well guarded and as inaccessible as the loot in Fort Knox. Being too tight-fisted about cash flow can seem oppressive to our partner, who almost feels he or she must ask for permission to spend. We can be insufferable cheapskates, even with our partner's income. We trespass into their financial territory too forcefully, and this can stir up much unspoken resentment. (Roles can reverse in the Seventh and Eighth Houses periodically, and sometimes it is our partner who will sound much like what's been said in these last few paragraphs.)

People shouldn't even bother to try to borrow things from us, as we can be sticklers about the way they handle our goods (similar to Saturn in the Second House). Our generosity can be highly conditional, and we resent it when we are suddenly put on the spot to give. We may be like this about lending because we have been the victim of another's irresponsible use of our possessions in the past (in this lifetime as well as in former lifetimes), so we are cautious and discriminating about what we let people have. Yet we also can take excellent care of other people's possessions entrusted to us for safeguarding.

We don't normally like to borrow things, but if we have to, we keep them well maintained, even in perfect shape (good to know when you are thinking about lending us your favorite astrology books). But the general policy here, especially with strangers, is that "What's yours is yours and what's mine is mine. So hands off what's mine!" We would rather buy you a copy than let you walk away with our original, but not out of any spirit of generosity.

SOUL SURVIVOR

What is great about having Saturn in the Eighth House is that we can end up being hearty old souls who have been through thick and thin, only to have our resilience strengthened in meeting the storms of life. We may find we are very resourceful and can make do with just about any condition without complaint. Hardships test our mettle and show us the depths of our resolve. Some of us may live a very long time (Saturn here can indicate longevity), so we are compelled to make peace with our earthly experience and deal with life on its own sometimes-perplexing terms. We learn wisely to stop fighting and struggling with inevitabilities. A secret to our success may be that we know when to withdraw from the hustle and bustle of worldly affairs whenever we start to feel out of touch with our inner selves (this is typical of Saturn in all the "water" houses—Fourth, Eighth, and Twelfth). We need stillness to self-rejuvenate.

Astro-lebrities with Saturn in the Eighth House

Sigmund Freud	Paul Gauguin
Elisabeth Kübler-Ross	J. P. Morgan
Salvador Dali	William Lilly
Franklin D. Roosevelt	Vanessa Redgrave
H. G. Wells	Jane Fonda

SATURN/PLUTO ASPECTS

NATAL

Saturn and Pluto share a common ability to give complete attention to whatever seriously engrosses them. Their powers of concentration can be amazing, and even more so when these planets are combined in aspect. Pluto evokes Saturn's capacity to apply the dogged persistence demanded when undertaking any enormously taxing feat. Saturn reinforces Pluto's talent for remaining singularly focused on an objective no matter how grueling or unsupported by others. Both planets test the limits: how far can we go with it? Saturn is associated with high achievement potential, while Pluto is the planet of mega-accomplishments ("mega" anything, in fact). Billy Payne, brainstormer and chief coordinator of the 1996 Atlanta Olympics, was born with a Saturn/Pluto conjunction. Perhaps we are born with a Saturn/Pluto aspect if, for our soul growth, we are to overcome great odds in order to reach objectives others would deem near impossible. It seems the more arduous the task, the more compelled we may be to self-reliantly handle all obstacles associated with it. This certainly fits Payne's experience in working superhumanly hard to bring the Olympics to the fabled "Phoenix" city of the South (Atlanta has natal Pluto in the First House). Our own squares and oppositions may also sharply bring these dynamics into play for us.

Both planets are driven to attack weaknesses, whether of internal origin (as in our character flaws) or of a more external source (as in faulty processes that block the functional development of something). Remember, both planets act as terminators, willing and able to end that which cannot support optimum growth. Saturn and Pluto know when something is unable to be salvaged, and each opts for that something to halt, cease, or die. Sounds dramatic, but we are dealing with two planets that do not wish to waste time or energy on whatever has no viable future. Pluto's urge is to recycle what it can, while Saturn will save any workable parts before throwing the rest out.

Accordingly, we can be very resourceful with the materials or supplies life gives us to work with. Although Pluto's oft-repeated keyphrase is "death and rebirth," rebirth in this context implies a talent for rebuilding, even from scratch if need be. This is something hard-working Saturn would support. Some of us with Saturn/Pluto have the guts to tear down parts of our lives when they no longer work for us, then pool all our inner resources to structure new frameworks that are well fortified to withstand future threats to our security. A few of us are forced by circumstances of a very fateful kind to let go of our past and start anew. Our mandatory rebuilding process can seem like punishment, but once the initial hurdles and fears are overcome we probably can look back and realize how we sorely needed to end a chapter of life and open ourselves up to a new and momentous beginning.

There are also a few points of contrast that can be found between these planets. A major one is that Saturn's mindset encourages energy and matter to take on permanent form. It inflexibly expects things to stay as they are, as long as they are serving a relevant purpose and are in good operating order. Pluto says nothing is indispensable, especially anything locked into rigid form. For Pluto, whether through biological mutation on a small scale or upheaval of drastic, global proportions, change is life's only real absolute. No matter how perfectly any Saturn structure is built, Pluto always has the option to annihilate Saturnian form while reclaiming the energy that held such form together. Pluto's desire would be to use that energy for another endeavor altogether. Such a highly impersonalized use of transmutational power may horrify Saturn, a planet already grappling with built-in insecurities about potential loss and deprivation. So how do we handle this conflict of interests when these are planets natally in aspect?

Many of us do not handle it well. We may be afraid we will not be allowed to set up anything lasting in our lives for fear that sabotaging elements may come in and take every-thing away by force—like when the Plutonian IRS swoops down and confiscates all our tangible assets because we've neglected or refused to pay our taxes (in fact, Saturn/Pluto aspects do suggest we get our legal financial affairs in order and not do anything underhanded). A Saturn/Pluto reaction would be to put up a fierce do-or-die struggle in opposing the actions of outside authorities, the law, or whomever we regard as dangerous invaders.

Perhaps we first felt the threat of oppressive power from our father or father figure. We may have been treated with a severe form of discipline or sensed a controlled rage that could erupt at any minute and attack us. Probably other factors in the chart need to set this potential off, but the possibility of experiencing brutality on some level is indicated for at least a few of us. Later on, if unchecked, we can become the brutal, authoritarian ones (in our stern judgment of others, if not physically and emotionally). But in most cases, we Saturn/Pluto types can seethe within while showing remark-able poise and composure on the outside. It seems to the world that very little really ruffles our feathers. People tend to see us as towers of strength, especially during times of crisis.

Arnold Schwarzenegger was born with the conjunction, and he certainly has played screen roles in which he has appeared to be more than human. The titles and themes of some of his flicks (*Predator, The Terminator, Eraser*) smack of Saturn/Pluto issues. His movies probably allow him to vent the enormous inner pressures typical of this planetary combination. While we may not seem as larger-than-life as Arnold, we can be very motivated, highly dependable, and quite able to carry a heavy load, especially if it's for some greater cause. Others may mar-vel at our endurance and respect our commanding authority (assuming we haven't taken a dictatorial route as did Stalin, with his Saturn in Aries semi-square Pluto). Some of us are probably destined for a special leadership role.

Still, our inner world can feel tumultuous as we battle con-trolling forces that keep us feeling anything but relaxed and content. With Saturn/Pluto stress aspects, we tend to be tightly wound up and always on guard. Paranoia can be a Saturn/Pluto trait. We are probably far more rigid than we realize, and much more unforgiving of those who trespass against us than we'd care to admit. At the same time, we can be hard on ourselves for giving in to our demons and losing control. We need to make sure we do not resort to devious, ruthless measures to achieve our desires, as we can be a formidable opponent who doesn't always play fair. Ethical standards need to be adhered to. Just because some of us can bully or intimidate the weaker doesn't mean we should. If we are to fight, let it not be "dirty" fighting. Total self-mastery can be an all-consuming goal for some of us, but enlightened self-awareness may be even more important.

Sextiles and trines are certainly not as problematic regarding much of what has been described. We probably have opportunities to show guts and courage when truly needed. We can be highly principled people who realize the power of discipline. We can achieve major goals without being obsessive-compulsive about the methods used. Our authority is firm but not threatening to others. We still need to ease up on ourselves when we get too single-minded in our aims, but life allows us easier outlets to rechannel our potent energies. We can release our Pluto power in small, practical doses rather than wait for a big build-up.

TRANSIT

How we register transiting Saturn aspecting our Pluto depends a lot on what we've been doing thus far to develop our need for power. When these two planets connect in any fashion, it can denote a time for us to take a cold, hard look at those elements in our life where we feel we're under someone else's thumb—if not an actual person, then some facet of the social system that has forced us to behave against our inner grain for a long time, as both Saturn and Pluto can symbolize old, ingrained patterns that control or suppress us in some fashion. Saturn now brings all this to our attention through outer circumstances.

If we have a history of defiant, Plutonian eruptions against authority in the past (and have earned our share of trouble due to it), Saturn is now warning us to exert greater self-control and discipline over our passionate responses to the societal powers that be. If we are not technically "the boss," we need to stop turning the tables on those who are our supervisors, or perhaps to try working more cooperatively with the law. It's time to follow the rules rather than risk fines, penalties, or financially jeopardizing lawsuits (all having an Eighth House ring to them). Sometimes serious criminal offenses are involved—even murder—but extreme manifestations are mercifully rare. Still, some of us need to be careful not to stir up animosities by engaging in futile power struggles. Why fight so fiercely when we have no chance of winning? Pluto might still want to do such battle, but Saturn wouldn't (and right now Saturn is setting the limits).

Most of us have not been too aggressive with our Plutonian drives during our lives. We have instead allowed the Pluto process to remain very submerged, buried deeply within our psyche in a manner invisible to our conscious, waking self. Pluto's power quietly lurks within us. It's not as immediately accessible as, say, Mars energy (and even that planet is hard for some to comfortably and assertively act out). In this case, defiance and rage have not been part of our repertoire in dealing with power and authority, so this Saturn transit allows us the transformative option of bringing more of our Pluto potential into a concrete, workable form—to give it form for the first time, in some cases. We get to manifest some of what has been typically kept under wraps because of hidden fears, internal taboos, shame, intimidation, or ignorance of our potential. This can be a "coming out" process where we finally show our power to be ourselves on our own terms, and take our chances living a more authentic life.

Obviously, we need to carefully examine the current dynamics of our Pluto house. We need to ask how Saturn, through situational unfoldment, can impress on us a desire to have a constructive Plutonian experience, fulfilling what both Saturn and Pluto stand for. These planets deal well with stark realism and want laser-beam clarity to help dissipate foggy perceptions. Therefore, we may find we are hyper-alert to the issues of this house we have long wrestled with, usually from the Plutonian perspective. It is typically here where we have not felt potent, and such feelings of powerlessness can make us attack ourselves in self-sabotaging ways. Pluto has a blind urge to annihilate when frustrated.

Saturn attempts to restore order by helping us better organize our power drives. When well managed, this can feel like a fresh sense of renewal. We become invigorated and ready to build new frameworks for vital living. Maybe we have been "the walking dead" for too long, just barely tapping into the energy of our spiritual core or our potential for fiery self-impassioned expression. Saturn, within limits, is trying to help us feel really alive and filled with purpose. This can seem like a special mission for some of us. If we are having a transiting square or opposition, we need to make sure feelings of certitude and absolute rightness of action do not degrade into fanaticism and unethical strong-arm tactics. We shouldn't have to get to where we want to be by becoming a human bulldozer or a high-powered tank, crushing all things that dare to stand in our path.

Maybe we are having to undergo a divorce as our only way to get back the Pluto power we let someone else mishandle (Pluto in the Seventh House or Scorpio on its cusp), or perhaps we have a showdown with a parent in order to become truly autonomous by cutting the psychological umbilical cord (Pluto in the Fourth House or ruling the IC). Even in these tensional scenarios, we cannot afford to be underhandedly manipulative, act treacherously, or be deliberately cruel. Saturn is not trying to evoke these reactions, it's trying to take hold of Pluto's energy and direct it more level-headedly— but with Pluto, you never know what garbage will spew forth from the bowels of the personal unconscious. Pluto tends to "vent now, repent later" (if at all). Saturn tries to prevent us from using shameful tactics we may regret afterwards when it may be too late.

In a less dramatic manner, transiting Saturn aspecting Pluto could simply be a time of hard work and steady application towards important objectives—usually those that cannot be put off too much longer. Both these planets hate procrastination and laziness. It would seem with a trine or sextile that we could not only tackle something significant to us, but finalize it. Saturn pushes for Pluto to complete something that can have long-range rewards (not necessarily monetary). It seeks to secure an awareness of enrichment. A deep sense of satisfaction for a major job well done can be the greatest reward here. Instead of being chronically pregnant with our goal's potential, we finally get to deliver the awe-inspiring baby. The timing could be ripe for a Plutonian renaissance, where we can enter a whole new vitalizing world of experience.

We over-achievers can really do some serious revolutionizing with these Saturn transits, since we already have the guts and fortitude needed to make many sweeping changes. We just need to be sure we don't engage in overkill. It's us self-inhibitors who will need to bite the bullet and draw deeply from our inner resources in order to feel strong and act decisively. No firm guarantees of security are given when we turn on our Pluto energy, and we need to come to grips with that fact. But attempting to stagnate and do nothing would be highly offensive to both planets, and will probably incur complications for us that further undermine our needs. This would be akin to being severely constipated, where we not only feel much discomfort but also run the risk of poisoning our body. Maybe we could view a well-handled Saturn/Pluto transit as a cosmic laxative or enema (having a high-colonic irrigation session would be a particularly symbolic way to facilitate the inner purging processes associated with Saturn transiting Pluto).

Lastly, it is true that we may have to deal with death, since both planets represent the end of life cycles where the essence of the cycle's meaning can be distilled, but not its outer packaging in terms of form and structure. These less permanent parts die away. Perhaps someone older (Saturn rules the elderly) may be ready to make the big transition into the afterlife, maybe after undergoing poor health. However this comes about, we are to let go and let the universal process take over. We may have forced separations with people we've outgrown but are still unwilling to let go, so life creates a situation where such relationships are removed from our pattern. It's best to see the wisdom of this rather than obsess about it. We must have the faith to move on and be open to new growth. Overall, this transit can be quite contemplative and thought-provoking.

Chapter Thirteen Endnotes

1. Paul Wright, *Astrology In Action,* CRCS Publications, 1989, p. 159.
2 Donna Cunningham, *Healing Pluto Problems,* Samuel Weiser, Inc., 1986, p. 130.

CHAPTER FOURTEEN

SATURN IN SAGITTARIUS

A TEST OF FAITH

Free-spirited, exuberant Sagittarius might initially seem at odds with level-headed, somber Saturn. Points of contrast between planet and sign are numerous. However, common denominators can be found. For one thing, they share a mutual concern for the guiding principles of social law. Both have a legalistic orientation, a sense of unconditional justice, an interest in broader social involvement, and a moralistic concern for collective conduct and behavior. Saturn and Sagittarius direct attention toward the development of relationships within the societal realm.

Due to Sagittarius' natural positive sense and its genuine desire for social betterment, many of Saturn's most wholesome and honorable qualities are encouraged to express openly. Our ability to sensibly develop enduring faith in something bigger than ourselves is put to the test. We develop a code of living that allows us to idealistically structure and define life's greater meaning. Sagittarius stimulates Saturn to focus serious attention on purposeful belief systems and effective social objectives, while Saturn evokes the more profound, philosophical side of Sagittarius, helping to harness its otherwise restless, free-wheeling temperament.

THE LAST WORD?

Our ego-security drives (Saturn) are here motivated by the soundness of our own world view or cosmology (Sagittarius). Since Sagittarius is a mixture of mutability and fire, it is innately driven to explore all of life's potentials with a high level of adventurousness and mental adaptability. Saturn, however, can be rigid in its orientation, highly traditional, and too inflexible or narrow in scope to adopt such a trusting, spontaneous approach. Saturn attempts to control life's continuous unfolding at every step. When mismanaged, this combination could easily denote a conflict of interests. Rigidity filtering through basic Sagittarian principles can create highly judgmental attitudes and biased viewpoints. We may become intolerant in our assessments of right and wrong, attempting to apply our view across the board. This is due to the way Sagittarius can generalize any concept and seek to apply it to everyone or everything. It's a "one size fits all, at least in theory" kind of sign. This is how many "isms" are created, for better or worse.

Our tendency to turn our sweeping moral/societal assumptions and judgments into absolute beliefs about reality can become a major pitfall. We might envision ourselves as the central authority concerning the proper ethical behavior or morality of humanity at large. In Sagittarius, Saturn's power and control issues are related to intellectual beliefs about humankind, God, and the Universe. We may be tempted to lay down the law and have the last word regarding proper conduct for people. If Saturn is also in a fixed house or in aspect to Pluto, it is particularly vulnerable in this regard. However, while Sagittarius may get on its soapbox and preach to the masses, it is not a dictator at heart.

ON CLEARER DAYS

Constructively, we can motivate ourselves to patiently seek a practical comprehension and acceptance of "reality" on the broadest of terms. Breadth of scope and magnitude of vision are Sagittarian attributes. The organizational talent of Saturn can make the vibrant idealism of Sagittarius more workable. This earth planet helps to tone down this fire sign's tendency to anticipate fulfillment through impractical or visionary goals. At the least, Saturn forces us to learn from our repeated disillusionments. The more it is involved in tensional patterns, the more Saturn tends to resist the grand overview Sagittarius has of life and its many unifying parts. Intolerance often becomes an issue to wrestle with. Our narrow-mindedness can block Sagittarius' typically expansive, lofty, open-ended viewpoints. Saturn can even unearth and underscore the often unrecognized judgmental quality in Sagittarius itself—the "holier than thou" syndrome.

But Saturn can also help us sustain our brilliant, fleeting mental enthusiasms to the point where aspirations are approached with greater maturity and self-assurance. Sagittarius' inspirational flow becomes better grounded and effectively directed toward concrete goals. Saturn gives this future-oriented sign a clearer picture of the present, which helps greatly when it's time for us to aim and shoot our arrows of inspiration.

ALWAYS RIGHT ON TARGET?

Because careful, analytical Saturn serves as a screening agent for this sometimes gullible, naive sign, we are better able to filter Sagittarian energies discriminately. One result of this is that visions, revelations, intuitive hunches, and prophetic outlooks (Sagittarius) tend to be more timely and reliable. When it is well integrated, Saturn's level-headedness enhances Sagittarius' keener faculties of judgment. When we allow ourselves to operate from a point of fear, deep self-doubt, or a lack of faith in life's basic goodness, our Sagittarian "revelations" turn negative and/or are misguided. Our visions or broad assumptions turn cynical, fed by a belief that life is more than just meaningless—it is also unfair and unkind. Saturn's potential for pessimism can be blown out of proportion or unrealistically exaggerated, and the Sagittarian principle is prevented from operating at its most spiritedly soaring levels.

PLAYING THOSE MIND GAMES

Sagittarius represents our capacity for abstract reasoning and speculative thought. It typically glorifies mind power and is especially enthused by seeing how far it can stretch its mental potential. Mind expansion is something real for this sign. Saturn helps provide sensible limits to our thought processes, preventing us from aimless theorizing or vague mental rambling. Left unchecked, Sagittarian abstractions can easily result in empty pseudo-intellectualism or irrelevant mind games. Its sometimes-scrambled kind of "logic" can drive Saturn or Virgo up the wall!

Accordingly, an important goal for Saturn in Sagittarius is to accept mental discipline. This placement can often lead toward scholarly pursuits for Saturn. It implies a deep respect for all worthy avenues of serious knowledge, plus a sense of duty and commitment concerning the pursuit of such knowledge. We may not always get the meaning or relevance of certain abstract ("far-out") concepts at first, but in our dedicated pursuit to know the Truth underlying everything, our overall comprehension can improve with maturity. Of great importance in this regard is the proper development and wise use of the "higher" mind. Saturn can then appreciate high-minded concepts even if they don't have practical application.

ETERNAL STUDENT

Saturn provides Sagittarius with the ambition, perseverance, and long-range planning ability to help us strive to excel in education. It promotes the mastery of a specialized body of thought. This is perhaps the only Sagittarius placement (besides Pluto in Sagittarius) with an interest in undertaking weighty, ponderous studies that require patience, time, and effort. It is less apt to become distracted or look for shortcuts to learning. The notoriously poor Sagittarian attention span is quite improved by the steady focus Saturn demands. At its best, Saturn in Sagittarius impels us to seek significant mental accomplishments that help our culture rather than merely secure our material power and social position. We may feel that our life quest is to enlighten society's mind in a responsible, well-informed manner. We often wish to impart our wisdom to our community on some level. Always desiring to feed our minds, we are truly eternal students of life, eager to be taught from a wide range of learning channels. Later on, we are equally enthused to impart any relevant information we have faith in. It could be that, due to Saturnian insecurity, we never think we know enough, so we press on to accumulate even more data. Perhaps we should remember this: sometimes it is the enthusiasm of the messenger that is more important than the details of the message.

DOES BELIEVING MAKE IT SO?

As stated previously, a poorly handled Saturn in Sagittarius indicates rigid or authoritarian approaches to belief systems. This can be a biased, prejudiced, bigoted Saturn whose faith can oppress others. Sagittarius, with its natural tendency to lump things together into loosely defined, generalized categories, only feeds the flames of self-righteousness typical of critical, condemning Saturn. The result can be an obnoxious "know-it-all," immune to objectivity or self-examination. We can become defensively resistant (Saturn) to all beliefs or theories that run counter to our firmly entrenched ideas about big issues such as God, sin, politics, capital punishment, abortion, genetic manipulation, etc. Our close-mindedness (often

214 • Chapter Fourteen

aggravated by our open-mouthedness!) suggests we often lack
a deep understanding of that which we strongly attack.

Sagittarius' sense of well-being and inner trust only makes
us feel more confident and certain about our assumptions or
short-sighted viewpoints. Essentially, this placement teaches
us to create boundaries in consciousness according to the
quality of our beliefs and suppositions. We are to exercise the
power of such beliefs with much thoughtfulness and common
sense. Life will demonstrate the value of careful, responsible
analysis of all that we deem to be true. We are to recognize
the need to become more selective concerning how and where
we put our intellectual faith in people or things. At best,
Saturnian impartiality helps us develop wisdom.

In Search of Lost Gods

A search for God is usually a major theme for Sagittarius, typically eager to pour its faith into life with an almost boundless
sense of fervor. But when working through Saturn, a degree of
doubt can be introduced. Any personal beliefs in a higher, universal power will need to pass the test of time before we establish firm convictions. We need to make our search a conscious
one, not exclusively the result of social pressures to conform.
Luckily, we live in a society where we can stand apart from
the congregation without being tied to a dunking apparatus
and nearly drowned by an angry and fearful religious community or burned at the stake as a heretic, so we needn't be
afraid to think for ourselves regarding God and other divine
matters. However, a mismanaged Saturn in Sagittarius suggests undue skepticism. We may fear any belief system that
requires placing trust in something or someone outside of ourselves. But without some measure of faith in something
beyond ourselves, the world we exist in can end up looking
like an unfriendly, untrustworthy place.

It is very Sagittarian to trust the goodness of people and
even the whole universal process of existence. Life unfolds in
bigger and better ways, and moving toward the future holds

the key. But for a poorly handled Saturn, pessimism looms on the horizon as well. We can develop a hard-edged, cynical view of the human condition, seeing few redeeming qualities. Our potential for embracing an enlightened cosmology is soured by our fear of the consequences of human imperfection.

Yet Saturn will always pressure us to work through our greatest resistances. Life will thus continue to introduce us to alternative ways of looking at its deeper meaning, either through the spiritual people that we meet, the thought-provoking books we read, or perhaps even our own uncanny experiences that defy logic and reason. Maybe it takes just one astounding miracle in our life to help us find our lost gods once again.

We should allow ourselves to be agnostic if we wish, or call ourselves atheists if we must, but it's wise to always keep in the back of our curious minds that maybe everything is indeed linked to everything else in a purposeful manner. We certainly shouldn't dismiss the whole notion because of an unfortunate religious upbringing. So what if the nuns scared God out of us? There are other routes available for exploring Deity. Nobody has all the keys needed to make the workings of the Godhead and the Cosmos fully understood, but why shut the door forever? As often said, Sagittarius is much more enthralled by the wonders of journey than by reaching the final destination point. We have great potential to be rich with wisdom later in our golden years, with eyes shining towards the heavens and feet firmly planted on the ground. One sure-fire way to get to this level is to never be afraid of knowledge, other people's opinions, or our own ethereal musings. Each provides us with the education our soul needs.

CHOPPING DOWN THE BIGOT TREE

From tiny acorns grow tall and sturdy oaks, given the right climate, the right soil conditions, and plenty of time. But if in early childhood our tiny seeds of emerging consciousness struggled to grow in a toxic environment of social prejudice and hatred for specific classes of people, we could end up stunted in our spiritual growth, and the fruits of tolerance and compassion could die on the vine. Bigotry based on unwarranted fears and an almost willful ignorance of the humanity of people who are ethnically different from us can be a symptom of a totally out-of-touch Saturn in Sagittarius. We may feel intimidated by other cultures and their peculiar mannerisms. We may feel frustrated and even anxious hearing them speak languages or dialects we cannot understand. We get cranky when foreigners do not quickly assimilate the customs, clothes, or food preferences of our country. But it is so important for us to work through this Saturnian block if we are to ever understand the essence of Sagittarius and its gift of universal consciousness.

Astro-lebrities with Saturn in Sagittarius

Abraham Lincoln   Edgar Allan Poe
Charles Darwin   Martin Luther King, Jr.
Evangeline Adams   Anita Bryant
Mohandas Gandhi   Maria Montessori
Grace Kelly   Michel Gauquelin

SATURN IN THE NINTH HOUSE

HEAVEN ON EARTH

Saturn in the Ninth House of collective inspiration and broad social awareness may urge some of us to direct our quest for ultimate meaning toward more practical, workable explanations. Universal ideals and religious concepts need to be well structured and made real if they are to provoke any sense of true belief for us. For those with orthodox views, God must forever prove His Almightiness in clear, black-or-white terms in a world where true believers get healed and sinners get punished for transgressions in this life as well as in the hereafter. Viewing God as a stern judge who rewards the obedient and the righteous may be appealing for some. Others of us, less connected to mainstream religious tenets, may have an ambition to thoroughly understand heavyweight life principles and profound theories. We can be deeply philosophical and contemplative, with a scientific bent. While we may also take religion seriously, we do so cautiously; much the way religious scholars do as they try to differentiate accurate scriptures from corrupted texts. It is important for us to have clearly presented knowledge devoid of cultural bias, which is very difficult to find in the field of religion.

Our earnest need to be exposed to Truth is mixed with skepticism regarding the human proclivity for misplaced faith based on ignorance and superstition, so our ability to appraise the worth of "higher" mental pursuits is put to the test. What seems to be a common challenge here is the need to sort out "the God issue" for ourselves, one way or another. Where are we to put our ultimate faith and trust? This Saturn rarely feels gullible or emotionally blinded regarding its belief systems about how divinity and the universal process works; we feel certain we know the facts, based on reliable established authority. When mismanaged, such a conservative Saturn leans toward a strict, dogmatic mindset more motivated by the fear of God without than an acknowledgment of the God within. Our vision becomes narrow and rigidly applied.

RITUALITY

Saturn in the Ninth House denotes the appeal of religious traditions that have proven the test of time, or ancient spiritual practices that have survived throughout the ages. Saturn trusts anything that endures over long periods. Some of us may depend on a religious structure that proclaims its core doctrines to be infallible, and, by implication, unalterable. That can make believing easy and uncomplicated. We put an unerring, unchanging God on a cosmic pedestal in a way that always keeps things absolute and unambiguous. Such a God may express idealized father traits that we otherwise had or have a hard time experiencing with our real father, who may have seemed remote and far away from us on some level. In contrast, we believe our God to always be very close and reachable, and that our personal relationship with Him will remain intact as long as we abide by the instructions laid out by His holy words in sacred bibles, tablets, scrolls, etc. Adherence to these rules and rituals provides true believers with a safety net that is very important, considering Saturn's need for security and predictability. Saturn can be a planet comfortable with solemn ceremonies. It can also depend on rituals using the physical objects of faith (crucifixes, prayer shawls, mandalas, rosary beads, Menorahs, altars, pentagrams, Madonna figurines—all types of religious artifacts).

Following traditional procedures becomes important. Even Tarot card readers with this position probably are good about keeping their cards wrapped up in a special silk cloth to protect their vibes. Eastern religion meditators will always want to light those time-honored sticks of sandalwood incense (not that fake strawberry kind). Catholics will give their prayer beads a workout while counting their "Hail Marys," and Jews will be mindful of the Sabbath and the dietary restrictions of their faith. Our willingness to unconditionally accept any such rituals depends on an unquestionable belief in the rightness of what we are doing. We approach our rituals with much respect, reverence, and dignity—but maybe a little too sanctimoniously. We need to not confuse religion with religiosity.

Fearing the God-Fearin'

Saturn in the Ninth House, due to a harsh and sometimes scary introduction to religion in our early years, suggests we can be blocked about the concept of God. If God has been presented to us as judgmental and exacting in His punishment of transgressors of His law, threatening fire and brimstone as eternal punishment in hell for temporary sins on Earth, this is going to seem unjust to Saturn (although "an eye for an eye, a tooth for a tooth" may sound a bit more fair in theory). We don't want any part of a God like this. We don't wish to surrender to any power higher than our own conscience. We believe ourselves to be the final authority concerning our own proper ethical conduct and morality. Defensive Saturn suggests we resist giving in to any outside control as pervasively intruding as the strict, omnipotent God of fundamental faiths. The same applies to our intellectual assumptions regarding society, the government, humanity at large, and even the universe. We do not want to be led by the nose according to any general consensus of opinion or mass indoctrination. We want to make our own rules to live by.

Some of us also wonder why, if there is a just God, innocent babies can suffer cruel fates while the truly immoral are permitted to prosper and live to a ripe old age without ever getting their comeuppances. It's this paradoxical inconsistency of divine "justice" on earth that probably troubles the Saturn principle within us the most.

Agnosticism and atheism can result. We can pull back from the faithful herd and remain separative from this collective experience. As a result, we may also feel like outsiders, cut off from the support of those strongly held suppositions about God that seem to give so many others peace of mind about this life and in the afterlife. There is a vexing dichotomy here, as one part of Saturn would welcome a total guarantee of certainty that God exists and that we are part of a master plan, but the "doubting Thomas" side of Saturn will only accept solid, irrefutable proof that continued consciousness awaits us after we die. Of course, such objective proof is not currently possible according to the rigorous standards an unconvinced Saturn demands.

POLITICALLY CORRECT

Politics is also part of the Ninth House experience, as are any "isms" that involve how the rights of a society impact on the personal liberties of the individual. Politics is a good example of social belief systems in action, whether we favor them or not.

Saturn in an earth or water sign would want to preserve the status quo, supporting the same political agendas decade after decade with only practical adjustments allowed to fit certain cultural changes. Nothing too radical here, no toppling of The System, and definitely no flirting with social anarchy. Saturn in air tends toward liberal policies, but only those well thought out and fair enough to satisfy a diverse constituency (with the exception of Aquarius, which is fixed and surprisingly dogmatic at times). But Saturn in fire can be willful and passionate in its political persuasions. If fundamentally conservative, we can be dramatically and emphatically so. If we are discontent or disillusioned, or if we have political axes to grind and are angry with government power, Saturn in fire can want to shake things up and push for quick, urgent reforms—a "throw out the bums" attitude. We are open to fresh leadership, as long as promises of change made during the campaign trail are delivered.

A few of us could even make a career in politics, though our overall tendency in most cases is simply to be responsible citizens who feel obligated to vote, do jury duty when asked, show civic pride, defend our country, wave the flag, and be upstanding and law-abiding.

But some of us can hold the darker attitude that governments are fundamentally oppressive, playing too much the restrictive "big daddy" role and trying to run everything related to our personal lives. Think of Saturn in Scorpio or Aries in a conflict aspect to Pluto or Uranus—this doesn't sound like someone who would feel safe and secure with powerful governmental structures. We don't trust that people in key political positions will look out for our welfare. We can be resentful about their authority, and may not want to be part of this collective framework. We feel very critical of federal policies or even laws handed down from the higher courts. We may project that politicians are selfishly ambitious, greedy, and over-controlling. We liberals may even think we see the dangers of unchecked patriotism very clearly, and it can scare us. But whether we battle God or the Feds, the deeper issue

is probably our fear of bowing down to any supreme authority, since a lesson of Saturn in the Ninth House is to recognize the spiritual power of our own inner authority regarding
personal Truth.

CANCEL THAT TRIP?

Saturn is usually a homebound planet, not often filled with
travel fever. It has no big urge to play the role of intrepid
world explorer. Saturn prefers the familiar, while wandering
too far away can put us in touch with the unfamiliar, creating
culture shock. Thus anything foreign, exotic, international, or
ethnic is not warmly embraced. Much of this could be a matter more reflective of our own early cultural background (like
a lot of our Ninth House matters), especially due to narrow
attitudes adopted by our family. Maybe we heard too much
bad stuff about "those people in Asia" or "the Mexicans" or
"the crazy Catholics in Italy" or "them sodomites in San
Francisco." It probably was pretty offensive material that was
broadcast within range of our sensitive ears—sweeping and
unflattering generalities applied to large groups of people. For
some reason, a few of us were taught to either fear or loathe
anything or anybody different or foreign. We may have been
told not to trust folks from abroad—not their culture, not
their religion, and certainly not their weird food! The implication was that we were to always stick to the ways of our own
country and "our own people," meaning those who are as
exactly like us as possible.

This is a sort of mind control that can last a lifetime for
some. It's a sad legacy that goes completely against the wide-
angled scope of the Ninth House, a house of universal proportions needing lots of room to spread out. If we have Saturn
here, we will need to overcome our provincial, xenophobic
ways and enrich our awareness of global reality. It's a big
world we live in and we need to understand more about it.

As we get older, we will have opportunities to mingle with
those whom our parents warned us against (perhaps a college

roommate who is of the Hindu faith, or a business associate from Denmark). Little by little, life can usher in people and situations that educate us about realities quite different from anything in our upbringing. We may learn to slowly appreciate those diverse elements that hold the world together. We may even someday get to write home that "New Yorkers ain't so bad after all," to the dismay of "our own people." It would be good to take courses in comparative religion or French cuisine, and even subscribe to *The National Geographic* just to give us an education as to what's out there. If all goes well, maybe we won't wish to cancel that trip to Bora Bora we won on "Wheel of Fortune" (not to worry, it's a round-trip ticket).

A LIFETIME EDUCATION

The Ninth House is an area where we can learn to feed our minds as much as it can take. Traditionally, it's the house of extended education, which can mean a stubborn case of Universityitis for some of us. We over-achievers can't help but take courses, pass exams, give dissertations, and collect our degrees and diplomas. Saturn here can take schooling all the way, since it has great patience and endurance. We probably figure we're only going to get older anyway, so why not older and smarter and armed with academic credentials? Often, we may not have been able to complete our schooling in our early years due to economic hardships, bad grades, or simply an urge to drop out, but we can make up for lost time once we have matured a bit and are in better financial shape. We also have a much better idea by then what we want to get a degree in.

We approach higher learning almost as if it is our duty to keep our mind working like a finely calibrated tool, well lubricated by knowledge. But the knowledge we expose ourselves to cannot be trivial or superficial in content. We gravitate toward subjects that are broad in their application or universally experienced on the mass level. Degrees in science, mathematics, engineering, and other technical fields could be a possibility for some of us. Saturn and the Ninth House also favor the study of history. Whatever we choose, our aim is to excel in our studies. We have the ambition to do something effective with what we have learned. We usually do not study out of boredom or sheer mental stimulation (that's more a Third House issue). We instead want to embrace knowledge that is far-reaching. The desire to keep on learning all we can may become a lifetime aspiration.

WHOSE MORALS, WHOSE ETHICS?

Morality and ethics are part of the Ninth House life department. When masses of people congregate and form cultural norms regarding appropriate conduct, a result is the broad acceptance of certain socially sanctioned behaviors or actions that uphold high community standards, whether on religious grounds or due to civilized, democratic principles. We are not to rob banks, because it harms people's securities directly and can later injure the economy, harming even more. The "head" tries to prevent this by enacting laws with penalties to be suffered, but the "heart" enforces inner law through morality, using shame as its tool. Saturn in this house can be very guilt-ridden, acting like a model citizen for fear of social condemnation—or it can resist such moral indoctrination and only live by its own code of ethics. It's an issue we may ponder on a large scale.

Astro-lebrities with Saturn in the Ninth House

Oliver Stone	Richard Nixon
Abraham Lincoln	Marcel Proust
John F. Kennedy	William Inge
Pat Buchanan	Evangeline Adams
Anita Bryant	Woodrow Wilson

SATURN/JUPITER ASPECTS

NATAL

Saturn and Jupiter share an awareness of those patterns of human interaction specific to the makeup of a community or a society. These are not planets whose agendas are exclusively personal, unlike Mars or the Moon, for example. This is not meant as an indirect criticism of our Moon or Mars, for we need them and what they represent in order to be aware that we are flesh-and-blood beings who first and foremost are separate individuals. Thus, the "inner planets," as they are called, are critical to our evolutionary growth, but at the next stage of development, Jupiter and Saturn symbolize life principles that help us get beyond our strictly self-absorbed approach to life, just as both lie beyond the orbit of Mars.

This is not yet a universal or transcendental orientation toward humanity at large—that's a matter for Uranus, Neptune and Pluto. Instead, Jupiter and Saturn deal with the necessary development of social consciousness, where we learn to participate in a larger field of human activity. Instead of just living for pure self-centered survival (including the urge to directly protect the needs of our immediate family), we are to experience a budding awareness that we can form units of individuals unrelated by blood ties who all share similar survival needs. We find there is safety in numbers and that the shared responsibility to look out for one another affords us even greater protection in the long run. It also feels good, as if we had an extended family. However, we are well aware that whatever associations are fostered under these socialized conditions are not necessarily intimate or as personal as what we experience with our own "clan" or "tribe."

This sounds like a course in Sociology 101; what does it have to do with our own birthchart? For one thing, having any aspect between Saturn and Jupiter suggests we are at an evolutionary point where we need to pay attention to how the world around us works, because we are likely to have to play an more active role in it. We are to study (Saturn) society and how it works so that we can participate (Jupiter) in improving its functioning. Jupiter is always interested in stretching the potential of something, while Saturn has a talent for refining anything in order to make it operate more perfectly. Together, they impress the need to fulfill our civic duty and become model citizens who can inspire others by our example. We can show people what social responsibility is all about as we work to build sound structures that can benefit the masses.

All this sounds good on paper, but how do we accomplish these uplifting ideals? First, we do our darndest not to break laws. Nothing scandalous. Jay-walking may be permissible once in a while, but being convicted of grand larceny certainly won't look good on our résumé or win friends at the country club. With trines and sextiles, we give the impression of being a "goody two-shoes" who does everything by the book, and who almost religiously follows rules and regulations. We appear as upright members of the community. Jupiter can put something up on a pedestal and glorify it; in this case, it can idealize law-abiding behavior, self-control, inner discipline, and all those other Saturn keyphrases astrologers love to use.

Trines and sextiles should have little trouble advocating that philosophy, since they tend to play it safe and not rock the boat too much. We can be regarded as honorable folks, filled with integrity and above-average honesty. Conversely, squares and oppositions can resist the limits society imposes through its laws. They look for loopholes, expect preferential treatment, or opt for shaky shortcuts to social success.

Another way to bring out the best these aspects have to offer is by being open and helpful to many. It sounds corny, but a well-managed Saturn/Jupiter is also the signature of "the good Samaritan." We feel dutiful in our ability to offer people our assistance, but we will need to take a closer look at our Saturn to make sure we also know how to appropriately protect ourselves from shams and scams and fast-talking con artists looking for a kindly soul like us to bamboozle (although Neptune/Jupiter is more problematic regarding naiveté and being tricked). Here's a case where a good old Saturn/Jupiter square in fixed signs can come in handy, since fixed Saturn can raise the caution flags and fixed Jupiter is not so quick to give without knowing what it's getting back in return. Putting the brakes on our urge to do favors for strangers is a wise thing to do until we are quite sure we have developed the powers of discrimination and good judgment that may come with maturity. We need to be careful until we've had time to size things up.

The conjunction, square and opposition are tricky because we are prone to feel both planetary principles strongly, yet their aims can be quite different. (The conjunction should work out its challenge more easily, however, since conjunct planets are committed to pull together.) Generally speaking, our expression of Jupiter never feels Jupiterian enough to those interacting with us (maybe we control our generosity inappropriately) while our Saturn sometimes fails to stick to its guns and build proper boundaries. Our sense of responsible action is interfered with by our need to be free to wander and play with opportunity in an unstructured manner. Jupiter, unsure of commitment, can stall even if Saturn's timing is technically right. But for the most part, we usually pull our forces together when it really counts, and succeed in our serious endeavors.

With stress aspects, many of the more unappealing traits of both Saturn and Jupiter can be evident. If Saturn seems dominant in our consciousness, some of us may always see the glass as half empty and discover the food at life's banquet to be merely a few cold leftovers. Maybe we arrived at this feast too late. Perhaps we do not anticipate that life in general will give us any special privileges, even if we work like a dog to prove our worth in society's eyes. Due to our inner philosophy of uncertainty and our shaky faith, we may sit and sit on our Jupiter potential, even when the time seems ripe to go for all the gusto we can get and gamble on ourselves big time. But do we ever really feel we are on a roll?

If Jupiter is more dominant, we've probably been to too many banquets already; we've pigged out and thought we were having a swell time until our material structure started to fall apart at the seams. We may tend to overdo momentary gratifications and all those feel-good experiences at the expense of building a solid backbone of discipline. Growing into healthy adulthood may be postponed. Nancy Reagan was giving us Jupiter-dominants good advice when she said "Just say no." We may attempt to do it all without any long-term plans of action. We may tend to promise more than we can deliver (typical for Jupiter anyway). But the difference here is that Saturn won't allow for sloppy, irresponsible behavior, where we leave others holding the bag, or fail to meet important deadlines, or come to work too late too many times. There's always a price to pay and we will wake one day to find Saturn handing us the bill.

A more face-saving way to explain our pattern to others is that we are "just late bloomers" who haven't found yet what we want to do in life (at age forty-eight), or we are simple not ready to settle down. We like to keep our options open. The reality is that our social skills are nothing to write home about if all we do is take the lazy, aimless, procrastinating route. Real success eludes as as we try to evade creditors, not doing either our Saturn or our Jupiter potential very well. We need to get a grip.

TRANSIT

My hunch is that I didn't cover the natal Saturn/Jupiter issues some of you might have been expecting (religion, travel, and making "the big bucks"), but they'll be touched on in this section. Remember, I'm writing these aspect reports in a way that natal and transit material can be fairly interchangeable, so see if you can apply this transit information to natal themes of Saturn aspecting Jupiter.

When Saturn transits Jupiter, something of a Saturnian nature is meant to influence the way we have been processing our Jupiter consciousness up to this point in time. This could be a period when we need to bolster our faith and make our beliefs more solid. We also may be expecting our faith to move mountains and give us manifest results. Saturn first is asking us to review those things we put great trust in, especially our biggest philosophical assumptions about the world we live in, whether based on religion or years of personal observation. If we believe society is basically good and most people mean well, then even the tensional transits of Saturn can allow us to put our ideals to the test in some positive social framework. If we work diligently toward this, we feel certain we will get sufficient and maybe even abundant social support—and we often do.

If we've been doing our Jupiter in too naive a manner or should we be too convinced of the complete rightness of our religious and philosophical views, Saturnian circumstances could force us to reevaluate our faith. Maybe we have an unrecognized arrogance in our pursuit of God and higher meaning that needs to be exposed and eliminated. Saturn would love to tackle this job in order to ensure our greater humility in the future. If we work with this aspect instead of fighting it, we will learn to temper our zeal or maybe even start to practice what we preach (Jupiter is the planet of the hypocrite, with its "do as I say, not as I do" tendency).

But if we are without any higher guiding principles, Saturn becomes the agent of ponderous contemplation about the meaning of life—more specifically, our own. Why are we here and what mission are we supposed to be fulfilling? This could be a crossroad for some of us, where we can take a path that leads to greater organization and clearer vision or one that leads to further aimlessness and a pessimistic outlook on our future. It would be much better to sensibly embrace a philosophical overview that uplifts our spirit but does not offer magical solutions to our worldly dilemmas. We are supposed to work at getting ourselves out of the predicaments we have put ourselves in, due to our unchecked Jupiter behavior in the past.

One of those predicaments may revolve around financial obligations. Venus may be our basic money planet, but

Jupiter is the concept of profit-making. Jupiter deals with prosperity and money-making related to luck and the ability to think big. It will gamble on a vision, whereas earth Venus (and Taurus) would not. Money becomes a material way for Jupiter to experience the expansion principle on worldly levels. When Saturn makes its transit, we normally need to look at our financial picture and see if we have been appropriately self-protective—do we save enough, are we investing wisely, do we purchase things of true value, or are we squandering our cash and unwisely wasting resources? Jupiter can buy with credit today and worry about paying tomorrow (or preferably even a year from now—maybe by then Jupiter will win the lottery). We need to be in touch with our fiscal habits at this time. If we are the impulsive shopaholic types, we can be in for a rude awakening.

With sextiles and trines, we experience a couple of close calls that make it clear we need to slow down and start keeping more money in the bank. We may try to set up a budget and a system that enables us to pay all our bills on time. The conjunction might even initiate a new cycle of frugality and wise spending for us where we don't deprive ourselves materially—we just get smarter with our purchasing power. On the other hand, squares and oppositions tend to suggest that financial burdens can start to mount if we have been too careless or extravagant in the past with money. We may have maxed out our credit cards, or taken out too many loans that have yet to be completely paid off. Anything that hurts our credit-worthiness can also jeopardize our social standing (a Saturn/Jupiter issue).

In this case, Saturn implies we may have to be cut off from further financial self-abuse by being penalized in a manner that gets our attention. If we've been on a spending spree, now Saturn demands we snap out of it! Some of us may have very serious issues here requiring legal confrontations (we owe money that others want now). No matter how deep a pit we have dug, Saturn is also trying to tell us everything is correctable. We just have to start living with less for a while and cut corners to pay for our daily necessities (milk and bread, that is, not Gucci watches and weekend trips to Aspen). We are to learn the philosophy of "less is more." Maybe when we cannot spend as freely on material temptations, we learn to enjoy more simple pleasures like walking down nature trails or going to the library to take out a few books about travels in Europe. Saturn aspecting Jupiter can be an important time to rebuild our financial status through the mature handling of our assets.

Speaking of travels in Europe, maybe Saturn is suggesting we shouldn't even be thinking of spending cash we really don't have on a few carefree days in Boise, Idaho, much less the Riviera. If a trip is not essential (to our business, or perhaps somebody very old and dear to us died and the funeral's out of state), then it is best to save our dreams of exploration until a more opportune period (even if Saturn trines Jupiter). Saturn is always asking about the intrinsic purpose of something. If we wish to get out of town only because we are maybe...oh,...a little bored with our current scene, now may not be the time. Saturn is probably certain it can find relevant things to keep us busy right in our own backyard (not what Jupiter wants to hear). It would make more sense to start stashing away a little bit of money on a regular basis in preparation for a wonderful major trip later on when we are on top of things financially.

In general, Saturn doesn't have to rain on Jupiter's festive parade. Our optimism simply has to be more grounded and based on real potential and not wishful thinking. Real potential can be determined by how much effort we are willing to make in order for a sensible dream to come true (Jupiter must have goals to shoot for). It makes little sense for life to crush our spirit at this time with a heavy hand of cold, brutal reality. That's not what we need for our growth. Saturn is more apt to act like a rudder, helping us steer our boat toward safer waters where we can remain buoyant instead of thrashed about on choppy waves where we can spring a leak and sink. We are to be directed in ways that can help us feel free to accomplish at a reasonable pace. As usual, the wisdom of patience and sensitivity to proper timing will help us make the best of this period.

If I have been a little breezier in this aspect report of Saturn/Jupiter than I have with some other Saturn aspects, blame it on the inspiration of Principle Nine—the power of humor to make its point. Besides, after undergoing Saturn/Pluto, we probably all need a laugh or two or at least feel we can smile again about our life experience.

CHAPTER FIFTEEN

SATURN IN CAPRICORN

CLIMB EVERY MOUNTAIN

Ambitious, hard-working Saturn operating through socially authoritative Capricorn might make this the most earnestly striving, accomplishment-conscious placement for this planet. Since Saturn rules Capricorn, the common denominators are plentiful. Both wish to earn elevated status in society by proving their worth to The Establishment, often at a slow but steady pace of development. Each is aware of limitations set up by life at different stages, and will abide by them, accepting paying your dues as a prerequisite to success. Both planets are very hardy and self-sufficient and will seek self-direction in their professional focus, without needing or desiring much supervision. With this placement, we tend to do whatever it takes to eventually be in charge of ourselves, as long as we believe that we will be honored and respected as we put our higher ambitions to the test.

Patience and outward humility can be part of this experience, but first and foremost, Cardinal Capricorn overtly seeks influential social standing and public recognition for its efforts. It shows a humble face to the world while assertively gravitating toward the limelight and going directly after positions of prominence and status. Capricorn fits the hectic, bustling pace of the high-pressured corporate executive who is decisive and quick to act (Ross Perot with Saturn in Capricorn appears to be this type; yet his apparent humbleness—at least in reference to the new grass-roots political movement he has spearheaded—comes through in full twang within his oft repeated phrase: "This is not about me!").

On the other hand, introspective Saturn seems more steadfast and fixed in nature, and more concerned with maintaining the status quo. Saturn tends to build fortified walls around itself in its attempt to ensure self-preservation. This can manifest as aloofness, lack of intimate involvement, love of solitude, and a strong need for privacy. In contrast, Capricorn is more movement-oriented (like all cardinal signs) and cannot keep still. It is driven to move upward and outward into greater areas of challenge and conquest with a pronounced sense of enterprise. Saturn is much more quiet, somber, reflective, remote, and monkish in nature. Note the difference in surface temperament between Capricorn rising vs. Saturn conjunct the ASC. The Saturn-ASC individual will typically show greater self-restraint, self-consciousness, and less animated surface expression than one with Capricorn ascending. A notable exception is Queen Elizabeth II, who not only has Capricorn Rising, but Saturn in Scorpio squaring practically everything!

DESTINY WAITING

Socially adept Capricorn (once it gets its true momentum) helps conscientious Saturn build outer worldly structures in an honorable, prestigious manner. Since both deal with proper timing and needed maturity, we are to learn much about patience, long-range planning, hard but rewarding work, and readiness for certain life experiences. This is one Saturn placement that can really feel pretty karmic. Saturn often undergoes trying and testing restrictions in Capricorn (as does Saturn in Pisces), and we are seldom allowed to deviate or ignore our limitations until we have sufficiently handled certain commitments and obligations in the world. Our chosen career, vocational aspiration, or general lot in life may be more "fated" and "predetermined" than it appears. Life makes sure we are led to this path carefully, as if appointed by destiny (sounds like a good time for some "Twilight Zone" music). Capricorn's utilitarian nature combined with Saturn's urge to control gives some of us the ability to shrewdly take full advantage of every social opportunity, no matter how seemingly insignificant, that may upgrade our public image. We tend to appear very sure-footed here, and indeed, we take calculated steps based on a realistic assessment of options at hand.

ON TOP

Saturn in Capricorn can be a most dynamic placement for significant achievement. It may take a while to reach the top, but we can deal well with any adversity while we push forward to attain positions of high level management, leadership, and supervision. We learn the ropes early, advancing quickly, and often taking on careers or authoritative roles (even in the family, due to the Cancer polarity) that are typically associated with someone much older. Business know-how, seemingly more innate than learned, is emphasized. The assertive cardinality of this sign gives executive drive, enabling some of us over-achievers to initiate large-scale operations systematically and with a keen insight into probable results. Note that while equally efficient, Saturn in Virgo, being less aggressive, does not seek to operate on as broad a scale; it has less of the required overview of matters needed to function like this.

Saturn's stamina reinforces Capricorn's ability to stick to realistic objectives and ambitions amid all opposition and struggles, persisting until such goals materialize. We are apt to confront obstacles more head-on than would Saturn in Virgo or Taurus. Capricorn can be a feisty earth sign—that is probably how it made its way to the very top of the Zodiac to begin with. We may show single-mindedness in slowly but surely rising to an elevated key placement where we can eventually wield great power and clout. But with this double dose of Principle Ten, there is a tendency to over-control due to the fear of losing any social ground. Since Capricorn can be overbearing and authoritarian, and Saturn harsh and unyielding when on the defense, some of us have to be careful not to resort to oppressive, dictatorial measures when trying to obtain our objectives. Honor and integrity are always the way to go for this combo.

SOCIETY'S TASKMASTER

Saturn in Capricorn can denote a well-developed (but sometimes too crystallized) social conscience. We may be prone to want to apply our personal moral structure to society at large rather than view it as simply representing our own chosen guideposts. Saturn in Sagittarius appears to be similar, but Sagittarius just broadcasts such attitudes from its soapbox. Capricorn, once landing in the power seat, can turn rhetoric into action by helping to pass conservative legislation or by enacting tough laws. Gotta watch that Goat! It wants certain collective values to become entrenched in the social fabric and believes in strict obedience to the rules and regulations. Following correct procedures and going through proper channels become important.

With somber Saturn involved, we may feel obligated to take charge and enforce our sense of law and order on our immediate environment. Such an urge can be constructively channeled into government service, civic affairs, playing the legal advocate, and politics in general. The motivation is usually noble: we wish to not just selfishly take from society but give something back that has long-term or even permanent value. Later in life, some of us make major contributions that benefit society, both now and in the future. This is how we show profound gratitude for our elevated status and social privileges.

COLD SHOULDER

We are likely to be class-conscious as a means of self-protection, even if we feel a little ashamed knowing that it's politically unfashionable. We tend to construct social barriers that separate us personally from those we consider to have less desirable status. There's a touch of this with Saturn in the Tenth House too, although Saturn by itself can identify more easily with hard-working people of humble origins. But Capricorn can be almost as snobby as Leo once its ego finally gets a chance to swell. Some of us may insist that others adhere to certain formalities, proprieties, and protocols. These social rituals can provide us with the proper distance we feel we must maintain in order to secure the control we desire in our world. A few of us, when mismanaging our Saturn in Capricorn, can behave in cold, dehumanizing ways and wear a thick coat of untouchability. Our cool veneer normally demands respect from others, but also tends to be intimidating. Obviously, this Saturn can be most chilly and austere when rubbing shoulders with the "wrong" people.

ALL WORK, NO PLAY

Fortunately, most of us do not behave like this all the time—we'd alienate too many people whose connections we may need to capitalize on later. Nevertheless, we display a great amount of caution and reserve in certain social settings. We are not your pushover types and are not easily taken advantage of, unless we are severely into self-inhibiting. We are more likely to use than be used, exploit than be exploited. But by striving too hard, many of us leave ourselves little room for true relaxation, recreation, and leisure. Where's the joy in living when all our time is eaten up running a business empire? Where's our peace of mind when we're constantly worrying about it (something we'd rarely admit to)? Both Saturn and Capricorn advocate self-discipline and the conservation of time and applied energy. We typically expend ourselves only when there is a well-defined reason for doing so, with the likelihood of succeeding in our efforts. Yet due to our inclination to organize our life according to strict, self-imposed standards, some of us may feel guilty and self-condemning whenever we deviate or are detoured by circumstance from such established order (especially in the activities indicated by the house Saturn inhabits).

RECLAIMING INNER AUTHORITY

We self-inhibitors can have a consistently difficult time cooperating with all authorities. This typically stems from poor interaction with our father or father figure in our early years, implying an underdeveloped relationship. This could be indicated by a father who dies early, who abandons the family while we were very young, or who was never there to begin with. Unfortunately, as a result, a few of us have taken this childhood experience and blamed it for why we thwart our ability to accept responsibility and personal control over the outcome of our lives. With no father to guide us and show us the way to deal with the outer world, we find ourselves blindly resisting self-control, or so the excuse goes. Of course in today's world, many kids do not have access to a father, yet they do not always become out-of-kilter adults filled with unchanneled anger, confusion, and lack of direction.

It might be different for Saturn in Capricorn, though, symbolizing as it does a double dose of the father archetype. If some of us do fit into this category, we may have a marked fear of social judgment or failure. We may seldom attempt to challenge that fear by attaining positions of responsibility and command. A few of us may expect life itself to manage our personal affairs with little effort or hard work on our part, or we may defensively defy all existing social restraints rather than feel bound and constrained by them. This could manifest as lawlessness. Of course, other factors would have to be present and operating on that level for this to manifest, such as strong mismanaged Uranus or Pluto themes, mishandled squares from self-willed Aries planets, or even prominent stress aspects to Mars. In this case, we need to realize that self-management is one way to obtain personal power in our lives, and that proper self-determinism is a great way to help fulfill our expectations.

But we first need to allow ourselves our great expectations. Otherwise, we can feel a frustrating sense of detachment and loneliness, a sense of being cut off from the social matrix and feelings of being ineffectual. We need to feel we count for something very important to the total structure of our society. By discovering or reclaiming our inner authority, we provide ourselves the focus to be a vital part of a larger human reality.

GOT THEM DHARMIC BLUES AGAIN, DADDY

We are probably undergoing a crucially important incarnation, and one in which we can lay a major inner foundation for future evolutionary growth. A prime issue is how we handle our current dharma (roughly translated as our social duty and observance of all levels of law). One Saturn in Capricorn individual who seemed to have fulfilled his special social mission was Charles Dickens, who bravely pointed out in his novels the grave injustices brought upon the lower ranks of society by the rigid class structure of his life and times. He certainly didn't look down on such people (of course, it also helped that he was born with Sun in Aquarius, along with a freedom-embracing Sagittarius Moon and Venus in empathetic Pisces).

Success for most of us inclined to fulfill our nagging sense of social obligation may come about only after much dedication, relentless effort, vigilant self-discipline, and the internal stamina to make it through life's testing periods. This can feel like heavy weight on our shoulders, and we may periodically get a case of the blues, thinking we'll never reach the mountain peak—alive. There's always those jagged rocks and crashing waves waiting below to worry about in case we slip and fall.

Nonetheless, we feel driven to see our commitments to the end with great dependability and little outward complaint as we grit our teeth and bear it. Once our true life purpose has been established, we can concentrate on the work to be done as if by cosmic decree. An evolved Saturn in Capricorn (anyone we know?) is not in awe of the temporal power he or she has been given. Some of us are thus less ego-attached to the honors and merits bestowed on us, no matter how deservingly. Nor are we unduly impressed by the stature of our social position in our chosen field or in the community at large. When news reporters shove cameras and microphones in our face and ask us how we can be so low-key about all our fame and acclaim, we can look them straight in the eye and honestly say "Aw, shucks, folks, it's just my dharma!" That should leave 'em speechless. But it may be true that we are more motivated by the innate rightness and timeliness of our personal social contribution to the world rather than by the mere immediate benefits of worldly power and privilege.

Astro-lebrities with Saturn in Capricorn

Marie Antoinette	Edward Kennedy
Emily Post	Dick Clark
Walt Disney	Ross Perot
Andy Warhol	Charles Dickens
Neil Armstrong	Sean Connery

SATURN IN THE TENTH HOUSE

THE WORLD IS WATCHING

Our Tenth House is not only a life sector associated with our outward contribution to society's structure, it also represents the fruits of our efforts resulting in our reputation—honor, social standing, and the name we make for ourselves via our achievements. It describes what motivates us to move up the social ladder in our attempt to fulfill our ambitions. Much of these dynamics can be gleaned by studying the sign at our Midheaven, our key to the somewhat less personal identity we develop to meet societal demands. However, any planet in our Tenth House does imply a personal drive that needs proper outlets for its expression. When that planet is Saturn (especially when it is close to the MC), we may feel in a semi-conscious manner that society is forever evaluating who we are in a worldly sense, and what we intend to do to add something important to this collective structure. We assume the world is not only watching and judging us, but is demanding we produce something tangible, solid, and enduring, so we feel pressured to emulate model civic behavior on some level.

By studying our natal Saturn's aspects, we can spot our assets and weak points in this context. Stress aspects suggest we may experience inner resistance to playing the game of fame and acclaim by traditional, expected means. I say some resistance because Saturn also willingly adopts much of the conservative behavior demanded of The Establishment, and acts accordingly in order to be on the winning side of the powers that be. But there is also a potential for deep resentment and criticism of authorities that exert control over us if they disrespect us or impersonally use us for their own ends. This won't work for Saturn and its ongoing need for honor. Saturn/Uranus also wouldn't go for this treatment and might rebelliously lash out against the freedom-robbing rules and regulations set up for the mainstream to follow. Saturn/Pluto could seek ways to sabotage such authority by acts of angry defiance, while Saturn/Mars might fight the heavy hand of authority openly and vigorously.

Saturn alone in this house does not guarantee that we will fall in step and obediently give The System what it wants of us, but some of us do sense we have a destined role to play that cannot be ignored. The world may be watching, but it's also waiting.

TOTAL MASTERY

We may set up very stringent guidelines for our own behavior, even when no one's around to study us and take notes. It seems we have a very well-entrenched conscience that acts as a stern inner judge, always devising a lists of "shoulds" and "should nots." Our tendency to be so self-disciplinarian is probably not always conscious. Since a part of us is fearful we will fail to live up to our rigid standards, we may not always want to be aware we even have them. Accordingly, we could delegate the role of overseer to more interior parts of our psyche, but doing so can give this dynamic a compulsive power, whereby we are eternally hard on ourselves. Actually, a few of us can be painfully aware of our shortcomings, and may overcompensate by trying to completely master all facets of ourselves—or just give up and never try to excel in anything.

Self-inhibitors tend to see all the challenges to Tenth House success as much too demanding. Of course, failure is dreaded—but less obvious is the fear of success. Fear of success? Yes, because when we are finally in a top dog position and everyone is expecting nothing less than our best (meaning we are to make few mistakes if any), the pressure to be perfect can be enormous. That's at least what we might tell ourselves now while we are still relative nobodies. Someone should tell us that time works in favor of Saturnian goals, and quitting prematurely before we've given it our best is courting much guilt and chronic frustration.

Over-achievers, however, are more the ones to watch out for. We on overdrive work hard at mastering ourselves through carefully polishing and presenting our strengths to the world in a highly professional manner. We also have ambitions to master the world itself, or as least as much of society as we feasibly can. Maybe this is what Napoleon and Hitler had in mind when flexing their Saturn in the Tenth House muscles. Saturn and Capricorn may both have a need to conquer in order to control, or make absolute, that phenomenon called predictability. It sounds like we may have a hard time accepting chaos with all its random unexpectedness. While maybe we do not behave like power-crazed dictators, we want to run a tight ship and avert disorganization on a grand scale. It's bad enough that we get all knotted up when we can't find our wallet or lose our keychain, but when the world we live in is crumbling due to faulty structures or no reliable structures at all, something inside drives us to want to take over and set things straight again. The trouble is that if we are good at doing this, we won't know when to quit and let someone else have a chance at holding the reins of power. We want to firmly lock in our authoritative position and will do whatever it takes to thwart others from taking over.

Astrologers have traditionally warned that engaging in any ruthless tactics or nasty power plays when Saturn's in the Tenth House can eventually lead to a great fall from a mighty place. Yet before we tumble from the mountain top and crash onto those aforementioned treacherous rocks and choppy waves below, we may first start showing signs of less sure-footedness and increasing incompetence. The wisdom of mature self-counsel fails us, while we also block the advice of others who could help us with our goals. We can shut everyone out and become autocratic in self-destructive ways. Life will demand we come to a halt. The one thing we cannot master is Fate, which in this case will conspire against us using all resources at its disposal. History bears this out, so it behooves us to grab for a little power when we have earned it, but not go hog wild with it and lose all perspective. Everything about Principle Ten revolves around recognition of the need for appropriate limits.

DADDY DEAREST

I keep hearing two opposite sounding reports from my clients with a Tenth House Saturn involving their father, no matter what their natal aspects to Saturn are. The one image we often make such a big to-do over is the cold, unsympathetic, highly restrictive dad who has seldom opened up to us emotionally or even shared his true nature with any member of the family. This kind of parent becomes a mystery to us (not necessarily in a Plutonian way; that seems to almost always involve elements of intimidation and a threat of danger). What makes

Dad hard to figure out is his highly reserved temperament mixed with resentment of those who dare try to pry him open. He could even harbor hostility toward a world he perceives as treating him dishonorably or holding him back. Our dad may be hypersensitive to being rejected, but defensively rejects us and others first. If the situation is more intense than this, our father might throw in an element of cruelty along with his strictness and attempt to squash our spirit or invalidate our worth. This can be very tough stuff for a little kid, who would turn cartwheels if needed to please his or her father and get his deeply craved approval. Of course, any child would wonder what he or she has done to deserve such treatment. Seeing such a father as a mean old ogre or a hard and unapproachable taskmaster is perfectly understandable.

Others of us with Tenth House Saturns know a father who had quiet dignity and easily received respect from others due to his dependable, reliable ways. He could be a role model in terms of patience, persistence, and stick-to-it-iveness. Because of his hard work and ability to develop productive habits, he probably reached a level of career success that impressed us and others in the community. We viewed him while growing up as a man of honor and integrity. But naturally, he still may have had a few flaws. For one thing, Dad may not have been the most openly expressive parent in the world, which could also mean we didn't hear him gripe or complain much no matter how bad the pressures sometimes got. He was of the "stiff upper lip" school of life who would not wear his heart on his sleeve. His mission was to offer his family security and safety in the material world while not burdening others with his own inner problems. We could have benefited by seeing his vulnerable side once in a while, but we didn't get to.

Our father may also have shown a bit of a cowardly approach when forced to fend for himself with others more aggressive than he. Why? Because his practical side convinced him there was little to gain from fighting, so why cause a big scene, say things that he'd regret later, and unnecessarily cause hurt feelings? From his point of view, it was wiser to shut up and walk away from a confrontation than to struggle unsuccessfully in the thick of it. We may have interpreted this as a parent who let himself be taken advantage of (sounds like Neptune in the Tenth House too), but our dad most likely did what he felt was the right thing. This is only a problem if we later on grow up and find ourselves in a panic when having to face others who either directly challenge or antagonize us. If we turn and run instead of holding our ground, we not only blame Dad on some inner level but also come down pretty hard on ourselves for acting like such wimpy fraidy-cats. Like the Cowardly Lion in *The Wizard of Oz*, we could use a dose of courage.

One other scenario: Some of us may not have had a father around at all, even during our formative years. Either he died before we could really know him, or left the family and kept his distance after a bitter divorce. In a few cases, he broke the law and wound up incarcerated, and now we feel that further association with him would create so much social embarrassment for us that we choose to keep our distance The theme of humiliation or social discomfort regarding our dad, because of something he lacks or is deficient in, can be a subtle issue even if he has been a law-abiding citizen. If he tries to reach out and love us, and we push back and stubbornly reject or dismiss him, it's obviously our problem, and one that may come back to visit us when it's our turn to become a parent.

Saturn in the Tenth House never misses a chance to teach us our karmic lessons regarding taking responsibility for our actions. The bottom line is that our experience with our father seems to influence how we shape our concept of authority, worldly responsibility, and commitment to duty, or how we fail to successfully interact with the world at large. At some point, we need to take charge of our own social direction without self-defeatingly blaming a parent's lack of acceptance as our justification for why we seem to never amount to anything or aspire to achieve our best.

OLDER BUT WISER

Many of us seemed wise and knowing about the ways of the world even when we were very young. We have probably spent more energy watching the dynamics of control and power exchange between adults than did the average child, and thus became introduced to realities other children did not confront until reaching adulthood. A few of us went to the school of hard knocks at a tender age, perhaps due to certain family hardships. Saturn in the Tenth House by itself doesn't confer emotional maturity (what if our Moon in Cancer were to also square Mars in Aries? That describes a volatile feeling nature showing very little detachment and objectivity). But even if the rest of our temperament enables us to run around and act like hyperactive little kids, there is one aspect of our psyche that is taking notes about the rules of the game of life. Many of us probably have shown a degree of reserve that is uncommon in young people, and a wise understanding of how effort and application can pay off.

When we finally do psychologically reach adulthood (usually at age twenty-nine or thirty, corresponding to our first Saturn Return), it seems we have established patterns of behavior and response that help us plant our feet firmly on the ground. A deep inner stability can be at work, keeping us on track and moving at a deliberate pace of unfoldment. We don't wish to make false moves or missteps, and patiently find ourselves biding our time and waiting for the right moment to turn on the ambition. We can be fairly steady in how we apply our will to achieve, but we also seem to have a philosophical acceptance of those times when opportunities feel ripe but bear little or no fruit. Our soil may be properly tilled and well fertilized, but the climate (outer world conditions) is sometimes just not right. Being denied one's proper place in the world due to delay after delay can be very disheartening, but we with Saturn in Tenth House can be so enduring in our material goals that disappointments fuel our committed determination to eventually succeed.

GOLDEN YEARS

No matter how many ups and downs we experience, we may find ourselves being in the world striving to reach the top while also not being of the world as we step back and realize the limits of material success. But after the heady experience of climbing to the mountain's peak and looking at the world from such a grand vista, where else is there for us to go? Well then, of course, we take to the limitless sky and learn to fly. As we age with grace and wisdom, we may find ourselves quite ready to pull back from our dense experience of living an earthly life. The time now becomes right for giving form to a different reality.

Saturn has been deemed the planet of the disciple on The Path. Most of us are not going to give up all our hard-earned titles and possessions in pursuit of a spiritual journey, because we know that getting to this worldly point has already been part of our spirit's sojourn. Old age can fill us with awe, as we put our attention on quieter, less public ambitions. Maybe we've ended up being a double Nobel Prize winner with all the acclaim and honor that comes with such achievement. But even if our golden years are spent contemplating something as small but wondrous as growing the perfect rose, we have earned a sense of completion. We close out our life feeling triumphant.

Astro-lebrities with Saturn in the Tenth House

J. Edgar Hoover	Adolph Hitler
Napoleon	Leonardo da Vinci
Malcolm X	Henry Ford
Bill Clinton	Nicholas Copernicus
Albert Einstein	Oscar Wilde

SATURN/SATURN ASPECTS

TRANSIT

Obviously Saturn cannot aspect itself in our natal chart, unless
you are considering secondary progressions (too slow) or solar
arcs (nice and zippy). But when Saturn transits its natal placement, we see how Principle Ten operates in a dynamic planetary mode. Saturn/Saturn transits are considered as life cycles
common to all people and occurring at about the same ages.
Although the information about Saturn Returns will be discussed at length, the remaining Saturn/Saturn phases will only
be briefly addressed.

OUR FIRST SATURN RETURN

From ages twenty-eight through thirty, we find ourselves at a
symbolic crossroads in life requiring major adjustments, a critical time challenging us to define the nature of our true inner
identity and to begin living out that identity as authentically
as possible. This period is called our first Saturn Return.
Everyone goes through it who makes it to thirty. Our daily
newspapers are wonderful sources of astrological data for
those with patience and sharp eyes. As long as a date is given
with a printed story, we get to play astro-detective: "Suspect
Billingsly is to be officially charged with the triple ax-murder
on Tuesday, just two days shy of his twenty-ninth birthday..."
It is common to see such daily reports of people having their
first Saturn Return who have done reckless things that have
landed them in big trouble. But getting into hot water with
authority is not what this Saturn transit is primarily all about.
It is liberating ourselves from the parental/societal yoke of the
past and testing out our real strengths on our own terms that
is really the goal.

We are no longer encouraged to allow parental, peer, or
impersonal social pressures to do our identity-structuring for
us, as we did while we were growing up and struggling to find

our place in the world. This can be a time emphasizing the development of maturity and the testing of our ability to be self-sufficient on all levels. Many of us are actually learning to simplify our lives by finally getting down to the basic fundamentals of who we are (apart from the inadequate images others have created for us) and what we need in order to actualize self-fulfillment. Only what is relevant to our real essence remains and flourishes. The rest has to go. We are to embark on a course of living that permits us to be what we were meant to be, whether or not this emerging identity meets approval from others in our past.

We are to take stock of ourselves in a sober, realistic manner that can eventually help us recognize and mobilize our own strengths into the world. This becomes a prime period for self-assessment and reflective evaluation of all our past achievements and failures—a time to attend to any existing gaps and voids in our life with concentrated effort and focus. If we have striven to dutifully fulfill Saturn's obligations in a productive and realistic manner, life is now ready to release the bonds of our past and usher in a world where we are permitted to perform with greater freedom of action. Often an area of our lives that has been deeply unfulfilling (typically indicated by our natal Saturn house position) can now undergo a timely and healthy change for the better. Long-term frustrating issues can be clarified and resolved. The only dreams shattered now are our most illusionary, non-productive ones. The aspirations that are well within our grasp are the ones to be sought.

On the other hand, if we willfully continue to avoid growing up by not taking responsibility for ourselves, this Return can be a depressing time when we become painfully aware of our stagnation, lifelessness, and insignificance. We are meeting the consequences of past negative conditioning that we have allowed to operate unchallenged. If we find ourselves passively enduring our discomfort and acute sense of lack during this critical period without making a strenuous effort to get out of our rut, we can find our strengths and inner support systems beginning to lose their effectiveness. We may then diminish our capacity to further control the external patterns of our life.

Sadly, some of us may approach our thirties with no serious objectives to aspire toward and no real sense of our life's purpose. Meanwhile, socioeconomic pressures can bear down on us even more oppressively. Such are the pitfalls of continuing to conform to outworn patterns. For a few, these are desperate times where drastic, self-destructive measures are sought. The fewer options we think we have, the more we try to kill off our Saturn consciousness in favor of the wild but temporary freedoms of lawless behavior—and we almost always get caught. Going to prison for a long time is one unconscious way to have other people provide us with a fixed structure complete with set routines and lots of rigid rules to follow; we don't have to decide or choose much for ourselves. Everything already comes pre-packaged. Prison inmates have given away their Saturn power for someone else to manage. Think of this next time you read of people in deep trouble with the law who happen to be between ages twenty-eight and thirty-one.

Should outer circumstances demand that we halt our current activities and submit to conditions that seem uncompromising, it is probably because we have not properly aligned ourselves with the Saturn (reality) principle during most of our experimental twenties. We have likely chosen to take the "easy" way out for the most part, content to drift along with the ambivalent tide of life rather than to cultivate self-determinism. Nobody is more at fault here than ourselves. If our life is now in shambles, it is probably due to our own lack of insight, foresight, careful planning for our future, poor timing, or general mismanagement of our practical affairs. We no longer are allowed the privilege of being casually noncommittal with our destiny. The dues we now must pay are those we owe both to ourselves spiritually and to our society.

OUR SECOND SATURN RETURN

Our first Saturn Return is a turning point when our potential to overcome the inertia of the past can be at its peak. By allowing ourselves to undergo all necessary alterations of character by way of honest self-appraisal, we can make breakthroughs in our development that foster our personal progress for the remainder of our lives. The more we can do during the first Saturn Return to improve ourselves, the easier life conditions might be for us during the second Saturn Return in our mid-to-late fifties.

This next Saturn Return is also significant in terms of defining what we are to ourselves, but at this point, self-definition regarding our place in the outer world becomes less of an issue. We now seek to define who we are according to our inner experience of ourselves from now until death (assuming we won't have a third Return). Most of us feel less obliged to perform on a social or professional level in any pressured manner. However, because of economic uncertainties, our company's attempt to downsize may suddenly leave us without a job. This sense of career displacement goes against our inner timetable, and many still unresolved issues (regarding security and self-respect) carried over from the first Saturn Return can be brought into play again. Times have changed and company loyalty can no longer be taken for granted, making this second Return trickier than it has even been in previous decades.

But let's say that under more ideal conditions we still want to impress society with our continued worldly accomplishments. It's just that we are less dazzled by the results of our efforts. This can be a "been there, done that!" feeling. Some of us are more concerned with doing things that make a deeper impact on our inner selves. We realize with retirement age just around the corner, we start wanting to achieve something that is meaningful to just us. When well handled, this Return can be the backbone of a generally stable life period. When mismanaged, the deterioration of our hard-won

self-concept since our first Return can result in a sense of res-
ignation. A lot of this has to do with how well we reassembled
ourselves during our mid-life crisis (when Uranus opposed
Uranus, Neptune squared Neptune, and for many of us when
Pluto also squared Pluto).

This second Saturn Return could thus pinpoint a "make-it-
or-else" passage for us where we either get another chance to
revitalize ourselves and build healthy new structures, or we
psychologically begin to dry up and calcify on mental and
physical levels during the closing years of life. In short, we
start aging gracelessly. How we deal with this Return and its
own challenges best establishes how we remain flexible and
adaptable in our later years. For those of us who rebuild ourselves as best we can, such "golden" years can remain vibrant.
We can stay lucid with a sturdy grip on reality and a wonderful sense of self-sufficiency. For those of us who cannot further
work on ourselves due to the toll our life-long doubts and insecurities have taken on us, we sadly end up withering, never to
blossom again. This does not have to be inevitable, since each
of us can make attempts both small and great to structure
ourselves with a nourishing sense of self-preservation. At this
stage, the Saturn Return works like a cosmic oil can ready to
lubricate parts of our psyche that otherwise start to rust out
on us. The Tin Man must have been having his second Saturn
Return just as young Dorothy was experiencing her first
Saturn opposition Saturn phase. And who knows just what
Toto was going through!

OUR THIRD SATURN RETURN

Trying to figure out the issues and themes of this final Saturn
Return in a normal life span is quite speculative. This
Saturn/Saturn transit occurs in the late eighties. Before its
arrival, those of us still alive first have undergone two other
life cycles that probably have helped us detach from most of
life's mundane concerns: transiting Neptune opposing our
natal Neptune (around the early eighties) and the Uranus

Return (at about age eighty-four). The Neptune transit, occurring just before the Uranus Return, echoes the awareness of disillusionment we may have experienced during our mid-life crisis (Neptune square Neptune), but we are now less willing to let some dreams go. Former distortions we have emotionally held onto with blind determination and false hope can now be recognized, enabling us to finally dissolve them in our consciousness. We can make peace with the past, as we grow nearer to being at home with the God within. This allows us to withdraw into our inner world with a sense of serenity and a tranquil acceptance of ourselves and others. We surrender to the greater cosmic process in ways that also help us prepare for our physical transition and the afterlife.

The Uranus Return symbolizes the end of the human socialization cycle on the mundane level. All the structuring we were able to develop from our interaction with society has been established, and now we are free to detach more completely and live out our remaining years functioning on the inner realm of the mind. We simply don't care what others think of our behavior at this point, since we are no longer caught up in mainstream living anyway. Our eccentricities become more apparent to others, but so what?

By the time we reach our third Saturn Return, our identity-structuring needs are more subjective than ever, as we are now giving form to our spiritual essence. The sense of being "in the world but not of it" has never been stronger. However, Saturn is a reality planet no matter what stage of life. Bottom-line realities at this age will probably revolve around health and energy loss. Our old physical parts are wearing out after years of dedicated service. Our vitality needs to be conserved for our most necessary activities (that for us could still be painting, music, reading, or anything that feeds the soul). We seek to establish steady rhythms in whatever we do. The threat of our worldly securities taken away from us by things we can't control (sudden hospitalization, landing in a nursing home, not being able to pay our utilities, etc.) can be strong. But Saturn is taking us to the end of the road and telling us to psychologically let go of our attachment to nearly everything physical, including people. We can still have all of our material comforts, but we realize that attention is now to be put on preparing for our new journey in consciousness after death. It's too bad society doesn't help us facilitate this next adventure with the same attentiveness it has applied to making us fulfill our earthly commitments. We, in typical Saturn fashion, are once again feeling all on our own in this area.

SATURN SQUARE/OPPOSITION/QUINCUNX SATURN

In general, these tensional phases allow us to stop and review how effectively we have been structuring our life according to its real demands. If we are off kilter, these become correctional periods. We typically need to let go of needless baggage that has weighed us down. Probably due to losses experienced, a degree of pain is often registered. Even fears not adequately addressed in the past may now crop up, demanding self-examination. But our scenarios usually unfold in ways that later prove self-educational and pivotal to future success. Timing is very important during these transits. We are delayed in our objectives for good reasons, although it can feel like punishment for past mistakes. Trying to push matters to reach fruition or conclusion prematurely does not ultimately work for us and can even further hinder our plans. We need to make small but sure-footed steps towards sound goals within our reach. Our options may be limited, but this helps ensure a singular focus in specific areas needing our attention the most.

SATURN SEXTILE/TRINE SATURN

These Saturn transits coincide with periods when we can retain what's productive about most structures in our lives while weeding out whatever is not working for us. We are encouraged, but not forced, to build new frameworks based on clear and well-defined goals. The sextile is more eager to try a variation on a theme than is the status-quo supporting trine. Thus, if we already have personal areas that offer us the right kind of security, this transit helps fortify and insulate these life sectors in small but practical ways. The affairs of Saturn's natal house are typically the focus of our attention. Our persistence and patience can pay off quicker for us during these industrious cycles than they do with the Saturn/Saturn stress phases, where frustration and delays are more likely. As with all Saturn transits, we are learning to be selective with how we apply our time and energy, but focus can come easily and we are more willing to delay immediate gratification for the security of long-term stability.

CHAPTER SIXTEEN

SATURN IN AQUARIUS

SOCIETY BUILDER

Saturn can operate on progressive social levels in humanistic Aquarius. Future-oriented objectives are more carefully formulated with thoughtful consideration for their practical application, particularly in terms of how they impact groups of people in society. The development of broad applications of thought and social organization is taken seriously. We have the endurance and patience needed to persistently work at manifesting such collective goals. Experimental Aquarius combines with conservative Saturn to urge us to seek untried methods and procedures with a patient level-headedness not always expected of Aquarian placements (especially if we identify more with the idealistic but unpredictable free-soul quality of co-ruler Uranus). Saturn's natural caution and insistence on practical functioning prevents Aquarius from unduly deviating from standards just for the thrill of trying something new or shaking up the status quo.

A common denominator of planet and sign is a focused desire to influence the structure of society at large. There can be strong sociological inclinations with Saturn in Aquarius. Social structuring is viewed from an impersonal, theoretical manner as we seek to apply our ideals for humanity on a large-scale basis, if only in our heads. The sometimes wild, erratic Uranian side of Aquarius does not get to express itself as easily due to the controlled, disciplined element of Saturn. The sporadic impulses of this high-strung, unpredictable sign tend to be denied expression that could otherwise prove reckless and destructive. Saturn encourages a more sustained and systematic release of Aquarius' famous electrifying energy. Constructively, this can be one of the most efficient, workable positions for The Water Bearer, with worldly Saturn contributing a practical realism to an altruistic sign often caught up in abstractions. Aspirations can be better realized and made tangible through enduring personal or group effort as a result.

BETTER TOMORROWS

Saturn's need for lasting frameworks combined with Aquarius' desire for mass enlightenment suggest our tendency is to revolt against obsolete patterns of social behavior or useless traditions, usually in an attempt to instigate new and effective structures within our existing society. We are less inclined to completely tear down or totally shatter things in our own lives if we feel we can utilize the structures of previous situations for the betterment of new goals. Reformation is mixed with a great measure of common sense and a streak of self-preservation. The utilitarian side of Saturn keeps freedom-fighter Aquarius from resorting to anarchistic means in order to sweep out old or oppressive societal patterns. Saturn will look for a less radical solution.

Keep in mind that Saturn is the traditional co-ruler of Aquarius, and as such has a strong attunement to many of this sign's principles. We could speculate that because Saturn has had a longer history dealing with Aquarius energy than Uranus, it knows how to better work with this sign, and evokes its more mature traits. Societies take a long time to reach complex levels of development, and social alterations worth pursuing similarly need to take time, according to Saturn.

MAD SCIENTIST?

This Saturn placement acts like a bridge connecting established social values with advanced modes of thought. We can bring our experimental but humane ideals to a down-to-earth level whereby such ideals can be made meaningful for all. Saturn gives needed substance and form to the airy, abstract reality of Aquarius. This helps make our theoretical visions of collective betterment realistic and attainable.

Saturn's capacity for precision, organization, and exactitude stimulate the strong scientific bent of Aquarius. Traditional scientific procedure owes much to the discipline and reasoning power of Saturn. Even when used for Aquarian purposes, science must involve Saturnian carefulness and patience. The approaches taken can be painstaking. Results demand utmost attention to detail. None of this sounds very Uranian, but Saturn in Aquarius is not the signature of the crazy inventor, manic about his or her discoveries and creations. Dr. Frankenstein was more an example of Jupiter or Uranus in Aquarius with tensional patterns from Pluto for an added dose of crazed obsession.

SAFETY IN NUMBERS

Both planet and sign have a high degree of detachment, which is important for intellectual clarity and unbiased reasoning. Both also show an aptitude for technological or social service skills. Aquarius' inventive ability can be utilized with a greater sense of responsibility, suggesting practical innovations or progressive thought that helps to quietly revolutionize the world.

However, our sense of obligation is aimed toward the community as a whole rather than toward each individual within that community. We probably believe strongly in the power of supportive teamwork. Saturn suggests we shrewdly take advantage of networking as we try to appeal to a wide range of temperaments existing in society. Aquarius is not afraid of strangers or strangeness, although Saturn is. Some of us will need to consciously work through our fear of people and things that seem "weird" or too far out. Often, we feel safer when closely bonded to a group or association where, oddly enough, everyone thinks alike or agrees with certain theoretical premises (and such premises can be very progressive and unconventional). We want solidarity with like-minded individuals who also will fight for certain freedoms. Pure Aquarius doesn't need the validation of others who always think the same, but insecure Saturn often does.

CLEAR BUT COLD

On a more personal note, many of us may be committed to improving social consciousness but still come off as aloof or lacking warmth on the one-to-one level. If we are a Pisces or a Cancer with lots of Venus or Neptune aspects, this can really be baffling to us, since we know ourselves to be filled with deep concerns about people.

But the detachment principle of Aquarius blended with the natural reserve of cool, unemotional Saturn can make us appear devoid of real human passion and feelings. Maybe we appear to cope with everything life throws at us without blinking an eye, removing ourselves from our humanness by exercising too much unbiased objectivity. Nothing seems to get us hysterical or filled with rage in a personal way. But don't try trashing our ideals and principles, because then you'll have a battle on your hands—though most likely a war with brilliant words and concepts rather than screams and flying fists.

While we seem like cold potatoes to some, we are blessed with an unselfish interest in elevating the collective mind. As a result, dutiful Saturn is steered far beyond the usual realm of personal, self-seeking ambition. We will need to develop better social skills and learn to have more fun within groups or crowds. Tact and diplomacy are needed, rather than our penchant for turning rooms silent whenever we forthrightly speak our mind. There are areas where we can be unknowingly insensitive, since we fail to realize how touchy many people can be about hearing certain "truths." But our motivation is truly humanitarian.

APART FROM THE CROWD

We can either comprehend broader, universal issues with much clarity and profundity, or with undue pessimism and doubt (aspects to Saturn in our natal chart should give clues to which way we usually go). The materialistic side of Saturn can strongly modify Aquarius' uncommon intellectual vision. A point of contrast is this: Saturn prefers either to work alone or exclusively control and regulate the work of others, while Aquarius seeks a democratic condition in that all parties involved are self-managed and independent from authoritative rule. We may attract managerial positions within group enterprises such as associations, societies, clubs, fraternal organizations, community projects, etc., whether career-related or not. When mismanaged, we can feel quite removed from any collective body we must associate with. We may not feel comfortable participating in many ordinary social functions, stand-offishly observing and analyzing from the sidelines. We are humane but sometimes have difficulty establishing rapport with society in its current state. It's the idealized vision we'd rather relate to.

Normally gregarious, Aquarius has some trouble filtering through a planet known for its crippling blockages. We self-inhibitors may be uptight about developing even casual social alliances. Aquarius says we need to have acquaintances, but Saturn may find such non-committal relationships too shallow and meaningless. We probably had bad experiences being rejected by cliques in school when we were younger. Group energy can now seem threatening to us, since it can stir up old wounds. At the least, we demand that most social interactions serve a serious, well-defined purpose. We're not willing to just mingle and let our hair down with masses of people we don't even know and who don't know us. Thus, some of us may always feel apart from the crowd. We cannot let ourselves experience the true sense of the camaraderie typical of

Aquarius. Life is teaching us to feel like a real member of our community, our society, and the Big World.

POWER PARADOX

Prestige and public significance become meaningful and motivational for us when we align ourselves with a great cause or crusade to enlighten society. We envision a freer world where the rights of each individual are upheld, and will work hard with others to initiate reform. However, if mismanaged, wayward Aquarius filtering through rigid Saturn can manifest as social intolerance. We may attempt to impose limitations on the social freedoms of those who resist our utopian outlooks. Saturn is trying to help us recognize and respect the limits of our own social idealism.

Although Saturn can show a mask of social respectability, Aquarius suggests we are seldom able to sustain such a facade if it intrinsically goes against our abstract principles. Aquarius wants truth to be known at all costs. Prestige and public significance become meaningful and motivational for us only if they are the offshoots of championing a cause worth the effort of our social involvement. We may need to discipline ourselves and refrain from assuming control over the "group mind," since we may not be as cooperative in real life as we imagine—Saturn can be unyielding, and Aquarius can show a headstrong stubbornness common to all fixed signs. We are to learn about practical compromise on the one-to-many level. Otherwise, we alienate those we need to coordinate with to get large projects done. We may not "interface" well with others when we become heavy-handed with the enforcement of reform, no matter how many people will ultimately benefit from such changes. Aquarius is teaching us to understand and tolerate the many disharmonious voices in society.

A REFORMATION OF HEART

Saturn is either motivated to act according to its safety urges and fear of being overpowered, or by its uncertainty about secure outcomes. Its presence in Aquarius suggests we tend to avoid establishing intimate contact with people who could put us in closer touch with our vulnerable, emotional self. If we are lonely, unfulfilled, and lacking meaningful fellowship, it is normally due to our own intellectual capacity to reject others who fail to meet our ideal standards (Saturn in Virgo struggles with this too). If we are not aware of this, we could project such rejection onto others, seeing them as unfeeling or indifferent in areas involving universal concern. We may even draw such people to us, only reinforcing this rigidly held blind spot. It will take the pure objectivity and rational power of Aquarius to help us understand why we are so disenchanted with our social environment. Although we often aspire toward a collective goal that could unconditionally benefit society, we need to be careful not to live out our own lives in a vacuum, removed from the reformative impact warm human contact could afford.

SATURN CO-RULES AQUARIUS?

It may not be easy at first to see Saturn's role as co-ruler of Aquarius. Many of this sign's traits seem more fitting of Uranus, especially when observing younger Aquarian types in action. Maybe as we embark on the Age of Aquarius, Uranus' influence will become more strongly felt in the social consciousness of those who break away from the pull of the masses.

However, since Saturn was deemed the sole ruler of Aquarius before the discovery of Uranus in 1781, its initial relationship to this air sign may have been based on historical realities. Before we knew Uranus existed, individualism in its unique and most open form was typically limited to royalty, the aristocracy, and the upper echelons of the clergy (even though they were all stuck in their own tradition-bound mindsets). The common man and woman (whose civil rights Aquarius has such concern for) was not allowed the social privilege of outwardly expressing his or her individualistic potential without the accusations of heresy or threats of imprisonment, ostracism, and even death. We had to at least

264 • CHAPTER SIXTEEN

go underground with our uncommon attitudes and keep our knowledge of inner things hidden if we were to survive. Occasionally, an artist or artisan of rare talent was allowed to vent eccentricities, and even to profit through them, but average individuals were not socially conditioned to stand out as different and special. We were limited by the oppressive dictates of authoritative rule, as well as the threat of mob rule spearheaded by superstitious neighbors. Not much was allowed to look out of place or weird.

If anything, Aquarian energy in past centuries expressed more through enforced group effort. Many individuals had to work together toward the fulfillment of a larger cause that usually only benefited the elite or those who held power. Group involvement, in other words, was not based on free will or the recognition of individual self-rulership. It was instead structured to strictly adhere to social duty and the will of those in control. The rights and liberties of each contributing individual were not considered important. It was how that individual could be used that mattered. Thus, Saturn's initial rulership of Aquarius does seem appropriate.

Of course, around the time Uranus was discovered, social revolutions began to erupt (particularly the French Revolution). Freedom for each individual was passionately sought. But even after Uranus' discovery, Saturn apparently held power for quite some time during the Industrial Age, considering the human abuses experienced in factories and industries. The birth of labor unions was needed to help reform the plight of the working class struggling in these slavish conditions.

Astro-lebrities with Saturn in Aquarius

Carl Jung
Gloria Steinem
Ayn Rand
Albert Schweitzer
Carl Sagan

Sir Winston Churchill
Yoko Ono
Howard Hughes
Greta Garbo
Ralph Nader

SATURN IN THE ELEVENTH HOUSE

CROWD CONTROL

Saturn in this house has a basic fear of the potential chaos large groups of people can cause. Mobs running wild or anarchists on an uncontrolled path of destruction could be two of an Eleventh House Saturn's worst nightmares. There is something about unregulated group energy on the move that repels this planet. We could at least get claustrophobic in crowds. The Eleventh House is where we find people coming together to support progressive and even futuristic ideals. Large groups of individuals get to pool their energies, form powerful alliances, and operate as an even greater social force, for better or worse, than any one person could alone. Saturn, looking at this complex of egos fortifying each other's power and will, starts to panic. That's because Saturn is a separatist at heart and is not eager to lose its identity to any group. It will not surrender itself unconditionally to any abstract cause, especially when in this house. Total, unquestioned loyalty is not what Saturn is willing to give (although Saturn/Neptune patterns might). Yet there are many other facets of the Eleventh House experience that can help Saturn feel connected to people in a broader and more purposeful sense.

While it's probably true that many of us with this position feel uneasy in crowds or being around throngs of people, we seem to be very observant regarding our peer group dynamic, starting as early as preschool or kindergarten. The Eleventh House invites us to participate in activities where we work together as a controllable unit with everyone on equal footing, no one with greater privileges. But Saturn doesn't buy this "all for one and one for all" approach, and we find ourselves wanting to back away from too much team involvement (even though no one on the team was all that excited to pick us anyway). We either reject or are rejected by the group, the clique, the membership, the gang, etc. We over-achievers usually don't like being rejected at all, and, determined not to be excluded, will try to prove our worthiness by doing whatever it takes to fit in and be accepted. But what the group may not realize is that we may also harbor ambitions to later take over the leadership role and be in control. Conversely, we self-inhibitors may take not being included too much to heart, feel crushed, and learn to resent anything dealing with groups, teams, networks, and other such alliances.

It is unlikely that we stood out among our peers as being highly popular and sought after. One reason, especially in our youth, is that we felt older and more mature than many others our age. This was very apparent in high school, when we probably were studious and conservative while many others were rowdy and unfocused. Yet it is ironic how some of us studied those wilder kids that both fascinated and scared us. There is something very alluring about those free-spirited ones who break the rules and still do not get struck by lightning (the way we assume we would if we stepped out of line). And so, a dilemma occurs: whether to conform to social standards, ensuring our safety and the approval of authorities, or to flirt with experimental behavior and be like those who thumb their noses at convention in favor of more original and defiant social expression. Saturn often feels caught in the middle of these contrasting urges when in the Eleventh House.

It would seem most likely during the school years that we were very picky about who we hung out with. Quality friendships are what we sought then and now. We may claim we have only a handful of real friends that we really can count on and who know some of our deeper facets.

JOINING THE GROUP

The types of friends represented by the Eleventh House are not the same shown by our Seventh House, who are more our bosom buddies—those best friends with whom we have established intimate, personalized relationships. These are our loving, long-term companions with whom we share so much of our real self. Such unions become a marriage of sorts. But such intimacy is not part of the Eleventh House or Principle Eleven in general.

When people claim to have invited about 100 of their "best" friends to their wedding, you know they are coming from their Eleventh House experience, not their Seventh.

Our Eleventh House friends are more correctly described as acquaintances. They can also be people we congregate with in structured group settings like clubs, monthly meetings, associations, political fundraisers, and even bowling teams (group therapy is more a Twelfth House issue). These relationships have an element of friendly impersonality that is nevertheless very enjoyable when everyone is networking smoothly. We just know enough about one another to keep things sociable and upbeat. Saturn needs to be exposed to such group harmony to know it is possible to achieve. But Saturn will not get chummy with anyone it still regards as having "stranger" status. Saturn realizes there is something about all group arrangements that lends itself to strictly surface interaction, where nothing gets too deep or too real, and the associations seldom remain permanent. Eleventh House people tend to come and go, replaced by new faces.

Saturn, not being a natural joiner, approaches these social setups with caution and reserve. We probably would like the secure structure of a well-defined group that has been established for some time (no crazy anarchists here!). We may feel safe with all those familiar faces we get together with on a regular basis. It will take us time to warm up to all these new but seemingly interesting people, but at least they believe in the preservation of the blue-throated mountain swallow or the red-spotted river chipmunk or are working to support serious social issues. Such activist groups calling for responsible action are appealing to us. If everyone gets together to fulfill a worthy purpose, rather than just wasting time casually mingling, this would justify our membership or participation.

VOLUNTEER SERVICE

Saturn could be drawn to volunteering time and energy when needed since its has a serviceable nature and likes to be put to good use. We might even sign up to head certain committees when asked, especially when others sense our above-average organizational abilities and our willingness to work hard for an important cause. But we really have to like and trust the group we serve before we let things get this far. We are not under Neptune's spell here, so our sense of service is tied in with our sense of realistic limits. The group has to make sure it doesn't push us too far with its demands, and most importantly to never take us for granted! We may look like we are humble, but inwardly we crave recognition for our good works, loyalty, dedication, and overall perseverance. The fact is the Eleventh House is not a zone where people get sentimental about things or huggy-kissy, especially with Saturn positioned here. If we do things just to get a special warm response from fellow members, it may not be forthcoming (unless we also have the Moon in the Eleventh House, but in a different sign and not conjunct Saturn).

Still, we could take on a dutiful parental role in those groups we do relate to. Many will depend on us to keep things afloat and bring order to the way things run. But again, if we are over-achievers, we may like controlling the show too much and others may sense we have a problem being truly democratic, or even flexible. Why should little changes in the club's monthly procedures bother us so much? There is something spontaneous about the way things like to go in the Eleventh House, but we have to be careful not to bring our own Saturnian rigidity to these experiences. Self-inhibitors may feel guilty not wanting to volunteer, but we either do so reluctantly or are pushed into it by others who try to pump us up with confidence or assurance that we can do tasks required. If we don't undergo a real attitude adjustment, we later may complain about how we are carrying too much of the load and not getting the right kind of team support.

Again, it's a feeling of being used without being appreciated by people who are somewhat detached from the sacrifices we undergo to fulfill our role. Some of us might simply quit the group and not seek such similar involvements again for a long, long time, if at all. It seems the lesson here is not to drop out, but to establish clear boundaries and let other members realize what we need in return for all the work we do. It's not selfish of us to ask for cooperation. It's sensible. We are only being unreasonable when we expect everyone to be mindreaders who should already know when they are imposing on us, or pressuring us too much, or piling on too many responsibilities. All they do know instead is that we seem to take on all the little jobs they shove our way and not gripe about it. If this scenario is not suitable, then Saturn says we need to squawk about things politely but firmly, and not just retreat and get our feelings hurt. Saturn can be such a touchy planet sometimes!

BEING DIFFERENT CAN BE GOOD

Saturn gets too easily unnerved by people who look too unusual or do things that go against tradition (think of the conservative bent of Saturn in Taurus, Cancer, or Virgo). The Eleventh House is one life department where we have an opportunity to meet a wide range of people from all walks of life (the United Nations is an Eleventh House organization, although ideally its politics are Ninth House issues). This house challenges us to readjust our thinking about finding security only through people who are familiar to us (that's why it quincunxes the Fourth House in the Natural Wheel). We have the potential to embrace a larger "family" of friends in the Eleventh House. Saturn actually is no big embracer of anything, but in this house it often hungers for solid connection with members of society. It doesn't want to feel like an outsider who observes groups only from a safe distance, not daring to participate. In fact, Saturn can be a loner, but it doesn't always like being alone when in this house. It's a contradiction we need to work out.

Many of us will probably find we have adopted certain assumptions from our parents (maybe father more than mother) that anyone who is different is weird, and that weird can be dangerous. We are not supposed to trust strangeness in any form, much less allow ourselves to associate with it. There are many Uranian elements of the Eleventh House that Saturn finds both fascinating and disruptive. It's a house of anti-Establishment activities and protest movements that defy the cultural status quo. Even defining what is normal becomes a big question for the Eleventh House. Saturn always thinks it knows without a doubt what "normal" looks like when it sees it, but the Eleventh House is where our culture has a chance to re-invent itself and try out new ways of looking and behaving. Ironically, what is called bizarre today may be passé a few decades later. So we with Saturn here are going to be getting an eyeful and an earful of what a progressive society can look like and sound like, and a lot of it will go against what we have been taught to reject while growing up.

The challenge is to find value in people and things different from ourselves and our background. We need to be more socially experimental in the Eleventh House. For example, if we have the chance to either go to an out-of-state university versus a local college only twenty miles away, we should opt for going out of state, because that might ensure that we get to have the culture shock needed to help us alter any rigid social assumptions. Even if we did choose to play it safe and stay local, the universe may surprise us by picking a roommate who comes from the opposite side of the country, has slightly magenta-hued hair, loves exploring virtual reality, or even was raised by a parent who is gay (Uranus could be transiting our Saturn at the time). The point is that if we need to be more exposed to different realities out there in the big world, the experience will come to us somehow.

Once we continue to have repeated encounters with unusual types with far-out views of living more freely, we get to listen to our inner critic who has so quickly sought to judge and condemn people who don't fit the mold. A lesson in true tolerance is to be learned with an Eleventh House Saturn, but it's a tolerance based on a deeper understanding of why certain people dare to live the ways they do. What Saturn can offer us here is real objectivity, where we play the social scientist who observes and records the unlimited variations of human behavior. We simply take it all in without feeling like we have to protect ourselves from such exposure. It would appear that the more we continue to educate ourselves and exercise our intelligence, the better. People with lots of planetary focus in this house (similar to the Third, Sixth, and Ninth Houses) usually want to feed their minds new data. Saturn may be challenged to do so to avoid being too narrow-minded to appreciate current social overviews.

OLD FRIENDS

Saturn in this house literally means old friends—as in the elderly, the aged, those advanced in years. Actually, older associates might be a more accurate term in most instances (people about seven or more years older than us). We might befriend such people because they represent for us stability, maturity, settledness, experience. We gravitate toward those who have been successful with their material objectives or have made a name for themselves in society. Maybe we have a few old *famous* friends. We feel safe relating to people who know where they are going in life and who don't waste their time or ours with nonsensical behavior. What may make these relationships work best for us is when both sides know their boundaries and observe considerate behavior. These would be people who just don't pop over for a surprise visit. Or ask us for inappropriate favors. Or talk about us behind our back. We need to trust that our friendship will be honored and respected.

Actually, much depends on our Saturn aspects as to whether such old friends are to be a source of security for us or a burden. Saturn/Moon or Saturn/Venus stress aspects do not sound like we are dealing with older people who are also self-reliant or confident in their outlooks. They could drain us with their sad stories of how life doesn't give them any lucky breaks. Of course, we could attract someone of any age who could sound like a bowl of sour grapes. So it's not as much a matter of old friends as it is a case of friends whose life patterns start to get old on us after a while. We take on some of their chronic problems and it can exhaust us. This could be a test of learning to be more selective in choosing acquaintances. With the right choices, our lives can be quietly enriched.

Astro-lebrities with Saturn in the Eleventh House

Lucille Ball	Queen Victoria
John Updike	Henri Toulouse-Lautrec
Princess Anne	Marlon Brando
Charles Manson	Laurence Olivier
Robin Williams	Joan of Arc

SATURN/URANUS ASPECTS

NATAL

Though Saturn and Uranus seem like opposites, they both rule Aquarius, implying they do have a few things in common or at least can work together better than traditionally assumed. First, the differences: Saturn crystallizes form and tries to keep it from undergoing needless alterations, especially drastic ones. Uranus senses when form and structure start to put a stranglehold on the spirit, and counteracts with a shattering force, shaking everything up in order to release trapped energy. Uranus is a natural law-breaker while Saturn is the cosmic law-enforcer. Uranus doesn't bend the rules, it ignores them. Saturn doesn't just lay down the laws, it upholds them with threats of punishments and penalties. Saturn is comforted by the familiar and the conservative, while Uranus is excited by anything uncommon and somewhat risky. Saturn is understandably frightened by this face of Uranus.

Saturn studies the rules and regulations of The System and abides by them, seeing this as the only way to ensure true social organization and collective sanity. Playing by the rules of the game is how society preserves itself, according to Saturn. Everyone who cooperates by behaving correctly gets rewarded with stability and security. This sounds good on paper, maybe, but it doesn't actually work in the real world. If we all did society Saturn's way, we'd act like robots or machines running flawlessly, stuck in our social positions for life with no opportunity to change in mid-stream and try something new. This sounds more like the enforced pattern of social structure before Uranus was discovered, when social roles were predetermined by our family's station rather than by our innate talents and skills. But Uranus came along to sweep out the old view of fixed societal destinies. A few pioneering types way back then realized we could break away from the strictures of unquestioned tradition and family status. Life was finally allowing people to follow their ideals and visions of playing out different, sometimes unique roles in the world. We learned to follow our hunches, strike out on our own, and reclaim our individualism. We still received varying degrees of social penalty, maybe even ostracism, but it didn't matter to us mavericks who were on such a different wavelength—and it still doesn't.

Although both planets have many contrasting themes, what they share is social awareness and truth-seeking. Saturn pays critical attention to those who are side-stepping the rules while Uranus is wary of those who do not. Each planet observes what is happening in society regarding how authority operates in the lives of the many. Saturn wants to run a tight ship while Uranus knows it's regarded as a loose cannon. Uranus calls for urgent reform, seeing quickly and clearly what's wrong with blindly submitting to rigid policies and time-worn traditions. Saturn carefully weeds out those social procedures that no longer work well, but will continue to support the established framework. But even in their opposite ways of viewing society, these planets feel a responsibility to help shape the future of lots of people and share impersonal goals, even from a scientific or technological perspective. They each support collective betterment, even while feeling very individualized and separate from the crowd. These planets cannot merge and lose themselves to mass consciousness. They are too identity-conscious.

We will feel the tug-of-war implied by having to deal with two motivational forces that often want to go in dissimilar directions. We start off with the usual manifestations of feeling different from others (Uranus), yet not liking to be singled out as peculiar or strange (Saturn). Maybe other children sensed we didn't fit in to the approved structures demanded by convention because we looked or just plain felt unusual to them. At home, we may have gotten mixed messages about freedom versus caution, or about being just ourselves versus molding ourselves to gain the acceptance of the community. Parents may not have openly argued these issues while we were at the dinner table, but on an unconscious level (the Outer Planets—such as Uranus—start to introduce personal and collective unconscious factors into the picture) we absorbed the notion that being unconventional will incur social rejection, or that being too strait-laced will suffocate our spirit. Meanwhile, we start to become aware that we are more willful and headstrong than anyone realized, and that we want to invent our own social path.

Most of us probably had to do our Saturn routine in our childhood, since everyone around us was some kind of authority figure who managed us. But in the 1990s, the trend has been for kids to jump into their Uranus potential much too soon while avoiding their needed Saturn lessons. This can create a wild, defiant energy regarding social structure. The lawless behavior of some youth has been well observed. Uranus seeks quick release of tension, suggesting explosive results, often without a sense of the consequences of reckless action. The lack of Saturn development implies that parental authority has been lax. Such children know little about their capacity for inner discipline, patience, delaying gratification until a better time, and respect for the boundaries of others. Stress aspects (including the conjunction) suggests problems with balanced Saturn/Uranus expression. Too much of one planet seems to trigger a strong reaction from the other (with too much Saturn, Uranus finds ways to force sudden change by bringing disruptive elements into our lives).

It seems many of us are more paradoxical than rebellious. We are not consistent in how we play out our role in society.

We tend to follow those rules that further our ambitions and assure our material security, but we also have other areas where we can be very unconventional and risk-taking (responsible civil servant on weekdays, nude sky-diver on weekends...wheee!). We can live two separate lives in a way that may surprise others. With trines and sextiles, some of us have a great way of merging the experimental with the tried and true. We don't polarize these energies inside us, but find easier ways to blend them in the outer world. A few of us even have a marvelous talent for appealing to both the old-fashioned and the ultra-modern without threatening either. We can sensibly unite the qualities each type supports in an ingenious manner. We can reach a wider gamut of society by presenting new visions sensibly or old ideas dressed up in refreshing ways.

One issue that can prove problematic is that of self-will and how we apply it. Both Saturn and Uranus can be quite self-reliant, not wanting to depend on others. We probably like to see what we can do for ourselves before anyone else gets involved. But in some cases, this can lead to an uncooperative spirit. We may willfully try to control everything that involves us, not wanting people to steer us in any way. Uranus is more self-centered than metaphysical astrologers would like to admit. Saturn is also a very self-contained planet that would rather exclusively take care of its own needs without the interference of others who could mess things up or perform poorly.

Together, Saturn/Uranus reinforces a disposition that doesn't give in to people easily if doing so means a loss of autonomy. We keep our distance and protect our space from being invaded. While authorities can suggest guidelines, their sales pitch has to be brilliant for us to agree to work within imposed limits. Unalterable mandates won't sit well at all, and we can stubbornly hold our ground and not give an inch—even if it jeopardizes our slowly built structures and puts our professional life in a tailspin. A part of us may feel that supporting our inner truth is more critical than bowing down to outside controlling forces we have no respect for. We probably don't even wait to get fired for insubordination—we dramatically quit! Obviously, we need to avoid hasty decisions by tempering our impetuous spirit with a measure of common sense and practicality.

TRANSIT

When Saturn transits our Uranus, we need to analyze our current state of affairs and determine how much Uranian activity we have allowed ourselves up to this point in our life. If we have sensibly experimented with our Uranus potential in the past and have made room for individualistic changes in small but constructively personalized areas of our life, Saturn is now telling us to give form to our current intuitional feelings and see what kind of fresh new mental structures we can build for ourselves. Something Uranian has to come out of a process that is being directed by Saturnian elements from the outside, such as our social environment.

This doesn't sound like we should end up frustrated, as might be the case if transiting Uranus were to instead contact our natal Saturn and we found ourselves too insecure to try different options. However, Saturn does suggest that what we can do at this time to galvanize Uranus is limited for various reasons. Maybe it's a critical time factor that forces us to make our changes efficiently and not try to put things off. We need to take action while everything is falling quickly into the place, since destabilizing factors are already at work and changeability is in the air. Too much needless delay could throw off this optimum timing, and we later discover that we lost a rare opportunity because of foot-dragging and indecisiveness. Sextiles and trines may allow us more leeway in terms of timing and action, but not much. Conjunctions, squares, and oppositions push for us to seize the moment and start organizing our new approach, though not rigidly. Adaptability seems to be important no matter what the aspect is. Both planets suggest we need to rely on ourselves to get an exciting project off the ground. Maybe Saturn helps us recognize our dormant genius. We should at least be better able to shape and define future goals.

Uranus is fickle and Saturn can only do so much to structure a situation that can free up our energies and usher in new features. Our reaction to having our natal Uranus triggered can be typically unpredictable. Saturn is trying to tone down our restless discontent as well as any urgent impulse to abandon existing securities. It instead favors using such unrest to awaken us to reasonable possibilities at hand with a degree of social cooperation, while working within an authoritative structure. This is not intrinsically a defiant transit, unless we were born with a stressful Saturn/Uranus aspect we have yet to resolve. In this case, the transit just sets off the natal dilemma. (Even a transiting sextile can set off a natal square or opposition.) Still, if the Saturn energy is viewed as antagonistic to our Uranian independence, and this provokes our law-breaking tendencies, there could be trouble.

What kind of trouble? Often, we can have clashes with people who control us professionally, legally, or psychologically. We project big bad Saturnian traits onto these people, assuming they are trying to overpower us and rob us of our liberties. We resist them with a fierceness we seldom have shown before. Saturn/Uranus tends to create a pressure-cooker kind of tension. Saturn tries to keep the lid on something that's beyond letting off steam—it's capable of blowing up. Uranus rules explosives, but Saturn rules the timer that controls the detonator device. For us, timing is very important to the success of our Uranian ventures if we are to prevent matters from chaotically blowing up in our face. Uranus does not like to be stifled by time limits, though. Uranus will try to do whatever it takes to outsmart Saturn and to escape Saturn's clutches. This can result in some pretty desperate acts. But like it or not, Saturn is in the driver's seat, steering this transit, and will win out in the long run. It doesn't pay to get too crazy about things happening to us at this time, or to destabilize others by our rash actions.

If we just play by the rules we find the outcome isn't as bad as anticipated, so why the big panic? Why the frantic rush? Saturn is offering us the wisdom of slowing down and concentrating on the details. We will need to compromise now rather than attempt to defy the powers that be. Remember, this advice is particularly pertinent for those having an opposition, square, or conjunction. If we are experiencing a trine or sextile, nothing escalates to such a tensional degree. We may even identify more with the Saturn role, meaning we impose certain controls and disciplines on ourselves as our best way to fulfill our brilliant and timely plans of action. We may find others being very supportive and even offering their Saturnian expertise. If so, we need to remember not to single-mindedly attempt to take charge of every detail of our master plan. Give-and-take is hard for us during this transit, but stubborn refusal to meet people halfway can lead to stalemates and impasses that eventually have an unpleasant Uranian ending.

What's good about any Saturn transit is that it forces us to take a clear, objective look at the real needs of whatever planet is being contacted. In this case, we are getting a chance to more closely observe and analyze the typically less exercised Uranian parts of our nature—facets of our personality that our routine-bound everyday world does not encourage or even understand. With Uranus, we often feel we lack personal role models to show us how we are to implement this planet's innovative principles. As a result, we often get a chance to invent things as we go along, experimenting here and there, trying stuff out for the very first time in some cases—pretty amazing stuff, at that.

Saturn can be a firm but caring guide ready to warn us of and steer us away from Uranian pitfalls. For example, violent outbursts of a random, unjustified nature are Uranian (like earthquakes, as opposed to Mars violence, which always has a definite target for its anger). That pressure-cooker potential of Saturn/Uranus could result in a sudden loss of control and a capacity for damaging whatever gets in the way of Uranus' tornado-like force. Saturn's suppression of such

Uranian turbulence can actually add to its fury, but Saturn is also trying to modulate this hard-to-control planet so that its energy becomes workable for us rather than destructive. A secret to success is learning to use this energy in impersonal ways, not self-centered ones. Neither of these planets is willing to cater to the selfish "me, me, me" side of our nature for too long before wanting to shift gears and tackle larger societal concerns. Doing something that can bring some facet of truth to the many can be a challenging but progressive way to use any Saturn/Uranus transit.

This often involves work (Saturn) of an uncommon nature (Uranus). Science and technology have often been mentioned in astrological texts as potential areas of focus. Such fields have been of interest to only a minority of individuals until recently, with the mushrooming growth of home computers and the expanding access to the Internet (and the lure of the World Wide Web, spawned by the recent Uranus/Neptune in Capricorn conjunction in the early to mid 1990s). Luckily, our children or grandchildren are more than willing to teach us how to navigate cyberspace if we are willing to stop blocking our ability to learn something very unfamiliar, but also very exciting. Brushing up on computer skills can be a marvelous way to channel a lot of Saturn/Uranus energy. In the world of computers, information is retrieved very rapidly (Uranus) but still the process of how to access the information is structured and is usually reliable (Saturn). If some of us are still pecking away at a manual or electric typewriter, a good Saturn sextile to our Uranus may be just what we need to get us on the information superhighway.

Even a square or opposition may provide the right push to get us curious and energized, but it is important to go at a slower pace and not try to learn too much too soon. Otherwise, we may feel unreasonably aggravated with the progress we are not making with anything new we are being introduced to at this time. We need patience to accept we cannot absorb everything there is to know in an unrealistically short period of time.

CHAPTER SEVENTEEN

SATURN IN PISCES

SURREAL'S SO REAL

As with any Piscean placement, Saturn in this sign can ascend to great heights of spiritual self-mastery, or it can plunge to earthbound depths of despair and darkness. Pisces is the most complex sign of the Zodiac, even more multi-faceted in its mysteries than Scorpio. Pisces is the end of a cycle of human experience on the evolutionary spiral, where we get to distill the deeper meaning of all those lessons we have had to deal with in the previous signs. Whatever injuries, confusions, losses, and alienations have not been successfully transfigured and integrated into the spiritual essence of our totality are to be dissolved and sacrificed to a greater pool of consciousness, where the energy pattern can be cleansed and reformulated.

Dissolving this residual crud is one way to divest these failures and incomplete experiences of their power over us, but if only partly dissolved, the essence of any failure or incompletion may remain, perhaps carried over from past lives (or into future ones). We may live with unresolved issues in this lifetime that weigh us down due to our lack of understanding and/or proper closure.

Saturn in Pisces can thus be a difficult position for this sign, which already comes into the world sensing unfinished business or a feeling that something from the past is haunting its consciousness—something that can't be easily defined. Yet Saturn is a planet that needs well-defined structure. On some level, Saturn can help the otherworldly Piscean imagination rise up from its nebulous ethers and find a home in forms of unearthly beauty and spiritual power. More about this soon—but meanwhile, we may carry within an irrational feeling that we still have obligations to meet or actions to atone for from our intangible sense of our past. This sounds like a case of karmic jet lag.

Saturn crystallizes experiences, making them very solid and real to us. Piscean experiences are often better left on the inner realms where we can silently engage in deep reflection and contemplation. But when made tangible, even some of our wildest fantasies can become problematic and nightmarish. We have a great tendency to feel that our inner life will take on a power of its own in our physical world, and if we are more phobic than creative, such fears become manifested through the people and situations we attract. If we think about killing someone we're angry about, and they get hit by a careening beer truck in noonday traffic the next day, some of us feel certain we caused it to happen, that our private fantasy had the power to control the details of the whole scenario. It can be especially tormenting when we hate a parent who then suddenly dies. Lots of therapy may then be awaiting us. In short, there can be something oddly superstitious about this placement. I say oddly because Saturn normally would never take the irrational route. It usually pursues anything to its logical conclusion.

Pisces symbolizes the endless kaleidoscope of images that inhabit our unconscious mind. Such imagery typically appears and disappears without rhyme or reason, beyond our control, so much of what we "see" is confusing or even revolting to our conscience. We need to detach and simply watch this surrealistic ongoing film festival in our heads, observing without unduly reacting. But Saturn wants to stop the projector and freeze on certain bothersome frames, so we can get stuck on images that were initially meant to be vivid, even bizarre, but relatively incidental. We now fixate on them, finding them all-consuming. We sensationalize them and give them magical potency over us. This is not a smart idea. Curbing the power of "negative" imagination will be vital for us in this lifetime.

A SAFER MAGIC

Actually, melodrama is not what Saturn in Pisces needs. If we do have a special ability to manifest our dreams, let them be good dreams. Pisces has a whole lot of heartfelt feelings for the world and all its struggling inhabitants. It wants to protect and envelop all forms of conscious beings by unifying all energy fields. That way, nobody or no thing ever gets left out in the cold or the void. Saturn typically fights such connectiveness for fear that nothing definable and recognizable will remain. Everything gets subsumed by the big blob of timeless unspace (or whatever else this inexplicableness may be called). Such a state of affairs, just like the concept of eternity, scares Saturn, so, it may block much of the true magic Pisces can provide. We somehow need to feel we can be safe (or at least safer) in Neptune's realm.

It is often best that we allow ourselves to feel empathy for our fellow beings and do what we can to ease the transition we've all made from the more sublime dimension of spirit to this denser plane, where everyone is seemingly on his or her own to create earthbound realities. The trouble is, Saturn doesn't sense much real cosmic connection on this level. We tend to shut off the finest images and inspirations this sign can offer us in favor of its darker spells and enchantments.

The all-inclusive mentality of Pisces can degrade into a sense of paranoia, where we assume everyone is unified in order to plot or scheme against us. Conspiracy fears can be big with this untrusting Saturn. Maybe it's a case of assuming all people are essentially cold and uncaring, which puts us into a trance of self-pity. Saturn already knows it's hard enough dealing with surviving in the material world. Why, on top of that, does it also have to defend itself against invisible threats? This is tricky stuff for Saturn. We need to find a sane way to make our Saturn understand that Piscean consciousness need not be scary or overwhelming.

Steady Sacrifice?

Some of us had a few bad knocks in life at an early age that pulled the rug under us, security-wise. Maybe devastating things beyond anyone's control left us with a few big holes in our heart. It is questionable whether or not our parental upbringing fulfilled many of our essential safety needs. Abandonment themes can be very common here, even if our parents were never out of our sight (but we were often out of their minds). Usually the dread of being left alone is all too real because of a tragic incident that gave birth to our gaping inner wound (although we may be the only ones who can still see that scar). Whatever happened or didn't get to happen to us has made us feel not very sure-footed with living on the planet. We sense that much of what others take for granted is inaccessible to us, and that pains us deeply. We've had to make emotional sacrifices at a tender age, and if not careful, may continue to feel we still have to as adults, when our suffering is no longer educational. This is a soul-damaging situation. It would be a godsend if, at an early age, we were exposed to belief systems that teach different ways to spiritual enlightenment or redemption than through victimization or martyrdom, but this often has not been the case.

On Our True Path

We need to avoid like the plague any authoritarian doctrines that focus harshly on human sinfulness, or our puny insignificance compared to The Almighty, or even non-theistic

philosophies that claim life is basically meaningless and pur-
poseless (nihilism), or that we are here to fight off a hostile
universe through sheer force of will and the utter acceptance of
full personal responsibility, without faith in a higher purpose
to it all (as suggested in some schools of existentialism).
Saturn might find a bit of this appealing due to its pessimistic,
cynical streak, but Pisces energy cannot deeply nourish the
soul on such hope-deficient paths of being and becoming.

Even when delving into more "new age" beliefs, some of us
will need to analyze the nature of rituals and dogmas others
teach or preach. Guilt can too easily enter the picture and
force us to behave in a passive, slavish manner that goes
counter to our best inner growth (it's Pisces doing that
"trance" thing again). Do we chant to be perfect or just to be
more open to the flow of life's fuller dimension? Are we trying
to force ourselves to get every karmic debt paid off and close
the account in this lifetime by not daring to break any spiritual "laws," or will we just "be here now" and serenely let our
karmic timetable take care of itself? Another very important
question is: Do we entrust all our Piscean needs for total healing and purifying transformation to the authority of some
charismatic person who plays the role of high priest or priest-
ess, cosmic channeler, esotericist, religious hierophant, psychic master, spiritual guide from ancient Lemuria, etc.? We
may be in for a tremendous disillusionment if we do not apply
Saturn's gift of selectivity and common sense to Pisces' power
to believe in anything that promises altered states of consciousness—even the subtle authority of mind-altering drugs
and the distorted hallucinations they produce.

SERVING THE UNDERDOG

Since healing is important to Pisces and fixing what's broken
works well for Saturn, together they can do wonders to help
repair others who are life's walking wounded. We may gravitate toward areas where behind-the-scenes service is in critical need. One of our greatest natural psychics, Edgar Cayce,

was born with this Saturn (plus Sun in Pisces). Serving others in physical or mental pain was the foundation of his whole adult life. But we can do our own kind of healing in an even more down-to-earth fashion by finding charitable ways to pitch in when the community is asking for help. Fundraisers and volunteer programs that aid people in down-and-out situations can be rewarding. Remember, on some level we can identify with people experiencing tragedies or special hardships, so our ability to render excellent (even magical) service is above average.

Before we sign up to work at the downtown soup kitchen or manage the hotline phones at the local AIDS center, though, we will need to make sure we can lovingly detach from our emotions and function from a point of inner strength. We need to be able to be humane without being overcome with sorrow and grief. Since Saturn here can magnify vivid images it can't easily let go, we may otherwise take our experiences home and feel very depressed or distressed about the ills of the world. Dramatizing life's most horrible conditions can deplete our energy and make us sick on some level. Inner resilience is needed for facing up to life's harsher realities and other people's sufferings. Getting depressed helps nobody, particularly ourselves. Saturn can function as a buffer here, allowing us to serve without feeling overwhelmed.

Quiet Time

Pisces supports the power of stillness and quiescence. Silent moments are very important in helping restore our energy, especially when we pick careers where people problems can easily tax or deplete our strength. The trick is getting Saturn to stop being task-oriented long enough to relax and get away from life's constant demands. Pisces itself has less trouble being idle, as it likes to escape into daydreaming and other forms of creative visualization. Pisces helps us clear the mind of pressing worldly concerns, but that is something Saturn doesn't do easily. We will thus need to discipline ourselves to accept mental unbusyness as an important part of our spiritual health. With Saturn, it would be good to allot a specific time each day when we can unwind in a private, tranquil setting. This does sound like a perfect Saturn placement for meditation. What is important is not so much the technique we choose, but the regularity of establishing that special quiet time.

If meditation is not appealing (let's say we have too much Gemini, Aries, or Uranus in us and just cannot sit still for twenty minutes at a time), we might find a level of inner composure and tranquillity with artistic endeavors like painting, sculpting, flower arrangement, tie-dye, or weaving. Working in a garden (preferably with a goldfish pond or a mini waterfall) is also calming. Photography can be an excellent channel, especially if we are able to set up a darkroom and do our own photos. We just need to make sure we don't spend too much time in the darkroom! It is likely that when we are at varying states of exhaustion, sleep is the easiest cure for our frazzled nerves and spent emotions. It would be interesting to know if folks with this Saturn can enter deep sleep states.

LIFE'S LITTLE REFLECTIONS

Saturn has come a long way from its first challenges in Aries. By the time it reaches Pisces, we could assume Saturn has learned a lot about life. It senses having been through the ups and down of earthbound living before. Now, the essence of all our worldly strivings is to be absorbed on deep levels of being and knowingness. In personal correspondence, astrologer Jeff Jawer has said, "Saturn is very wise when passing through Pisces." Jeff is pretty wise himself for realizing this. Wisdom gained from suffering could be a common trait of both planet and sign, but wisdom gained from being real with life and open to all its experiences in a non-judgmental manner is also indicated. Perhaps this is one of the most grounding placements for Pisces. Saturn tears away the veils of illusion that otherwise lead us into confusion, but it still takes much of our effort to sustain clarity. Saturn shows that Pisces can bring a dream into manifestation and nurture it through love and devotion. Saturn offers Pisces enough detachment so that we don't retreat and withdraw at the first hint of rejection and conflict.

Staying power is not normally a Piscean asset, but with Saturn the Fish can ride even the roughest waves and still show a determination to heal a needy world in turmoil. Some of us will undoubtedly draw from the power of Saturn in Pisces and create a few social miracles. We know it's partly the workings of a wondrous universe, but also partly due to our human sweat and our innocent gumption to actually do the "impossible"—to move mountains and part seas rather than let ourselves block our visionary path. Still, humility seems to be something that we, in our wisdom, know better than to abandon.

Astro-lebrities with Saturn in Pisces

Isaac Newton	Vanessa Redgrave
Edgar Cayce	Alexander Graham Bell
Karl Marx	Glenda Jackson
Jane Fonda	Woody Allen
Thomas Edison	Henry David Thoreau

SATURN IN THE TWELFTH HOUSE

SANCTUARY

It's well established that the Twelfth House is the perfect place to retreat when we want to get away from the bustling, hectic world and find a little tranquillity. Peace and quiet are what much of this house is all about, even though paradoxically the Twelfth House also drums up nightmarish images of bedlam where the insane howl and the disoriented abound in a hellish place of jarring noise and chaos—and that's just of our own inner demons! But for Saturn, it's the silent places of the soul that are most sought after. Neptune in the Twelfth House is much like this too, except that Neptune has a special talent for zoning out—meaning it closes its eyes and flies at the speed of mind to other dimensions where time and space pose no barriers, perfectly unaware of its everyday mundane surroundings. Neptune is quite a trance-maker.

Saturn can never get that far away from its ability to be aware of form and limitation. Saturn retreats to the Twelfth House to deeply contemplate why things turn out the way they do. Saturn will dig deeply to understand the purpose behind the endings of situations and relationships, especially when they've ended badly or without sufficient explanations. The Twelfth House is where we hide a lot of our loose ends, but Saturn always finds them and gets very anxious. However, its strong point is organizational power, which is no easy feat in this house of formlessness and anti-matter. What could be suggested is soul structuring, where we learn to build consciousness carefully on our most internal levels. Saturn is learning not to fear the limitless world of the spirit within. By establishing a meditative atmosphere where stillness is emphasized, we can learn to recognize the reality of our spiritual self and feel its constant, protective presence. Saturn always wants a solid connection wherever it's located, and in the Twelfth House, we have an ability to bring more of our Higher Self into earthly manifestation, perhaps through the power of visualization. But first we have to dissolve a lot of barriers that block our path to such self-awareness.

HIDDEN WEAKNESSES

Some of us may have to deal with burdensome situations as part of our karmic plan for growth in this incarnation. We can suffer in solitude—at least, our pain is invisible to those we deal with in the day-to-day world. We learn to become excellent concealers. But since this is the house of behind-the-scenes activities or hidden circumstances, we are reluctant to come out and expose our more serious problems to others without feeling inexplicably guilty or more embarrassed and humiliated than is reasonable. A few of us opt to lock away and guard our troubling fears (Saturn rules locks and bolts), while moping around like a martyr or victim of fate, figuratively wearing a "kick me" sign.

Maybe we don't even mope but instead show a false self-assurance and an assertive drive to accomplish that keeps others from prying into our hidden parts. We over-achievers may try to conquer the hypnotic pull of the unconscious by putting all our energies into establishing ultimate values of the earthly kind. Winning the game of material life is then the ideal we put on a pedestal, while our soul needs are little understood or woefully neglected. It's not a common manifestation, but it can occur. Actually, Saturn does call for a sensible embrace of both spirit and matter. Making peace with being in the world while doing what we can to bring peace would be a goal to envision, but Saturn needs to know how far it can realistically fulfill this dream to avoid disenchantment.

Retreating for purely escapist reasons, to avoid people contact rather than to confront the great Oneness of life, can be the unwise way Saturn deals with anxiety. We can be hyper-vulnerable to our own crippling doubts or plagued with self-pity. We hardly want to realize that we are so fearful, much less have strangers or loved ones know this about us. We will need to do some honest self-confrontation to determine if we are allowing imaginary limitations to hem us in. Are we assuming certain negative Saturnian responses from others ("they loathe me...they really loathe me!") while being too chicken to get the facts straight by being direct and addressing certain issues face to face? If so, we choose to remain blind to the real truth, and thus hurt ourselves. Being in the dark about anything is not what Saturn's all about, but the Twelfth House can symbolize covert enemies, and that includes us engaging in hidden self-destructiveness.

For some of us, our interest in self-preservation (Saturn) or our preoccupation with unconditional safety (Twelfth House and Saturn) can be almost morbid. Inhibitive Saturn helps foster psychological repressions that can hide away and incubate for long periods of time. If not broken down and released through an active attempt at self-realization, these repressed parts can become chronic problems for our psyche, contributing to a bitter sense of loneliness and social alienation. Who really wants that kind of life? Apparently, some do. The soul is trapped in a steel cage and can only face out into a bleak world where darkness dwells.

But this is only one part of the puzzle for Saturn in the Twelfth House. There are redeeming elements as well, since the Twelfth House in many ways exists for the hope of soul renewal and the affirmation of the fresh and innocent cycle soon to be experienced in the First House.

INNER STRENGTHS

This can be a house of sacrifices, made more karmic by Saturn's presence here. Saturn tests character through restrictions and denials, and here it falls in a sector of private sorrows and disappointments. Life can be a painful experience for those of us who lack or refuse to develop spiritual knowledge, or at least deep psychological awareness. Simply living on the surface of the physical world and never delving within to examine and reflect could cut us off from a main source of inner comfort and universal meaning, and we might end up feeling drained or defeated by the mundane world.

We need contact with our Twelfth House to help renew our soul whenever we have become too immersed in our material roles and weighed down by our practical responsibilities. To be disconnected would rob us of opportunities to restore ourselves by recharging our spiritual batteries. But when this combination is handled well, we can draw from inner psychological strengths that enable us to courageously endure personal and collective hardships with a mature understanding that somehow, something purposeful is behind whatever otherwise appears to be senseless failure or tragedy. Saturn is a planet that can help us develop true wisdom.

But Saturn also demands justice, and often we see too many injustices in the world that do not get corrected, which can lead to cynicism or a lack of faith in any higher power.

Still, Saturn can imply that as we grow and experience more of what the world has to offer, we can show a determination to pierce through the illusions of our lives and seek a clearer comprehension of the external realities of existence. This could be an excellent position for the serious, scientific study (though not necessarily the active application) of psychic phenomena, mystical awakening, or any cosmology that helps better explain the mysteries of consciousness itself.

Researching the mind-body connection may also be compelling for some of us who wish to explore the healing theme of this house. In fact, researching anything complex or deeply hidden is a great way to use Saturn in the Twelfth House (or in the Eighth House). Maybe for some, the alien inner worlds being contacted are on the micro-cellular level, which is as removed from our daily lives as are the nirvanic planes. It is essential that we have something of interest that allows us to penetrate layer by layer until we uncover its hidden features, and it's best if these features tie into universal awareness or the underlying unity of all life. Then we can feel we are not as isolated and cut off as it appears; that we instead belong to a greater structure that will not exclude or abandon us. The fear of abandonment is typically strong here, and we need to pursue whatever knowledge that helps us feel we are an important part of the Whole.

Vague Ambition

The more competitive our culture and the stronger its message to push to the top, the more many of us feel bewildered and out of sync. The is not a place that feels like home to the worldly go-getter, because Twelfth House ambitions can lack clear definition. We can have a feel for what we want to do, but can't fill in certain essential details. But with Saturn as our astrological key to career and professional performance, what we do for a living needs to incorporate a few Twelfth House values. What are our best assets here? A serious concern for community welfare and even global peace is typically found. We can feel for the plight of the underdog and are typically upset about social inequalities and the destructive side of class distinctions. Careers that help remedy the conditions of the socially disenfranchised or the "rejects" of society may appeal to our idealistic sense of duty and obligation. People trapped in very turbulent situations due to economic hardship or personal instability may be those we wish to help restructure or rehabilitate. Of course, many of these jobs can be hard on the psyche for those who have not begun their inner Saturn work early in life. We'll need to toughen or loosen up a bit so that we can flow with the currents of a higher, inspirational power.

The sad truth is that many of the service-oriented careers that do excellent Twelfth House healing do not pay well, unless we are willing to strive to reach top-level positions of administration and executive power. But we often are less driven or committed to reach key positions, especially when the unfoldment of our path seems fuzzy to us to begin with. What if we feel plagued by professional uncertainties and want to later bail out? It's easier to quit a career when lots of people are not counting on us for both their direction and their livelihood.

If we desire to be self-employed in one of the many available healing arts, we'll need to be careful not to undercharge or do too much exchanging of services—such as our deep muscle massage for an aura cleansing session. Once in a while is fine, since it shows we trust the Universe to support our economic needs, but only real bucks will pay our very real bills. Our business instincts are potentially not the soundest.

If our material ambitions are more immaterial to us than we recognize, or if we never seem to be getting anywhere with our time and efforts, it could be that our true security comes more from intangibilities. That's fine for our inner soul growth, but not so good for the practical realities of living. We need to look at any unrealistic expectations we have regarding our career potential. Some of us may float from job to job in hopes of miraculously landing the perfect career some day. It can happen, but not necessarily by dumb luck. We need to visualize our capacity to realistically help society in a humanitarian way. If we turn our backs on people in dire need, a part of us feels more than guilty—it feels a nagging sense of discontent and chronic aimlessness. Humanity needs to be the object of our concern in some fashion. Saturn says we can help build powerful structures for the support of many in need. Quiet but competent service without much fanfare or publicity is to be sought.

GONE WITH THE EGO?

Saturn is a very self-contained planet, but the Twelfth House is where we engage in more selfless activities in which our ego and our "I"-consciousness often take a back seat. Saturn does what it can to protect our ego, which has a right to shine in each and every house. So here is a point of conflict: Saturn can put the brakes on Twelfth House attempts to dissolve our ego's boundaries. This is where we try to block the flow of universal currents that might otherwise help us become part of a unified field of consciousness and feel connected to others at an essence level. The threat of losing the sense of self in the process frightens Saturn.

But it could also be that we need to fortify our ego to protect ourselves from the uncontrolled flow of images and energies from the unconscious. These could prove overwhelming and disruptive to the functions of "normal" waking consciousness. It would be like never coming out of the dream state, and that could really terrify Saturn. Losing a grip on reality or going mad are high on the list of this planet's worst fears, so we may not allow ourselves to be susceptible to altered states of awareness. Even if we don't believe in higher consciousness at the moment, we do guard our here-and-now consciousness and do not trust having it tampered with.

However, when very well managed, some of us are able to keep our sense of selfhood intact while being open to universal energy and collective currents. We can become steady and reliable vehicles for social enlightenment. We may learn a lot—maybe the hard way—about spiritual love and humility. What we probably most need to learn on the ego-level is how to serve people uncomplainingly and without petty criticism of the imperfections of others (think of the challenge of having Saturn in Virgo in the Twelfth House square Mercury in the Third House). Maybe fear, doubt, over-analysis, shame, mistrust, coldness, aloofness, and defensiveness are just some of the Saturn manifestations that the ego needs to let go of and dissolve for good. We can be much needed comforters for the sick and the weak, as long as we don't make ourselves sicker and weaker in the process.

Saturn is interested in the closing of life cycles, as is the Twelfth House. Maybe we do have some serious karma to work out. We may need to repair our soul foundation from past life damage or harm we did to ourselves and/or others. Atonement is needed on some level, but harsh punishment and self-condemnation only perpetuate the worst this Saturn placement can attract. The discipline of unconditional self-love is probably the hardest lesson of all. People we have put our faith in may have betrayed us, or let us down in some fashion again and again. We are to witness all this during our life and make a few mental notes, but not identify with such low quality treatment. Constantly carrying such heavy baggage on our shoulders during our soul's journey can break our spirit. Learning to develop all the structure we need from within keeps us feeling safe and sane, and we find we are strong enough to give much of ourselves to the world for all the right reasons.

Astro-lebrities with Saturn in the Twelfth House

Galileo	Lily Tomlin
Indira Gandhi	Walt Whitman
Margaret Thatcher	Pope John Paul II
Mark Twain	Charles Darwin
Emily Dickinson	Robert Redford

SATURN/NEPTUNE ASPECTS

NATAL

This planetary pairing is not easily synthesized due to the strongly contrasted natures involved. Some common denominators focus on downbeat themes. Both planets can feel the heaviness of living on Earth with all its physical limitations, although Saturn plods on and endures while Neptune seeks avenues of escape. Saturn tends to bring out the ponderous, weighty side of Neptune while Neptune underscores Saturn's sense of social duty with its own feeling of collective obligation. Both are sensitive to themes of social oppression and injustice, strongly aware when people are mistreated or enslaved on some level. Both planets can experience sacrifice and loss, and both can be in denial when their weaknesses and shortcomings are pointed out. Saturn and Neptune also can react with fear and distrust when threatened, whether or not there is any real danger. Neptune can get the blues and feel very sorry for itself, while Saturn can get depressed thinking it's been given a raw deal. Together, they can reinforce a defeatist attitude, or at least a very thin-skinned reaction to criticism. Both planets resort to defensive shielding during times of vulnerability. Saturn is an expert at putting up walls and barriers to protect itself from losing its structure and form. Neptune simply retreats into a state of emotional withdrawal, making it unreachable and inaccessible.

Saturnian fears are typically based on objective reality and the probable consequences of action taken. With Saturn, we sense we are paying our dues or getting what's coming to us for past indiscretions or errors in judgment. Our conscience tells us we've over-stepped our bounds or have broken certain rules or laws, and now we must face the music and pay the price. Neptunian fears and forebodings are often more the product of distorted thinking or an over-worked, emotionally charged imagination. Such fears can be vague in content, not easily contained by common sense analysis, and seldom related to current reality. Nonetheless, they are real and potent in terms of the invisible grip they can have on us. Saturn/Neptune stress aspects can emphasize all the above.

When mismanaged, Saturn/Neptune implies we do not easily trust that anybody or anything will give us solid support. We worry that nothing will remain permanent once we surrender ourselves to any experience in good faith, that the rug will be pulled from under us. Saturn has seen how Neptune can make things evaporate or disappear, and thus cannot feel firmly grounded the way it needs to. Neptune also has sensed how Saturn's negativism and pessimism have aborted many of the beautiful ideals that Neptune yearns to fulfill. Saturn's cold splash of reality has often dashed our Neptunian high hopes, or perhaps many of Neptune's unworkable pipe dreams have left the sober Saturnian side of ourselves feel used and cheated. It's no wonder that some of us feel like pawns of fate, even though we are not. We can be deeply uncertain about life's intentions for us, especially as we get older and keep finding ourselves going down dead-end roads.

If we take the defeatist path and assume we are too unlucky to ever get a fair break, we run the risk of becoming increasingly suspicious of the world and ultimately of God and the Cosmos. Maybe, we reason, there is no God to hear and comfort us. We could deem existence itself as essentially fraudulent, feeling that nothing has the higher meaning or divine purpose the masses fool themselves into believing. Such a bleak world view can create further loneliness and alienation for us. Obviously, we are identifying in this case too much with negating Saturn and not enough with faith-inducing Neptune. But Neptune adds to the problem by its capacity to inflate a concept and make it all inclusive, so that if a little bit of our life is rotten, all of existence is too! Anything contacting Neptune can balloon and become overwhelming.

But when masterfully handled, Saturn/Neptune can indicate we have a strong and unwavering faith in the orderliness of a compassionate universe. We come to recognize our fears as misunderstandings of the divine process, due to ignorance and an awareness of reality held back by the organic limitations of a physical brain. Fear becomes more a by-product of limited vision or no vision at all. With sextiles and trines, we are prone to accept the part that pain plays in sensitizing us to empathy and universal concern. Suffering (not necessarily our own) helps open our eyes and hearts to the value of real responsiveness to living. A degree of detachment is required, but this is not to imply coldness and remoteness. It simply means we learn to pull back and see the overview which may help put things in a better and broader focus.

Regarding the issues of social duty and obligation, these planets do not cater to exclusively egocentric needs. Saturn and Neptune are better suited to implement needed collective values and ideals—helping to make the dreams of a society real. Saturn's ingrained sense of ethical integrity and moral responsibility can be uplifted to loftier levels by Neptune's vast perspective. Neptune permits us to see the world as a unified ecosystem, held together by love and human understanding. The trine seems to especially comprehend this. To make these aspects work for us, we should strive not to undertake dutiful commitment based on pure emotionalism or blind faith. Are we continually giving more than we get back from others, leaving us perpetually drained and silently resentful? If so, we could easily slip into a dysfunctional, martyr-like mode without realizing it. What could have started out as selflessness may end up as severe ego-denial. The resultant emotional and physical burn-out that results is not a pretty sight. Anyone with Saturn/Neptune in a hard angle pattern (including the conjunction) needs to learn plenty about the art of self-preservation if he or she is determined to embark on the rocky road to sainthood.

At their best, both planets are motivated to serve the greatest social good possible (not always an easy thing to determine). But when poorly handled, Saturn/Neptune aspects mean we can undergo emotional disappointments and material disillusionments to the point that we end up feeling like failures. We can lose faith in ourselves or rob ourselves of our honor and dignity as we spiral downward, and become vulnerable to being swindled and cheated by others with unsavory motives. Life can turn into one big rip-off, and the role we often play is that of the gullible victim. Will our hard luck stories never cease? Even those who look glamorously successful and accomplished on the outside could still feel victimized on the inside. Keeping our dark secret to ourselves is also a sure way to continue feeling imprisoned. Shame can take control of us if we don't reach out for help, which is not easy for some of us to do. But Neptune is the planet of miraculous conversions and Saturn is very much into rebuilding what is salvageable. Together, their message is "keep the faith."

Another common trait of Saturn and Neptune is a monkish disposition. These planets can turn away from gregarious lifestyles in favor of quiet seclusion and privacy in an environment free of human chaos and dissension. They don't need a lot of noise and movement. A hermit-like temperament can result, especially if we feel we've been beaten down by life enough and need to get away. Some of us apparently can survive and function without the intensity, excitement, and passion others crave. An ascetic streak can prompt us to materially possess little. Such instincts could give us the necessary time and space to structure our spiritual/mystical side, resulting in self-mastery. Meditation may not even be as important for us as is pure silence. We can thrive when relating to nature's wonders, which can renew our soul.

TRANSIT

Saturn transiting our natal Neptune might be easier to handle than having Neptune contact our natal Saturn, but it all depends on what we do with the challenges involved. How have we been using our Neptune thus far? Beautiful dreams for humanity sound marvelous, but what if instead we have been sleeping a lot, drinking cheap booze instead of eating right, or loafing around in a non-productive, semi-vegetative state? Have we perhaps been parasitic, leaning on too many others for all kinds of support? Is ours an addictive or deceptive approach to having what we want in life? If any of this is so, then Saturn has its work cut out for itself—and so do we. Remember, Saturn loves to take out the trash. How much trash have we allowed to pile up lately?

Neptune can get caught up in tracks of self-destructive behavior that mindlessly repeat again and again. We may feel helpless to stop these addictive cycles, but Saturn is saying this is not so. Control is on the way, even if from external sources. Life will usher people and situations that may come down hard on us if that is the only way we can wake up from our stupor and pay attention to what we've been doing or not doing. Brushes with the law are common for those of us who been breaking the rules too often and too easily. A dose of reality is needed for those who have had big visions but have done nothing relevant to help their dreams take flight. Either we get things off the ground now or dreams will die on the runway. Are we hungry for spiritual food but very confused about our direction? Saturn can now help us put the pieces together and direct our energy so that we can be clearer about what we really believe in—those deeper values that mean the most to us.

The common denominator is a willingness to commit to whatever it takes to restore our faith in self. Even going to jail for a while can help some of us clean up our act and stop abusing our spirit. Saturn thinks of the beneficial, long-range results in its attempt to stop us from doing negative things. Melodramatic Neptune may view the matter quite differently at the time, thinking it's all pure punishment or karmic torment, but we can start to see a flicker of wisdom once we've withdrawn from whatever has been keeping us stagnant or paralyzed. So, in some area of our current life (check your natal Neptune house for clues), we are giving form to whatever has been nebulous and ill-defined for too long. We are ready to build something we have secretly longed for. We are taking responsibility for reclaiming parts of ourselves that we've chronically disowned, which can include the goodness we really have in us, or the beauty of our inner self and our physical body. It's funny how some out-of-touch Neptunians can love all the baby hippos of the world but still despise their own bulging bellies. We especially need to recognize how very worthy we are of all the love and inner peace the universe wants to feed us. It's time to open wide and take a few bites.

In real life, many of these transits do not always end up enlightening us. Maybe this is because few of us have given our Neptunian needs conscious attention, and typically do not know how to skillfully use Neptune energy. This could be the fault of living in a materialistic culture (this whole book is written from an American perspective) where business and profit are more important than people and creativity. Neptune is quite at home with creative vision, but too many of us have been told at a young age not to take our artistic side seriously, as we couldn't possibly make a "real" living from it. Ironically, now it's rock bands and haute couture models (Neptunians) who rake in millions while school teachers and other public servants (Saturnians) are still underpaid. The truth is, Neptune vision can pay off if we know how to feed the public's imagination what it needs at the moment. But using Neptune—the planet of fads—for quick commercial profit only ensures the transient interest of the fickle masses. Once the trance wears off, the public can abandon us.

This planet has a lot more to offer regarding eternal values, as we find with certain indescribably beautiful works of art and music. Here something of the spiritual dimension has been brought into an earthly form that can be understood by the physical senses. Our parents were wrong. People who totally trust in their vision have been making a living doing their Neptune for centuries. Michelangelo was born with Neptune trine his Saturn, and not only did he excel in various artistic media (marble sculpting being a favorite, which is an appropriate Saturn medium), he became one of the wealthiest artists of his time. He put his complete faith in his Neptune (and God) while satisfying his Saturn/Jupiter worldliness at the same time. Artists need not starve or be poor (symptoms of Neptunian distortion) in order to maintain the purity of their inner vision.

But where does that leave the rest of us who are not the new Michelangelos of the world? We certainly could use this time to explore our hidden creative talents. Stress aspects may emphatically urge us to relieve our worldly weariness through the visual arts, music, dance, or any of the other outlets available. What about photography or maybe even furniture building? The Saturn influence suggests we should learn from an expert, perhaps in a structured class or workshop. We bring our own Neptunian inspiration to the experience, but we are to learn reliable techniques from others who dedicated themselves to perfecting their craft. It would be important at this time not to spend money we don't have (we'd best forget that three-weekend workshop in jewelry making if we know we'll probably need to have our car's water pump repaired at the end of the month). Saturn now must run the show, and will not support frivolous spending—that would in itself become a form of escapism—but buying an inspiring book or two that introduces us to the art of creating beautiful jewelry would fill the need. Better try the local library first, advises practical Saturn.

Saturn's transits to Neptune have been known to be phases when we feel we are losing touch with our everyday world, going bonkers, feeling very trapped, or suffocating on some level. Life can get psychologically messy. What could be happening is that Saturn has given sharper form and focus to those hidden emotions and fears that have remained up until now confusingly vague. Our unaddressed Neptunian parts seem to pop out from our depths and take root in our real world. But things at this time are not as bad as they appear, since Saturn is trying to prevent the total collapse of structure and the utter sense of powerlessness this would entail (though some of us may come very close to the edge of the abyss). Prescription drugs will not remedy this situation, nor will escaping into illusionary romances with people who really have no intention of ever knowing or loving us the way we need. We simply have to sustain our faith in a loving God force and Universe while we pull ourselves through this surreal, dark gothic novel our life has become.

Saturn gives Neptune permission to be real about its secret hurts and wounds. Life says it's okay to be holed up in our homes for an entire weekend just to cry and sleep if that's what feels best, rather than attempt to dutifully attend to a demanding list of practical chores. Eventually, being overwrought with angst and anxiety will prove exhausting (wise Saturn will make sure of that), and we may try alternating between a little work and a little weeping. Some of us may soon find that being busy with something like cleaning out a closet, which brings immediate order to our lives, has a soothing effect on us. Our outer efforts to restore organization help us to feel less disjointed and chaotic. If we have been doing Neptune negatively for too long before this Saturn transit, we likely have allowed external clutter and mess to take over, and there's probably a lot of tidying up we can do. Housecleaning per se will not heal our wounds, but being productively busy doing things that are within our grasp (while putting those "impossible dreams" aside for a while) affords us some sense of control over something we can manage here and now. It becomes a symbolic act of our willingness to straighten out our inner world.

OTHER FACES
OF SATURN

ESOTERIC SATURN

Some of us earthy Saturnian types will need to put on our Jupiter-Neptune space goggles before reading about this level of Saturn, since the cosmic-metaphysical view of this planet's role may seem too awesome and fantastic at times. But according to Theosophy and other esoteric schools of thought (see the writings of Helena Blavatsky and Alice Bailey), all life in our solar system, and thus all consciousness, is considered to originate from the Creative Being (Solar Logos) whose most dense vehicle of expression (physical body) is the Sun. The Solar Logos is that Exalted Consciousness (esotericists like to use capital letters a lot) that humankind calls God. When our solar system was ready to reappear in physical form (apparently it has manifested twice before, countless eons ago), Saturn is said to be the first planet to be constructed. The first of the seven Planetary Logoi to adopt a vehicle of matter was therefore that Great One who now ensouls the planet Saturn.

Thus, Saturn is the Elder One who had the initial responsibility of imposing the basic framework of earthly limitation through the condensing of energy (atoms) to a point where

time and space could come into being through our consciousness. Some occult schools have called Saturn the Keeper of
the Records, since it is said to record all impressions of energy
made on the Akashic ethers from the physical plane. That
means all impressions, no matter how seemingly insignificant—all on one gigantic cosmic CD-ROM. Saturn uses this
data to protect the evolution of life by enforcing the exacting
laws of karma. Saturn acts as our divine agent of ultimate
justice, balance, and wisdom, teaching us to endure all self-
perpetuated hardships and frustrations until a state of soul
perfection has been reached.

During the involutionary arc of experience (creating a
plane of manifestation), Saturn increases and concentrates
our sense of separate identity. This helps us establish a basic
sense of personal ego-consciousness. During this phase of
Saturn's influence, we are to experience a dualistic awareness
of life. Because of this necessary human learning cycle,
Saturn adopts the highly misunderstood role of Satan—the
apparent Slayer of the Knowledge of the One Life.

Satan—as Saturn—becomes the Testing Angel. Those
evolved souls who were trained in the Mystery Schools of the
past realized the necessity for humans to be grounded on the
Earth plane, with all its purposeful restrictions. Such disci-
ples understood the true nature and function of the Satan
(Saturn) force. They realized Satan was a fallen angel
(Lucifer?) cast down from heaven or Unity-Consciousness to
serve a mighty task for God the Father: that of building a
level of density through which Spirit could be self-realized
and allowed to devolve, gather experience, learn lessons, and
then evolve. They did not perceive Satan-Saturn to be an eternal enemy of God or Spirit, and they accepted Satan-Saturn's
function in the educational development of Spirit. Therefore,
we now can feel better about stating that although Saturn is
The Cosmic Taskmaster, it is also our "Great Teacher."

While it seems true that Saturn does rule the laws of
gravity and crystallization, seeming to weigh us down by having us acutely sense our limitations, Saturn also retains the

essence of all efforts toward true spiritual growth within the consciousness of each struggling entity. Saturn is continuously building for each soul a solid foundation through which self-actualization can become a reality. The difficult trials of life are essential prerequisites for the attainment of this self-knowledge. They should not be misread as evil, unjust, or threatening to our well-being. They are a necessary part of working out the Cosmic Plan of our Divine Creator.

Hindu Astrology associates Saturn with the Destroying Angel Shiva. Hindu devotees have long had a high regard for the function of Shiva. They accept the need for all material form, hardened and well defined by Shiva-Saturn, to eventually reach a peak of usefulness as a "container" of energy, and then begin to break down, decompose, and die. This allows the energy locked up in matter to release itself and merge once more with the Great Sea of all-pervading Consciousness. If Shiva-Saturn did not perform this divine operation on the dense physical plane, growth and transformation of matter would be impossible. Shiva also symbolizes procreative forces, so the "death" of form through the regulation of the organized matter's disintegration is truly a process that ensures the "rebirth" of physical form, as well as the eventual liberation of our spirit on the more subtle planes of awareness.

Lastly, Saturn has been called the guardian planet of Earth. It seeks optimum development of the physical form side of life. It constantly recycles matter and, through the gradual but exacting process of evolution, guarantees that Spirit will find conscious vehicles through which it can express itself. Saturn is the most crucial planet of our evolutionary development as ego-centered individuals and as a separate human kingdom. At any particular stage in life, this Dweller on the Threshold exhibits the wisdom to provide us with the most suitable testing experiences designed to allow us a clearer understanding of that which still must be developed or fulfilled in our consciousness.

Earthy types may now take a deep breath and remove your goggles! Hope you enjoyed the view from way above and beyond.

KARMIC SATURN

Beginning students of Astrology are initially taught to associate the Saturn principle with personal limitations, material obstacles, psychological roadblocks, and a restrictive sense of loss and denial. Many of us observe Saturn's symbolism in our natal chart with some measure of inner uneasiness and anxiety, even while we intellectually proclaim Saturn's higher purpose is that of our "wise teacher." Viewing Saturn in its traditional role as a limiting agent is not actually all that "negative." Saturn does indeed operate in this manner within the human experience, but to only see Saturn from this perspective creates an incomplete, unbalanced image of its prime contribution to our soul development. It is a question of intent. Is this planet truly the "Greater Malefic," as centuries of astrological tradition have suggested, grinding us down for no apparent reason? I believe instead that Saturn's limits serve a constructive, higher purpose, presenting challenges intended to develop our souls.

Interpretations about the karmic meaning of Saturn are speculative, so I'm offering my take on this planet and its connection to past lives, keeping in mind that karma may work in some very mysterious ways. Most karmic interpretations of Saturn are pretty dreary, the kind of stuff that makes you feel you've had your hand soundly slapped. The message always seems to be "Whatever you did then, just *don't* do it again!" We can't help thinking that when we were bad a long time ago, we must have been very bad. The actual situation is much more complex than this. Besides, isn't it ornery Mars that usually does most of the "bad" stuff while Saturn takes on all the guilt and regret?

I feel a main source of Saturn difficulty in this lifetime is due to karmic imbalance. This would explain a proclivity to enter the world willing and able to operate in self-inhibitor or over-achiever mode. We don't even have to learn to do so from our family or outside environment. What makes it karmic is how automatically we swing into such (re)action, and at such a tender young age. We either act in a manner that blocks our self-will and ego-assertion (self-inhibitors), or we try to take charge over the world and set up the rules based on our perspective and our needs (over-achievers). Both modes are compulsive and subjective. In general, Saturn squares and oppositions in this lifetime tell us we now have much opportunity to resolve such Saturn karmic imbalance—unless we wish to further sidetrack our growth through a resistance that will only perpetuate fear, pain, and a sense of futility. Unfortunately, self-ignorance keeps many of us defensive and unwilling to penetrate such layers of resistance.

Saturn-style karma is probably bestowed on us from a specific series of past lives that are not necessarily consecutive (Saturn is patient and favors a slow build-up). These are lives in which we have chronically attempted to avoid having our soul growth tested—especially so when Saturn is in fixed signs, long known for their resistance to change. Saturn karma tends to be precise, exacting, and sometimes harsh in ways that can appear unwarranted and unfair. The karma that results in the self-inhibitor's dilemma might indicate we have unknowingly allowed faulty ego-structuring, at some phase of our spiritual evolution, to reach a degree where we now feel awkward and uncomfortable when displaying many of that sign's or house's traits. Over several past lives, we have consistently underplayed our Saturn, taking the passive or ineffectual route rather than the active, dynamic approach. We haven't had enough of the Saturn experiences that would support lives of self-sufficiency and autonomy. Due to underemphasis, we may feel vulnerable and powerless in this incarnation regarding the natural processes of Saturn's sign and house. Our unduly sensitive response to failure only further retards or thwarts the ego defining we need to master self-awareness. This is a lifetime in which we are pressured to deal with our Saturn issues more assertively and openly. Fear and self-doubt tend to be our worst enemies.

If karmic imbalance results in the expression of over-achieving, we may have done our Saturn a bit too well in the past. We are not scared of whatever Saturn may mean for us in this incarnation. Over-achievers have learned to use Saturn aggressively in the past, but perhaps did not learn how to work within limits imposed by society or one's conscience. We often did our Saturn as if nothing could stop us in our tracks! We may have learned to use people and situations shrewdly in the past, and now tend to ignore limits and assume obstacles are meant only for others. We are more uptight about defeat than we are about limitation. But in this life, the rules are different. It's doubtful that we will get a chance to continue ignoring social restraints.

If we are over-achievers and our natal Saturn makes nothing but sextiles and trines, perhaps we can continue to move into the world assertively and try to directly control as many elements of our life as permissible. We are eager to meet life's challenges and flex our Saturnian muscles once more. We have no wish to avoid life's challenges. In contrast, Saturn squares and oppositions (and sometimes the conjunction) combined with the over-achieving mode can mean we are too forceful when displaying our built-in Saturnian traits. We put too much emphasis on supervising the world rather than constructively managing ourselves. Here's where we can adopt domineering traits that alienate people, who then may withdraw their love and respect for us. Getting love and respect are two things we cannot control in people by acts of sheer will—demanding obedience is easier.

There is also a possibility that some of us have the Saturn position we do merely because it represents qualities and experiences natural and appropriate for our present soul growth cycle. I call this karmic necessity. It's kind of a cosmic take on the concept that "Somebody's got to do it, so why not us this time around?" This is a timely incarnation for us to be (re)introduced to the principle of the sign and house expressed through Saturn. In this context, Saturn is not representative of any significant imbalance or distortion from the past, but strictly a here-and-now thing, not evoking any particular level of difficult stress or tension. Maybe this is what is behind an

unaspected Saturn. It is to be experienced sheerly for its stim-
ulative, educational value.

Perhaps our soul at this stage has had little relevant experience in the past dealing with Saturn consciousness according to the interests of its current sign and house (let's say it's
the first time we've come back with Saturn in Pisces in the
First House in 1,300 years). Many things about this sign and
house position have not been brought to our attention to any
significant degree, unlike the more sensitized, troublesome
levels of experience implied by karmic imbalance. Many
awarenesses here may still be dormant or in their budding
stage until we undertake further experiences in this lifetime
to unearth such potential.

Why should this be so? Perhaps previous life conditions
might not have been suitable for us to best comprehend the
primary "lessons" of the sign or house involved—at least with
any depth and conviction Whatever the scenario in the past,
any inner and outer understanding of our present Saturn
dynamics was at best superficially registered. Along with the
environment not being ready to provide us what we needed,
we also may have shown a lack of readiness to undertake the
experiences symbolized. If airplanes were not yet invented way
back when, it was okay since we wouldn't have been psychologically prepared to leave the ground anyway—even if angels
tried to lift our bodies skyward!

Yet should we now be in such a state of readiness, karmic
necessity impersonally dictates that we will be tested in our
ability to begin to integrate our Saturnian interplay more
responsively and actively. The time is ripe. We may not come
into this incarnation feeling overly oppressed or even
strongly impressed by the issues of our Saturn placement.
We are somewhat neutral in attitude, which enables us to
express ourselves here in very natural, spontaneous ways
(although I realize a spontaneous Saturn sounds oxy-
moronic). We approach our Saturn needs on a trial-and-error
basis, often from a point of naiveté and innocence. This
allows us to experience our Saturn sign and house without

undue fear or resistance. We are perhaps allowed more leeway in our actions and reactions than normally would be the
case with Saturn. We are held less accountable for some of
our Saturn actions in this lifetime.

However, there is no cut-and-dry formula for knowing if
we are working with Saturn on this level of karmic necessity.
I'd guess not many are born with this predisposition. A clue
could be if we show no strong reaction to hearing about our
"positive" and "negative" Saturn traits. We don't appear
defensive nor do we show a marked aversion to these qualities. The point here is that we may not be reaping what we've
sown or "paying our dues" as a result of past-life misdeeds.
The karma of retribution need not apply here. Instead, we are
simply offered a special opportunity to continue building fundamental structure in our consciousness as a normal conse-
quence of our own cycle of spiritual unfoldment. The spirit is
ready and the environment has evolved to a point where we
can dig a little deeper into our Saturn potential, and consciously so.

Our Saturn placement can take on a transcendental
dimension of vast importance concerning soul fulfillment if it
is seen as an indicator of spiritual liberation. Few of us are
born already experiencing Saturn on this rarefied level.
Before we get to this elevated place inside ourselves, there
may come a major turning point in our soul evolution where
ego-resistance to Saturn challenges reaches an almost
unbearable pressure point. No longer can we endure the rigidity of our ego-security needs or overbearing attitudes within
ourselves that result in dead-end roads and broken human
connections. Our attempts to avoid difficult confrontations
have been stymied by our tendency to repeatedly attract
them, due to the intense magnetism resistance can create.
Our inner defenses eventually become exhausted, weakening
their grip on our consciousness. If we do not succumb to this
heightened pressure, rendering ourselves neurotic in our
Saturn expression, we then begin to realize we have set ourselves up to undergo these lessons the hard way. We also

begin to understand that what we are seeing as coming from the outside is primarily rooted within.

At this critical juncture in our spiritual evolution, we start to acknowledge the healing, liberating aspects of Saturn. What a wonderful awakening this becomes! Now we may truly be at a stage in which we no longer negate the inner purpose of our Saturn sign and house interplay or attempt to battle against its often threatening outer manifestations. We instead open ourselves up to Saturn as an "Angel of Light."[1] Saturn becomes an enlightening force that finally enables us to close gaps in our psyche's structure that have previously left us disconnected and incomplete. We have effectively learned to mature and stabilize facets of our being that have been underdeveloped or overemphasized. Saturn can liberate us from the false concept that the world of appearances bears its weight on us without any sense of purpose or justice. Once we understand how to best tap into the spiritual resources of our Saturn placement, we may become better equipped to deal with the main purposes of our current incarnation with the greater self-confidence and inner fortitude suggested by our Sun sign and house. Our ego is then flexible and malleable to the point that, due to our masterful self-understanding, we can deal with reality in all its testing variations.

MYTHOLOGICAL SATURN, GRECO-ROMAN STYLE

In Greek mythology, Saturn is referred to as Cronus, the God of Time. Cronus was the offspring of Uranus (god of the airy, heavenly realms) and Gaea (goddess of the Earth). Gaea's giving birth to Cronus suggests that time is specifically a product of physical manifestation. Time comes into being through the existence of form and matter, which in turn springs forth from an undifferentiated primal state, just as Gaea herself sprang from primeval Chaos. Perhaps Cronus' connection with time is further emphasized by the fact that he was the last-born child of Gaea—implying that he had no choice but to wait to manifest. Saturn has eventually become associated down through the centuries with both delays and timely arrivals.

In the Greek myth, Cronus overpowered Uranus and achieved dominion by castrating him. The act of castration vividly symbolizes an occult principle: when the great cosmic impulse of Deity requires manifestation on a physical plane of existence, human awareness and understanding of chaos (timelessness and spacelessness) is rendered impotent and devitalized. Our awareness of the finite, if anything, increases to the point where the power of the intuitional function (Uranus) becomes diminished. Thus, as long as we operate consciously on this earthly plane, Saturn is in full command. Of course, unconscious factors seem always eager to break through the barrier of consciousness and make known their awesome power.

The Greek legend goes on to indicate that Cronus devoured all of his offspring except Zeus, a.k.a. Jupiter (apparently, even in those days, Jupiter was quite the lucky one). The act of consuming his own children hints at the Saturnian function of recycling or reassimilating the products of manifestation through the dissolution of form. In our own life experience, Saturn regulates this principle through the inevitable aging process, which proves time indeed devours all. Yet Cronus was not permitted to swallow Jupiter. Cronus' mate Rhea did a switch-a-roo and gave her husband a stone to swallow instead. A deeper reason Jupiter was spared may be that without Jupiter in active operation, Saturn cannot hope to reach perfection through ideal form in the physical realm. Jupiter is a planet that freely encourages the expanded growth and development of Saturnian form through clear mental vision—mind over matter. Obviously, Jupiter needs to be free from rigid definitions of time and space in order to allow Saturn to function at its optimum. Saturn cannot afford to swallow Jupiter's vision and rob life of all hope. Young Zeus/Jupiter eventually overpowered and dethroned Big Daddy Cronus (sounds like karma coming home to roost considering what Cronus did to his daddy), and went on to receive great reviews as the king of gods and men. He also bought a splendid mountain-top villa overlooking the Mediterranean in which he lavishly entertained his many out-of-town guests, according to celebrity-watcher Robin Leach!

Whereas the Greeks focused on father/authority/paranoia themes, for the Romans, mythological Saturn was more a god of agricultural concerns. This is when many of his earthy traits were developed. Related to the growth of products of the land, he was more work-associated than in the Greek myths. Still, he was intimately linked to cycles of time, although the cycles were more attuned to nature's seasons. Saturn symbolized abundant crop yield (a clue to the wise!) and the harvesting of produce after the labor of serious sowing. Somehow, this aspect of Saturn has been underplayed in today's astrology. The Roman Saturn (an abundance yielder?) sounds almost too Jupiterian and not at all like the Grim Reaper image made famous centuries later—the one we've grown to loathe.

As mythical ruler of Italy during its fabled "Golden Age," Saturn was said to help establish civilized social order, paving the way for prosperity. Saturnalia—a popular annual festival dedicated to this god—was a time of unrestricted feasting, freedom of self-expression, reversal of power-authority roles (servants got to get drunk and became masters for a day), and other forms of joyous, uninhibited self-release. No downbeat self-inhibitors hanging around during *this* festival! Everyone's duty was to let it all hang out and be celebratory.

It is interesting that here we have two contrasting views of the Saturn archetype. The Greek version puts greater focus on Saturn's heavy, oppressive qualities while highlighting the more impersonal elements of time and fate. The Greeks were good with their weighty dramas. Saturn as dutiful Cronus certainly seemed like a power-driven over-achiever, eager to topple authority in order to take full control over situations (but his mom swears it was for a good cause)! Such imagery can be fear-producing and anxiety provoking. However, the Roman version of Saturn reminds us of an important facet of this planet's principle: the natural regularity of time can provide us with enrichment, whether the abundance of harvest or rich experience. This image is more suggestive of the fruits of Saturnian maturity. Time is not the great enemy that threatens to swallow everything in sight. It can be our protector insuring us when life conditions will be ripe and ready for picking. The Roman Saturn archetype also makes clear the virtues of hard work and its eventual rewards.

PSYCHOLOGICAL SATURN

On a very human level, Saturn's sense of law operates through the self-imposed limits of conscience (our internal moral regulator). Conscience becomes the guardian of the psyche, setting up prohibitive boundaries to our instinctual expression, while also defining our necessary ego-limits. For Freud,[2] Saturn corresponds to his concept of the superego. Freudians tell us the superego is that facet of our psyche seeking to enforce moral standards as a way to control or inhibit the energies of both the ego and the id. The superego is especially interested in clamping down on the id, representing the most instinctual, irrational, and pleasure-seeking part of our psyche. Hmm...sounds like Freud saw a correlation between pleasure and irrational behavior. After all, he did have Saturn in the Eighth House in Gemini squaring his Jupiter in the Fifth House! Anyhow, Freud's superego does sound like an uptight Saturn.

For Jungian analysts, Saturn—at least in its darker expression—sounds like the shadow. Liz Greene set us straight about all that in her convincing 1976 bestseller *Saturn* (see my Preface). Jung[3] viewed the shadow as representative of qualities within our psyche that we persistently deny. With such denial comes a lack of access. As these qualities remain repressed within the unconscious, they eventually give form and power to an autonomous shadow function. It is assumed that the shadow expresses most readily through the projection mechanism, where another individual is perceived as having those very disturbing qualities we have difficulty claiming as our own.

Saturn has been associated with scapegoating. When we project our most undesirable traits onto others unconsciously, those people tend to become our scapegoats. What we refuse to recognize and accept within ourselves, for whatever reason, becomes precisely that which we acutely sense in others—often in a highly judgmental manner. The shadow is not the same as the superego. Rather, it tends to represent those very attitudes and desires the superego would eagerly attempt to snuff out. Apparently, both schools of psychology are addressing a valid, albeit different, facet of the Saturn complex. Perhaps we're talking about two sides of the same psychological coin.

What Saturn, as the shadow, may pressure us to do is embrace and come to terms with this planet's less desirable potential. By learning more about Saturn's underground (shadow) nature, we may become more conscious of all the moral dilemmas we need to ferret out within ourselves. Jung felt that the self-knowledge we gain from open confrontation with our shadow involves dedicated and often painstaking work, extending over a long period of time. Astrologers typically view Saturn in similar terms.

Abraham H. Maslow,[4] the "father" of Humanistic Psychology, would most likely have labeled Saturn as symbolic of safety needs, which is one of his hierarchy of basic drives. For Maslow, safety needs correlate with that which is stable, predictable, protective, lawful, and orderly. Safety needs help us ward off chaos and physical instability. Our safety needs can, however, turn neurotic when ego-security becomes a compulsive concern. I suspect Maslow would also liken Saturn to the need for self-esteem. Maslow apparently felt that our sense of prestigious self-recognition is important. Any drive urging us to feel worthy of status and social importance adds to our sense of self-pride. Although much of this sounds like the principles of the Sun and Leo, it nonetheless is also Saturnian to want recognition from a society that honors our efforts and achievements. Saturn just is less beaming and self-promotional about its accomplishments than is the Sun or Leo.

Fritz Perls,[5] the innovator of Gestalt Therapy, would probably have recognized some features of Saturn symbolized in his Ego Mode concept. For Perls, the Ego Mode explained a way in which the self functions in the world. It is associated with structure and discipline. It helps us become aware of form and make distinctions through form. While there is also some Mars symbolism to be found with this style of behavior, Saturn's separative tendencies are certainly emphasized. Perls talks of four types of contact or ways in which we connect with ourselves and our surroundings. One form of contact is called retroflection. This is done in the Ego Mode, and it represents the self-control we exert in order to accomplish an objective or clearly defined goal. By this definition, it is easy to see the Saturn correlation.

Gestalt Therapy also speaks of Safety Functions. The one that seems most Saturnian to me is desensitization, which is basically a protective strategy we adopt in order to numb us to conditions we psychologically are not ready or willing to handle. Safety Functions also appear to be a bit Neptunian in that they all share in common the need to escape from the pain of the here and now. If taken too far, desensitization can result in withdrawal, making us hard to reach. This sounds much like mismanaged Saturn/Neptune energy.

Dr. Eric Berne[6] and followers of Transactional Analysis would have little trouble seeing Saturn as descriptive of The Parent (one of TA's three major ego states)—especially The Critical Parent, a facet differing sharply from The Nurturing Parent (Moon). Berne's Critical Parent possesses all the classic Saturnian traits, with a tendency to be negative and fault-finding. Yet an underdeveloped expression of the Parent (called exclusion) can result in a lawless mentality or the absence of ethical guidelines and a weak conscience. Berne's Critical Parent is very fitting of the traditional father image Astrology associates with Saturn. Here are to be found conditional love and the evaluation of another's performance. Like Saturn, the Critical Parent is tuned into what is right and what is wrong. Anything not found acceptable is rejected.

These are just a few schools of psychology that—according to their own theoretical assumptions—affirm the principles of Saturn that astrologers have known about for centuries. Obviously, a general psychological trait of Saturn is guilt. Perfectionistic Saturn is the critical, nagging part of ourselves that never feels it's done enough, or makes us feel what we've done was far too inadequate. We tend to respond to all this by either punishing ourselves in both overt and subtle ways, or by engaging in flat-out denial. Denying shortcomings and purely human deficiencies paves the way for repression and suppression. It is certainly not the healthy route to take, but it is probably protective at times in order to ensure that other parts of the psyche are not damaged, as in a horrifying trauma, when we often go into shock and later remember little of the incident. The fact that our denied thoughts and feelings remain unconscious even gives them added strength.

Saturn is also a planet depicting our fears and dreads. All phobic tendencies are varying degrees of Saturn's reaction to the unknown, and sometimes the known—will my neighbor's chihuahua Gomez, who took a nip at me bit before, want to viciously bite me again? The unknown enters the picture by the fact we have to question this future possibility. During anxiety attacks, the feeling that something dreadful is impending is very Saturnian. Phobias and anxieties share one thing in common: they are reactions to situations that show a lack of trust and security. Saturn is not responsive to an all-accepting, unconditionally loving Universe. In essence, Saturn is the part of us that feels separated from whatever we are nonetheless drawn to. We have a hard time dissolving our barriers and feeling unified with whatever is outside if us wherever Saturn is in our chart. It is a planet of encapsulation. Psychological encapsulation means we deflect the impact of other people who could otherwise assist us in all forms of self-release. We unwittingly create our own vacuums, and suffer from the consequences of being so distant.

Depression is typically considered to be the result of a mismanaged Saturn. Psychology has suggested that depression is one result of repressed anger or held-in rage. Obviously, depression may involve Mars and Pluto symbolism as well. The experts claim that depressed people are anything but passive about their feelings. They simply choose not to let their volatile emotionality emerge (although it's not often a conscious choice). Perhaps they fear they will be condemned for their hard-to-contain passions. Depression is quite Saturnian due to its characteristic quality of lethargy, mental listlessness, and a lack of desire to face up to challenges (self-inhibiting expression to an extreme). Saturnian depression makes us feel any situation we fixate on is hopeless, unresponsive to change, a punishment, and all our own fault. But again, depression may also involve Mars symbolism in the chart (maybe Mars "squashed" by Saturn in various forms of Principles One and Ten).

ASTRONOMICAL SATURN

For centuries, an unparalleled physical property of Saturn was its five or six distinct rings (the number estimated until 1980). Saturn's rings were astrologically a traditional confirmation of its restraining principle. These rings are still considered symbolic of self-imposed boundaries we construct, as well as forces pressuring us to work within the limitations society has structured for us. However, we now know Jupiter has one thin ring around it, Uranus has about eleven, and even Neptune seems to have four very diffuse rings. What's going on? Does any of this take away from Saturn's special astrological status as the planet of life's restriction? Most likely not (but maybe it shows Saturn can be contagious).

For one thing, Saturn's ring system is unique, and even more so than previously considered. In November 1980,[7] Voyager 1 gave us physical evidence that Saturn has close to a thousand rings (we are talking serious restriction-symbolism here). Instead of the half-dozen major rings assumed, Saturn actually has innumerable "ringlets" that collectively give the effects of grooves on a phonograph record—appropriate for a god considered to be the Recorder of Time or Keeper of the Records. Interestingly, Saturn's rings look solid but are very insubstantial, as they are composed of millions of tiny "moonlets" a few inches across. One of these rings, called the F-Ring, is apparently formed by wispy, strand-like particles of dust that wrap around each other in braid-like fashion. This braiding effect sounds much like Saturn, a planet long associated with weaving.

There are some rings that do not align themselves as evenly as the rest, giving them a lopsided look. There are also dark, spike-like features in the rings that are baffling to astronomers, who have little idea whether these "spokes" are solid material or gaps within the rings. Another unusual feature is that the inner rings, closer to the planet itself, move faster than the outer ones. This differential rotation should theoretically keep these rings from holding their shape collectively. But that's not the case here. Why is everything holding itself together for so long, including the mysterious spokes? Well, after all, this *is* Saturn we are talking about!

Three new Moons were discovered by Voyager 1, making the count in 1980 fifteen in all. But since 1993, the number has risen to eighteen confirmed moons, with still others suspected to exist. Two of these new moons are not only in the same orbit (making astronomers wonder what keeps them so orderly and well behaved, since they should have collided by now)—they also are located in the ring system itself! Seems like everything in the ring zone is holding up pretty well. One moon is just outside the rim of the flukey F-Ring, which is the outermost ring. Since two moons orbit on both sides of the F-Ring, maybe that has something to do with its peculiarities. Another notable discovery is a giant "white spot"[8] in the planet's southern hemisphere (oh no, Saturn has a pimple! There goes that theory about Capricorns always having flawless skin). Jupiter's Giant Red Spot has been determined to be an enormous hurricane-like storm that has been whirling around for three centuries. Saturn's spot could be a smaller, more compact version. Why waste space?

Perhaps all these new astronomical revelations about Saturn will allow us to break away from clinging to the old traditional image of this planet being very plain and predictable. Of course, some could argue that the findings of dark spokes, lopsided rings, and irregular strands (like split ends) could emphasize that Saturn still relates to our own imperfections and blemishes on all levels. Still, this new look at Saturn is fascinating. Both Saturn and Jupiter have large amounts of satellites hovering around them, and both are planets symbolic of society-centered urges and needs. Perhaps the multitude of moons implies Saturn's sense of responsibility on the one-to-many level. The two moons embedded within Saturn's ring system sound appropriate for a planet known for its control tactics. It's almost as if Saturn cannot let go of its holding power over anything that is in its care.

Saturn Intercepted

Saturn intercepted is a little like Saturn retrograde in that there can be reticence regarding outward activity. Here is a face of Saturn that is typically turned away from public view. Situational affairs operating in its house are less overt, or perhaps we read into them certain nuances that are normally not associated with such affairs. This can suggest deeper Saturn responses to the everyday circumstances of that house; we don't always live on the surface of life. Due to this, our Saturn needs may be less apparent to others. How we react to things may be more important to us than how we take action. Many of our Saturn attributes are used to better structure our inner levels and less to bring order to our external conditions. This Saturn operates more subtly, which would seem better suited for self-inhibitors, who tend to be hesitant in using their Saturn openly in the outer world, but very frustrating for the average over-achiever. Saturn may appear to operate like any non-intercepted planet in this house, except that it registers experiences less superficially, for better or worse. That can make us more ponderous about the house matters in question than Saturn would already suggest. We first work on the subjective plane of consciousness before we turn attention to the outer plane of the material world.

SATURN'S GLYPH

The one face of Saturn we do get to quickly see in every chart is its glyph (planetary symbol). It looks like a stylized "H" but it is actually a mix of a cross and a crescent, with the cross rising above and to the left of the crescent. In planetary glyph symbolism, the cross signifies matter or the manifestation of form and structure within the boundaries of time and space. The cross defines physical plane realities and concrete expression, so naturally it has to be part of Saturn's graphic symbol. The crescent or semi-circle is said to signify the "personality," which means our emotional and mental components as they operate within ego-consciousness. The crescent has been called the soul and symbolizes the facet of our being that perceives life in terms of duality and separateness. Unlike the full circle (symbol of spirit, infinity, timelessness, unity, wholeness), the crescent implies incomplete awareness or limited perception.

Saturn's glyph reminds us of the necessity to undergo the limitations of manifestation so that the personality becomes well experienced in the principles of matter. This is a prerequisite before we can be free from the binding, exacting laws of the material plane, and before we can later safely function on supra-physical realms. The linking of cross and crescent reveals a spiritual truth: our incomplete awareness of unity makes us at least partly responsible for the restrictions we attract. This is the principle of "matter over mind." We set the circumference of our influence in life through our mental and emotional structures.

The degree of weightiness that we feel coincides with our finite understanding of cause and effect. Metaphysical Astrology would view this symbol as the crucifixion of the soul on the cross of matter, suggesting the Saturn glyph visually demonstrates the principle of karma, especially our karmic debts. Our external, mundane environment tends to objectify our internal atmosphere. All we send out into the world is to finally return home to us with the same degree of intensity and with similar intent. Because the semi-circle is being sub-jugated by an overpowering cross (it's a longer cross than the ones Venus and Mercury have), this might denote that only the personality (not the spirit) falls under the influence of the fixed laws of manifestation. Unenlightened, we feel the heavy pressure of the world. Yet once we make progress with self-realization, the power of the cross diminishes and we might even feel lighter in spirit, more gaseous like planet Saturn, and able to float on the waters of the Infinite.

Chapter Eighteen Endnotes

1. Isabel Hickey, *Astrology: A Cosmic Science*, Altieri Press, 1970, p. 49. This book has been reissued in softbound for-mat by CRCS Publications in 1992.

2. Maritha Pottenger did an interesting series on the leaders in the field of psychology in her "Maritha on Counseling" feature in *The Mutable Dilemma* (1979–1982). She began with Sigmund Freud in the March 1979 issue, pp. 3–17.

3. Maritha Pottenger, "Maritha on Counseling," *The Mutable Dilemma*, September 1979 issue, featured article "A Landscape of Jung's Thoughts" by Tony Joseph, pp. 9–21.

4. Maritha Pottenger, "Abraham H. Maslow: Proponent of the Healthy Human," *The Mutable Dilemma,* September 1982 issue, pp. 35–50.

5. Maritha Pottenger, "Be Here Now: The Message of Gestalt Therapy," *The Mutable Dilemma*, March 1980 issue, pp. 47–64.

6. Maritha Pottenger, "Maritha on Counseling," *The Mutable Dilemma*, September 1981 issue, pp. 47–64.

7. "Visit To a Large Planet," *Time Magazine,* Vol. 116, No. 21, Nov. 24, 1980, pp. 32–35 and 39–41. Saturn even made this issue's cover of *Time* (a magazine with a fitting name for this great planet).

8. In September of 1990, Saturn's large white spot appeared and spread in size. It encircled the planet by November. Astronomers blame this "blemish" on Saturn "burping" hot gases from its interior (gee, how embarrassing for Saturn). Smaller white spots have been observed and recorded in 1876, 1903, 1933, and 1960, suggesting this phenomenon is periodic. As this "burp cycle" repeats every twenty-seven to thirty years, it coincides with Saturn's orbital period and, for astrologers, the Saturn Return. It sounds like Saturn is having a case of indigestion every thirty years—much the way *we* sometimes feel during our Saturn Returns! Sources: "New White Spot on Saturn Grows, Changes," *Science News,* 138:325, 1990: and "Giant Bubble of Gas Rises through Saturn's Atmosphere," William Brown, *New Scientist*, p.22, October 20, 1990.

END OF THE TRIP

Whew! If you think it takes a lot of stamina to finish reading an entire book strictly about Saturn issues, try writing one—ha! Actually, now that I've finished this work, I feel like I've attended an intensive Saturn seminar sponsored by the Lords of You Know Who! This planet's principles and themes have been churning in my head for quite some time, and will continue to do so for a while. Writing *Twelve Faces of Saturn* gave me an opportunity to think about how The Ringed One has described parts of me and my life up to this point. Saturn is now going through my intercepted Twelfth House while I'm truly finishing up a few loose ends and closing certain life chapters (as of the summer of 1996). I hope indeed I have become a bit wiser than I was before starting to commit my thoughts to the printed page.

I suggest that from time to time you reread those parts of this book that specifically apply to you. Try not to let anything I've said become unduly discouraging. Not everything I've stated is even supposed to apply to you anyway, just some of it. Remember that you're reading about Saturn's sign and house placement unaltered by other factors in the birthchart (for example, what if Venus and Jupiter were also found in the same house as Saturn? That could certainly change the tone of things). Still, take in all the information and thoughtfully weigh all sides. Do not attempt to force the information to describe your inner/outer life if deep inside you know it just doesn't sound right (especially if you have strong mutable emphasis to begin with, since this mode can be quite suggestible). But at the same time, note which Saturn statements you are quick (perhaps a bit too quick) to dismiss. Your passionate responses to those parts of my material you outright reject could be a clue that you are unconsciously identifying with what you're reading, and that there may be unresolved issues to be ironed out: famous last words— "I'm never critical of people!" (Saturn in Virgo,) "I couldn't care less about the spotlight; give someone else all the attention!" (Saturn in Leo,) "But I have tons of close friends and have never had a problem being accepted by my peers!" (Saturn in the Eleventh House). Maybe all this is true for some, but still we need to dig a little deeper into and be a little more honest about our motivational dynamics when analyzing our natal Saturn.

In closing, I hope that from here on that you'll think twice before dumping on your Saturn, my Saturn, or anybody's Saturn. This is one planet that will always work with you if you willingly work with it and play by some of its sound and sane rules, and realize that time is often on your side. Be patient, but don't lose focus. Learn to recognize when something is really not meant to work out, and drop that something or someone in due time. Sorry, folks, in this world you really cannot have it all, no matter what you heard at those crowd-pleasing Jupiter/Neptune pep rallies. And this from a Scorpio with Mercury in Scorpio and a Sun/Pluto/ASC T-Square (whom you'd think would always demand to have it all, and then even try to have all of yours too!). Always be willing to make adjustments to your sense of reality. One last piece of advice: this may sound corny to some of you hard-core Plutonians, but Saturn is your friend if you let yourself be a friend to Saturn (that's right, take ole Saturn out to lunch!).

Shake hands with this planet and even try a warm hug (but nothing too mushy). You'll find that, at least on the level of character development, this will prove a worthy alliance providing you with inner rewards for a lifetime.

Well, the ride is over and we've made the trip in fairly good shape, considering some of the bumps, potholes, and detour signs along the way. Now, one last thing to check—did we leave the key in the ignition and lock ourselves out again?

BIBLIOGRAPHY

GENERAL REFERENCE

Avery, Jeanne. *Astrology and Your Past Lives.* New York: Simon & Schuster, 1987.

Binder, Jamie. *Planets at Work.* San Diego, CA: ACS Publications, 1988.

Cunningham, Donna. *Healing Pluto Problems.* York Beach, ME: Samuel Weiser, 1986.

Dobyns, Zipporah. *Expanding Astrology's Universe.* Los Angeles, CA: TIA Publications, 1983.

Greene, Liz. *Saturn.* York Beach, ME: Samuel Weiser, 1976.

Hickey, Isabel M. *Astrology: A Cosmic Science.* Sebastopol, CA: CRCS, 1992.

Mayo, Jeff. *The Astrologer's Astronomical Handbook*, 2nd ed. London: L.N. Fowler & Co., 1972.

Miller, Casey, and Kate Swift. *The Handbook of Nonsexist Writing*, 2nd ed.,New York: Harper & Row, 1988.

Pottenger, Maritha. *Complete Horoscope Interpretation.* San Diego, CA: ACS Publications, 1986.

Pottenger, Maritha and Mark, ed. *The Mutable Dilemma*. Los Angeles, CA: LA-CCRS, 1979–1981.

Smith, Huston. *The Religions of Man*. New York: Harper & Row, 1965.

Tierney, Bil. *Dynamics of Aspect Analysis*. Sebastopol, CA: CRCS, 2nd revised edition, 1993.

Wright, Paul. *Astrology in Action*. Sebastopol, CA: CRCS, 1989.

Sources of Astro-lebrity Saturn Sign/House Placements

Binder, Jamie. *Planets in Work*. San Diego, CA: ACS Publications, 1988.

Cunningham, Donna. *Healing Pluto Problems*. York Beach, ME: Samuel Weiser, 1986.

Erlewine, Stephen. *The Circle Book of Charts*, Ann Arbor, MI: Circle Books, 1972.

Gauquelin, Michel and Francoise. *The Gauquelin Book of American Charts*, San Diego, CA: ACS Publications, 1982).

Rodden, Lois M. *Profiles of Women (Astro Data I)*. Tempe, AZ: AFA, 1979.

————. *The American Book of Charts (Astro Data II)*. San Diego, CA: ACS Publications, 1980.

————. *Astro Data III*. Tempe, AZ: AFA, 1988.

————. *Astro Data IV*. Tempe, AZ: AFA, 1990.

Wright, Paul. *Astrology in Action*. Sebastopol, CA: CRCS Publications, 1989.

LOOK FOR THE CRESCENT MOON

Llewellyn publishes hundreds of books on your favorite subjects! To get these exciting books, including the ones on the following pages, check your local bookstore or order them directly from Llewellyn.

ORDER BY PHONE
- Call toll-free within the U.S. and Canada, 1-800-THE MOON
- In Minnesota, call (612) 291-1970
- We accept VISA, MasterCard, and American Express

ORDER BY MAIL
- Send the full price of your order (MN residents add 7% sales tax) in U.S. funds, plus postage & handling to:

  Llewellyn Worldwide
  P.O. Box 64383, Dept. K747-1
  St. Paul, MN 55164–0383, U.S.A.

POSTAGE & HANDLING
(For the U.S., Canada, and Mexico)
- $4 for orders $15 and under
- $5 for orders over $15
- No charge for orders over $100

We ship UPS in the continental United States. We ship standard mail to P.O. boxes. Orders shipped to Alaska, Hawaii, The Virgin Islands, and Puerto Rico are sent first-class mail. Orders shipped to Canada and Mexico are sent surface mail.

International orders: Airmail—add freight equal to price of each book to the total price of order, plus $5.00 for each non-book item (audio tapes, etc.).

Surface mail—Add $1.00 per item.

Allow 4–6 weeks for delivery on all orders.
Postage and handling rates subject to change.

DISCOUNTS
We offer a 20% discount to group leaders or agents. You must order a minimum of 5 copies of the same book to get our special quantity price.

FREE CATALOG
Get a free copy of our color catalog, *New Worlds of Mind and Spirit*. Subscribe for just $10.00 in the United States and Canada ($30.00 overseas, airmail). Many bookstores carry *New Worlds*—ask for it!

Visit our website at www.llewellyn.com for more information.

Instant Horoscope Predictor
Find Your Future Fast
Julia Lupton Skalka

Want to know if the planets will smile favorably upon your wedding day? Wondering when to move ahead on that new business venture? Perhaps you're curious as to why you've been so accident prone lately. It's time to look at your transits.

Transits define the relationship between where the planets are today with where they were when you were born. They are an invaluable aid for timing your actions and making decisions. With a copy of your transit chart and *Instant Horoscope Predictor* you can now discover what's in store for today, next month, even a year from now.

Julia Lupton Skalka delivers an easy-to-use guide that will decipher the symbols on your transit chart into clear, usable predictions. In addition, she provides chapters on astrological history, mythology, and transit analyses of four famous people: Grace Kelly, Mata Hari, Theodore Roosevelt and Ted Bundy.

1-56718-668-8, 6 x 9, 464 pp., softcover   **$14.95**

To order call 1-800-THE MOON
Prices subject to change without notice.

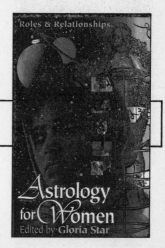

Pluto, Vol. II
The Soul's Evolution Through Relationships
JEFFREY WOLF GREEN

From the great mass of people on the planet we all choose certain ones with whom to be intimate. *Pluto, Vol II* shows the evolutionary and karmic causes, reasons, and prior life background that determines whom we relate to and how.

This is the first book to explore the astrological Pluto model that embraces the evolutionary development and progression of the Soul from life to life. It offers a unique, original paradigm that allows for a total understanding of the past life dynamics that exist between two people. You will find a precise astrological methodology to determine the prior life orientation, where the relationship left off, where the relationship picked up in this lifetime, and what the current evolutionary next step is: the specific reasons or intentions for being together again.

In addition, there are chapters devoted to Mars and Venus in the signs, Mars and Venus in relationship, Mars and Pluto in relationship, and Pluto through the Composite Houses.

1-56718-333-6, 6 x 9, 432 pp., softcover　　　　　　　　　**$17.95**

Prediction in Astrology
A Master Volume of Technique and Practice
NOEL TYL

No matter how much you know about astrology already, no matter how much experience you've had to date, you'll be fascinated by *Prediction in Astrology,* and you'll grow as an astrologer. Using the Solar Arc theory and methods he describes in this book, the author was able to accurately predict the Gulf War, including the actual date it would begin and the timetable of tactics, two months before it began. He also predicted the overturning of Communist rule in the Eastern bloc nations nine months in advance of its actual occurrence.

Tyl teaches through example. You learn by doing astrology, not just thinking about it. Tyl introduces Solar Arc theory in terms of "rapport" measurements, which you begin to do immediately, without paper, pencil, or computer, dials, or wheels. Just with your eyes! You will never look at a horoscope the same way again!

Tyl, in his well-known, very special way, also gets personal. He presents 30 Aphorisms, the keenest of maxims, the most practical of techniques, to create predictions from any horoscope. And as if this were not enough, Tyl then presents 20 Aphorisms for Counseling. Look for Tyl's "Quick-Glance" Transit Table, 1940-2040, to which you can refer more quickly than a computer. The busy astrologer will use this Appendix every day for many years to come.

0-87542-814-2, 360 pp., 6 x 9, softcover   **$17.95**

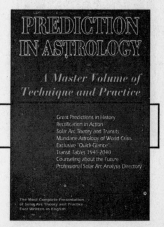

To order call 1-800-THE MOON
Prices subject to change without notice.

Meet Your Planets
Fun with Astrology
ROY ALEXANDER

Astrology doesn't have to be mind boggling. Now there is a playful way to master this ancient art! In this book, the planets are transformed into an unforgettable lot of characters with very distinctive personalities and idiosyncrasies. Maybe you're the Temple Dancer, a temptress oozing with exotic flair... the Tennis Champion, with his win-at-all-costs attitude ... or maybe the Math Teacher, an unrelenting stickler for proof and accuracy. Furthermore, the twelve signs of the zodiac are turned into 9-to-5 jobs; if a planet doesn't like its job, it will complain, procrastinate, throw a temper tantrum—typical human behavior. Now you can relate to the planets as people you know, work and play with. Finally, astrology doesn't take itself so seriously! You'll be amazed at how easy and fun learning the art of astrology is ... seriously!

1-56718-017-5, 224 pp., 6 x 9, 142 illus., softcover $12.95

Mythic Astrology
Archetypal Powers in the Horoscope
ARIEL GUTTMAN & KENNETH JOHNSON

Here is an entirely new dimension of self-discovery based on understanding the mythic archetypes represented in the astrological birth chart. Myth has always been closely linked with astrology; all our planets are named for the Graeco-Roman deities and derive their interpretative meanings from them. To richly experience the myths which lie at the heart of astrology is to gain a deeper and more spiritual perspective on the art of astrology and on life itself.

Mythic Astrology is unique because it allows the reader to explore the connection between astrology and the spirituality of myth in depth, without the necessity of a background in astrology, anthropology or the classics. This book is an important contribution to the continuing study of mythology as a form of New Age spirituality and is also a reference work of enduring value. Students of mythology, the Goddess, art, history, Jungian psychological symbolism and literature—as well as lovers of astrology—will all enjoy the text and numerous illustrations.

0-87542-248-9, 382 pp., 7 x 10, 100 illus., softcover $17.95

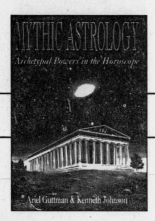